41, 44, 46-47, 48, 53, 56, 58-60, 63, 65,
76, 81, 85, 87, 91, 95-97, 99, 102,
107-08, 111, 116, 130, 136, 141,
143-46, 172, 178, 183, 186, 200,
203-06, 213, 215, 223-25, 228-30, 232,
246, 252, 254-60
Vo Nguyen Giap, 240

Wage Labor and Laborers, 109-12
War, 5-6, 12, 30, 49, 83, 92-93, 123, 125,
130-31, 133-34, 151, 163, 165-66, 189,
192, 200-01, 214-15, 233-34, 237, 245,
258, 268
Wars of (National) Liberation or Inde-
pendence, see Revolution, Types of,
Anti-colonial Revolution
Washington Conference, 153
Washington, George, 269
Watergate, 260
Weber, Max, 18-19
West (Western), 23, 33, 49, 60, 74, 102,
108, 116, 123-24, 132, 136-37, 141,
143, 149-51, 153, 155-57, 166-67,
209-11, 222-23, 226-27, 235, 237-39,
243, 247, 250, 253-54, 257, 262
Women, 75
Workers, see Proletariat
World Revolution, see Revolution,
Types of
World War I, 123, 130, 136, 142, 153-54,
243
World War II, 166, 204, 222, 236, 239,
243, 255
Wren, Matthew, 72

Yemen, 52
Youth, 247-48, 256-57
Youth Movement, 17, 22-24, 30-32

Zapata, Emiliano, 178
Zeeland, 68

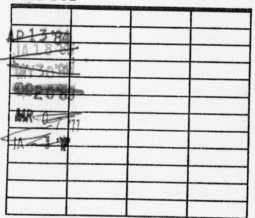

Revolution and the Revolutionary Ideal

Revolution and the Revolutionary Ideal

Robert Blackey and Clifford Paynton

SCHENKMAN PUBLISHING COMPANY
3 Mt. Auburn Place
Cambridge, Massachusetts

Copyright © 1976

SCHENKMAN PUBLISHING COMPANY INC.
Cambridge, Massachusetts

Printed in the United States of America

Library of Congress Catalog Card Number: 74-20484

ISBN: 87073-986-7 cloth
87073-987-5 paper

Dedication

To the memory of my parents, Ruth (1912-1963) and Joseph (1911-1968) Blackey, whom I shall always remember with love.

To my parents, Thomas and Selma Paynton, for many fond memories.

TABLE OF CONTENTS

	Preface	1
1.	Introduction	4
2.	Violence and Strategy in Revolution	11
3.	Social Institutions and Revolution	29
4.	Social-Psychological Factors in Explanations of Revolution	39
5.	Urbanization and Revolution	48
6.	On Eve of the Modern Concept; The Greeks to the Glorious Revolution	62
7.	Age of the Democratic Revolution	74
8.	Revolution in the 19th Century	85
9.	Revolution According to Karl Marx	101
10.	Lenin's Concept of Revolution	114
11.	The Russian Revolution	129
12.	The Non-Left Revolutions: The Irish Revolution Gandhi's Revolution The Nazi Revolution	140
13.	China in Revolution (I) Sun Yat-sen, Mao Tse-tung and the Cultural Revolution	149
14.	China in Revolution (II) Sun Yat-sen, Mao Tse-ung and the Cultural Revolution	159
15.	Latin America Revolutions and Revolutionists: Mexico	172
16.	Latin America Revolutions and Revolutionists: Cuba, Castro, Che	182

17. Latin America   196
    Revolutions and Revolutionists
    Che in Bolivia, Debray, Chile
18. African Revolutions and Revolutionists: 208
    Guinea-Bissau and Cabral
19. African Revolutions and   221
    Revolutionists:
    Algeria and Fanon
20. The Vietnamese Revolution   233
21. The New Left in America: 243
    Marcuse and Mixed Company
22. Conclusion: Some Observations   262

    Suggestions for further Reading   271

    Index   287

Preface

Revolutions—physically, intellectually and emotionally—have been among the most dramatic social experiences to have consumed the energies of mankind. Revolutions are not only experiences of times past but of the present and, we daresay, the future as well. In *no* society can the possibility of revolution be completely excluded as a means or cause of radical social change. When the vital institutions of a social system fail in some important respect to meet the needs of the people who live within it the potential for violent reaction and revolution exists.

The course of civilization has been altered by revolutions from the time of the Greeks, but it was not until the age of the "democratic revolution" at the end of the 18th century that revolutions began to take the form with which we are familiar today. In the last century, as revolutions became more frequent and the ideas of Karl Marx, Friedrich Engels, the Anarchists and others were developed and popularized, the modern concept came of age. In this century revolutions are not only commonplace occurrences, but are rarely simply national phenomenon limited to the borders of any one country.

1

This book is not a history of revolution. The history of revolution is, in fact, the history of the world in change, and that is a task that extends far beyond the framework of this volume. The focus here is on the concept of "revolution" and the changing nature of the "revolutionary ideal"; we have interpreted the term "revolutionary ideal" rather broadly to include ideas, ideologies and models. Only brief and cursory attention is paid to the concept before the period of the American and French Revolutions. This is not to minimize the significance of, say, the Renaissance and Reformation as periods of revolution, but to define the limits of the present study. We propose to examine our topic from both historical and sociological perspectives. The historical perspective begins with the late 18th century and traces the course of the changes in the concept. Simultaneously, we will discuss the revolutionary writings of the leading theorists and determine their influence on the revolutionary ideal. For the late 18th and the 19th centuries we will concentrate on Europe and North America. For the 20th century we will expand our examination to include Asia, Latin America and Africa. The sociological perspective examines aspects not only of the conception of revolution itself, but of the social and interpersonal phenomena typically associated with the revolutionary process. The inclusion of both the historical and sociological orientations permits us to take into consideration two crucial elements in the explanation of events. The historical view provides the critical dimension of "time", while the sociological concentrates on the "process" of social events; by itself the latter often neglects "time" as an important explanatory factor in the happenings of people.

Although the subject of this book may be considered a limited one in the enormously broad spectrum of human knowledge it is nonetheless significant in that it covers a time span of two centuries and a geography that is global. The authors, like most scholars, have expertise only in rather narrow fields and, as such, must rely heavily upon the work of other historians, sociologists, political scientists, anthropologists and philosophers. Much of this work, therefore, is a product of synthesis and interpretation. The primary and secondary material for the period covered in this volume is so vast as to be beyond the realistic grasp of any one or two individuals. The authors, therefore, recognize and acknowledge their debt to the works of literally hundreds of scholars they consulted. As such, some of what follows is second and third-hand, but there is no other feasible way when dealing with such a subject. No doubt many readers will take issue with the comparative brevity and, at times, superficiality of the various components of the presentation. To remedy this situation a list of suggested readings appear at the end of the book to provide a guide to readers interested in probing more deeply.

We wish to thank our families and students for the time we might otherwise have given to them, and while this project has not helped to make us better husbands and fathers we think it has helped us to be better teachers and scholars. We also wish to thank the library staff of California State College, San Bernardino, especially John Tibbals, Johnnie Ralph, Michael Brown and Frances Ekaitis for their patient assistance and the invaluable time they saved us. Our special thanks goes to Corinne Schnur who typed the manuscript so quickly and efficiently, and to our college's Faculty Professional Development Fund and President John Pfau for the grant to cover typing costs. Finally, we wish to express our gratitude to our colleagues and friends Frederick Campbell, Elliot Barkan, Robert Smith, Mike Persell, Stephen Graham, Marcia Graham, David Decker, James G. Nutsch, Brij Khare, J. C. Robinson, William Ackerman, Michael Darkoh and Paul Johnson for taking the time to read portions of the manuscript and giving freely of their expertise. For all that follows, however, the authors remain solely responsible.

1

Introduction:[1]
Background of the Concept

Revolution is an ideal as much as it is a process, or a call to action, or a way of life. Revolutionists and non-revolutionists alike have their own notions of what revolution is. But revolutions frequently change course and the leaders who emerge from a successful revolution are not always the same as those who initiated and carried it through. If they are the same their positions and ideas have often been altered (e.g., as with Fidel Castro). It is important to know what the nature (or meaning) of the concept was at the start and at the peak of the revolution when it served to motivate followers. Further, since revolutions mobilize large numbers of people, we need to know what it is that inclines some people to favor the interests of the revolution over the established government.

Revolutions are as old as recorded history and as contemporary as this morning's newspaper. But to echo the sentiments of the German Socialist Karl Kautsky, there have been few concepts over which there

4

has been so much contention as that of revolution. To simplify matters it may be stated that in a general sense there have been three phases in the evolution of the concept. The first has been called the *natural* or *astronomy* phase: borrowing the word "revolution" from astronomy it was applied in politics to refer to a non-human force, history moving in cycles regardless of human activity. Perhaps this view may best be summed up in the response of a courtier to Louis XVI of France who, upon hearing of the storming of the Bastille on July 14, 1789, is supposed to have exclaimed, "But good God, that is revolt!" The reply was, "No Sire, it is a revolution"—implying that revolution was a force of nature outside of human control. At the end of the 18th century the second phase, labeled *humanistic* or *romantic,* came into prominence: revolutions were believed to be initiated by the actions of man asserting his will. Thus, the course of history, it was held, could be changed by individuals. Much 19th century thought reflected this view. The third phase emerged with Karl Marx. This *scientific* or *realistic* phase was in many respects a synthesis of the earlier phases: revolution is a human activity and the human factor is crucial, but at the same time society must be ripe for human activity to be effective. The contemporary world sees revolution as a calculated, somewhat planned, long-term process and not a sudden, unexpected event governed primarily by the laws of nature.

In his *Theses on Feuerbach* (1845) Marx wrote: "The philosophers have only *interpreted* the world, in various ways; the point is to *change* it." This not only sums up the meaning of revolution for Marx and Engels, but for all revolutionists as well; that is, its purpose is to change the world—or at least a part of it—radically. In this regard, there is a strong parallel between revolution and religion: each has its own dogma, ideal and saints. Basic to most revolutionary ideals, as with most religions is the creation of the perfect man. Both stem from man's imperfections and are fired by his hopes for freedom and his dream of a utopia. And both call followers to create rather than merely to destroy. Revolutions, "create new time-spans for our life on earth. They give man's soul a new relation between present, past, and future; and by doing so they give us time to start our life on earth all over again, with a new rhythm and a new faith. . . . A revolution must overwhelm us as other passions do."[1]

Revolutions are as basic to human society as wars, and they are probably more crucial because, more than wars, they raise the question of the type of society which should exist. As compared to revolutions, wars do little to change the order of a society; depending on victory or defeat, they either expand or contract that society. What wars attempt to expand, revolutions have previously created (Napoleon's wars and the French Revolution are examples). In spite of the havoc they bring, revolutions are the positive movements of history, the "larva of civilization" according to Victor Hugo, because they establish new standards for society.

What is revolution? Like many concepts that are used to characterize rather complex phenomena it is overused and underdefined, and the study of revolutions has been riddled with a tradition of imprecision. In addition to the events of 1789 in France and of 1917 in Russia—which are more or less consistently labeled "revolutions"—there are other upheavals marked by revolutionary activity but referred to by other names: the Taiping "Rebellion," the Sepoy "Mutiny," the Paris "Commune," and the American "Civil War." Scholars differentiate between "great revolutions" and "mere rebellions," whereas journalists, politicians and law enforcement authorities are often ready to designate local disturbances or riots as revolutions. We therefore cannot begin to talk about the ideal of revolution until there is some clarification of terms.

But can we present a complete definition of the word which will be satisfying to all concerned? Probably not. In fact, it is really quite impossible to define revolution as one would most other words. To define it, as with a dictionary definition, is to limit what it is, and thus go against the grain of history. To assert that a given event is not a revolution because it does not meet *our* interpretation is to say to the people who experienced it (both revolutionists and counter-revolutionists alike) that what they perceived to be a revolution was not. This, it seems to us, is neither fair nor scientific. We ought to regard the reality of the past as much as possible in the way the participants perceived it at the time. Thus, what we shall present now are descriptions and definitions of revolution which we wish to b guidelines, not restrictive boundaries.

Leon Trotsky defined a revolution as "a political movement which attempted to substitute one ruling group for another and, in the process, shifted the balance of power from one social class to another."[2] George Pettee saw revolution as "a change in the constitution by illegal means."[3] For Peter Amann, "revolution prevails when the state's monopoly of power is effectively challenged and persists until a monopoly of power is reestablished."[4] Revolution to Louis Gottschalk is "a popular movement whereby a significant change in the structure of a nation or a society is effected."[5] A more grandiose definition by Sigmund Neumann sees revolution "as a sweeping, fundamental change in political organization, social structure, economic property control and the dominant myth of a social order, thus indicating a major break in the continuity of a development."[6] A psychologically oriented view by Charles Ellwood sees revolutions as "those convulsive movements in the history of societies in which the form of government, or . . . the type of the industrial and social order, is suddenly transformed."[7] And lastly, Eugene Kamenka calls a revolution "any sharp, sudden change or attempted change in the location of political power which involved either the use or the threat of violence and, if successful, expressed itself in the manifest and perhaps radical transformation of the progress o government, the accepted foundations of sovereignty or legitimacy, and the conception of the political and/or social order."[8]

Each of these descriptions suits the particular preconceptions of its author and adherents. But each can be restrictive in that for every one there are no doubt countless exceptions which might either void or detract from our presentation. We would prefer, instead, to leave our definition openended and somewhat vague to be able to examine a wide variety of events and theories related to revolution. This includes the Russian Revolution and the revolutionary ideas of the New Left. At other times we will discuss phenomena associated with the revolutionary process, such as violence, revolutionary leadership and followership, the potential for revolution and so on. Let us say, therefore, that revolutions generally have in common a number of characteristics or traits which may serve as the basis for a broad, comprehensive framework: revolutions are a challenge to the existing political—and perhaps social, economic and cultural—system with an aim at redirecting and restructuring; they occur when the legitimate means for effecting changes break down or function poorly; they often involve the use or threat of violence against some or all aspects of the status quo (that violence may be internal, external or both). They generally disrupt society sufficiently so that after they are over, the victors, either revolutionists or status quo, must engage in a significant effort to reorder and reorganize society. Revolutions tend to include references to the past, but these are often only rhetorical tools. More often than not, revolutions tend to involve more than one country and to become international problems. Therefore, a good, working, but by no means definitive, description is as follows: a revolution is a political and/or social and/or economic and/or cultural upheaval which calls for a fundamental change in the existing order; it is relatively rapid and generally employs the use or threat of force; it is directed against principles and institutions, not individuals.

The person who is dissatisfied with the conditions of his life usually has created, in his mind's eye, better conditions. To describe these "better conditions," to conceive ideas that will translate those conditions into reality, and to succeed in the execution of those ideas requires skill and even genius. Where those ideas are in direct conflict with the existing order and there is an attempt nonetheless to execute them, we have revolution. It is those ideas that motivate men to actions which the revolutionary ideal comprises.

Generally, prior to the 18th century men sought to resurrect an ideal out of a retrievable past ("Freedom by God's blessing restored," read the 1651 Great Seal of England after the Puritan Revolution) or a discoverable new land. But with the advances in science in the 17th century and in industry in the 18th and 19th centuries, men could better control nature, and new ideas and technology enabled them to claim further rights. Concurrently, they sought those rights and a better world in their own time, rather than in a restored past or in a heavenly world beyond.

A recent book described why the Chinese Communist Party succeeded: "Agonizing as the national and social problems were, there would have been no revolution but for the existence of an organized revolutionary movement armed with a doctrine, long-term objectives, and a clear political strategy susceptible to common-sense adjustments in times of crisis."[9] It seems to us that this sentence is a fair description of the role of the revolutionary ideal. That ideal must describe a future close enough to people's wishes, values and peculiar historical situation for them to identify with it as well as dramatic enough to excite and encourage them to action by pointing to both the viciousness of the enemy and his weaknesses. In addition, the ideal must be far enough away in time to make them work at a maximum, but not so far that setbacks or temporary defeat will cause despair.

The revolutionary ideal encourages and perpetuates commitment. Without an ideal there will be little motivation for revolutionary groups to band together. An ideal must appeal to diverse groups faced with different exigencies and minimize the differences between them by emphasizing common characteristics (e.g., the native versus the foreigner in nationalist revolutions). Without an ideal, the energies of revolutionary groups will be dissipated with a minimal effect on the social and political order. Without an ideal, the chance for success is greatly reduced. This is not to imply that an ideal will ever be fully realized. Often it becomes prostituted—sometimes, ironically, in the name of the revolution. To weigh or analyze the differences between an ideal and the ultimate revolutionary settlement goes beyond the scope of this book. The reader should beware of glorifying revolution or its ideal without first examining the complete story. However successful the revolution may be, after it is politically and militarily over, its ideal tends to take on different dimensions. Ambiguities become more apparent and a conservative tone is stressed. The ideal must now act as a cloak for the new society, covering its imperfections.

When does the ideal of revolution become fused with the reality of revolution? When does the revolutionist become one with the actual revolution? One view holds that the true revolutionary spirit is grounded in an idealism which alone can inspire sacrifice. Another view is that when the revolutionary spirit is merged with a revolutionary situation the passivity ends and the action begins. We recognize the differences between the making of a revolution and the actual revolution itself, between the potential for revolution and the real revolution. The conception people have of revolution does not necessarily remain the same between the preparatory stages and the actual event. Revolution is like a piece of cloth; the many factions and groups that comprise it are like threads that criss-cross and are woven to make the whole fabric. The authors recognize that every revolution is composed of several revolutions, of revolutions in the revolution. We recognize that often the secondary revolutions and ideals help to mold and transform the primary one, but to discuss all these complex facets and the ideals of each would be an impossible task. Therefore, our concern here will be with what we consider the central and most crucial ideals and essential elements that give the whole fabric of revolution its general quality. What we have tried to do in the chapters that follow is to isolate or zero in on key factors and ideals of revolution.

As scholars, we must always be watchful so as not to permit contemporary values and biases from coloring interpretations of the past. This is an especially difficult task for students of such an emotional issue as revolution, whether we are sympathetic or hostile to it. Nevertheless, it seems clear that most revolutions have resulted from the consciousness of men and women who rec gnize that life on earth can and ought to be improved. With advanced technology the demand for change has intensified and we expect change to continue.

A sobering note, however, should be added to this expectation for change. Any complete examination of revolutions should reveal that they have invariably achieved less than was hoped for, and they have often defeated and devoured their own supporters. Revolutions have produced evils sometimes matching and even exceeding those against which they were directed. Hoping to cure human misery, revolutions unfortunately have often added to the history of man's inhumanity to man. But this is not to say that revolutions are evil and we should do all in our power to prevent them. Rather, it is hoped that by studying revolutions we may learn about them, about their benefits and their excesses. History seems to indicate that revolutions are inevitable as long as human potential is not fulfilled.

NOTES

[1] E. Rosenstock-Hussy, *Out of Revolution* (New York, 1938), pp. 14, 128.

[2] Louis Gottschalk, "Leon Trotsky and the Natural History of Revolutions," *The American Journal of Sociology*, XLIV, 3 (November 1938), 340.

[3] George Pettee, "The Process of Revolution," in Clifford T. Paynton and Robert Blackey (eds.), *Why Revolution?* (Cambridge, Mass., 1971), p. 35.

[4] Peter Amann, "Revolution: A Redefinition," in *ibid.*, p. 59.

[5] Louis Gottschalk, "Causes of Revolution," in *ibid.*, p. 103.

[6] Sigmund Neumann, "The International Civil War," in *ibid.*, p. 122.

[7] Charles Ellwood, "A Psychological Theory of Revolutions," in *ibid.*, p. 151.

[8] Eugene Kamenka, "The Concept of a Political Revolution," in Carl J. Friedrich (ed.), *Revolution (Nomos VIII)* (New York, 1966), p. 124.

[9] Lucien Bianco, *Origins of the Chinese Revolution, 1915–1949*, trans. by M. Bell (Stanford, 1971), p. 203.

2

Violence and Strategy in Revolution

I

In the popular mind, violence is associated with revolution probably more than any other characteristic. Many definitions of revolution include violence as an integral part of the revolutionary process. While our evidence demonstrates that significant changes have occurred in the concept of revolution and the revolutionary ideal in the 19th and 20th centuries, violence has virtually always been associated with revolutions. It is especially true in the modern revolutionary process. Mao Tse-tung, for example, said that anything can grow from the barrel of a gun.

Yet even violence in revolution appears to have undergone significant alterations. Revolutionary activity in the 19th century took place largely without recorded instruction and explanation on the conduct of violence. But in more recent times the use of violence has become

11

very systematic as revealed by the developing literature specifying explicitly how violence can and should be used to accomplish revolutionary goals. George Sorel, Frantz Fanon, Che Guevara and others have promoted and instructed in the use of violence. Handbooks on revolution explain in very precise detail the necessary procedures for the most effective utilization of violent tactics. In other words, the role of violence has become not only systematic, but overtly recognized as such.

Violence is sometimes thought to be a result of a distinctly rational approach to the redress of grievances. That is, even where extensive property damage does occur, crowds have shown a remarkable ability to select targets for destruction that are directly related to their grievances and enemies. For example, the violence of the anti-war movement helped to block President Johnson's re-election and to reduce President Nixon's options for de-escalation and U.S. troop withdrawal. Blacks in the U.S. have discovered that channels of access to those in authority were opened and resources and reforms were enacted and enforced, only after they took to the streets. This is in contrast to the view of those who have generally explained collective violence as a result of unplanned, spontaneous, uncontrolled reactions to some particularly provocative situation. We would contend, however, that the very recording and systematizing that has occurred, has had a significant impact not only on violence but on revolution itself. The entire process of revolution has become more of a planned affair. Men are more easily able, assuming they are clever enough, to direct it to serve their own ends. But this is not to overlook the fact that many other variables intervene and affect the course of revolution and revolutionary violence, often to the dismay of participants on both sides.

Although the study of the role of violence tends to be recent, at least at the sophisticated level we have today, violence has remained, as we have suggested, a consistent companion of revolution throughout the ages. Perhaps this is so because there exists no known rational alternative as effective as violence in accomplishing the goals of revolution. Violence can be seen as serving to forge and preserve national identities. As such it binds a society together in that conflict with an outgroup and increases the solidarity of the in-group. It helps to dramatize grievances and injustices, bring them to public attention and create a new social consciousness. Fanon, Sorel and others have described violence as a purifying force having a kind of mystical property. Violence, as they describe it, when applied to the revolutionary scene, may act as a unifying force for the revolutionary group binding its members together, making them willing to sacrifice everything for the cause. Does their view lead to a glorification of violence? We think not. These men accepted violence as essential only because they saw no other possible way in which the equality of the disadvantaged and deprived could be attained. We feel they would accept the view that violence can have no utility for the new man and his society; that what is needed in a new society emerging from revolution is the development of new motivations, social and economic incentives, as well as a progressive technology and revitalized institutions.

If the conduct and manipulation of violence is sometimes more systematic in today's revolutionary activity than it has been previously, it is not always so, even today. Variables intervene and render its control difficult, or in many cases completely impossible, by anyone, including the instigators of the violence or other current leaders in the situation. One important variable determining or influencing violence, and probably the extent of violence, is the degree to which each side (in a conflict situation) defines or perceives the other as different. These differences may occur at various levels, such as between races, social classes or ethnic groups. In these types of situations, groups or individuals may believe the others to be a *threat* to their own desires and goals. For example, conservatives and revolutionists see their interests in opposition, and as a threat to each other. Once a confrontation occurs between them, a climate of violence is almost certain to develop, irrespective of peaceful professions on both sides. On the revolutionists' side is often a "prophet" who nourishes a climate of violence to achieve a desired end. On the conservatives' side is the fear of being destroyed by opponents who are intent in wrecking what they do not understand and who refuse to accept traditional procedures.

This concept of in-group and out-group relationships has great significance for the understanding of revolution, including violent revolution. The tendency to define inter-group relations in terms of "we-they" is essentially a method of dehumanizing members of the opposition group. "Dehumanization" obviates the need to justify acts of violence. Killing an animal is generally not considered an act of violence, but good sport, as well as healthy, manly, and an honorable and even exciting pastime. Apparently man is able to dehumanize his fellow man in a similar way. The enemies then become defined as legitimate objects of attack, to be killed, mutilated, destroyed. Slaves, women, heathen, members of ethnic, religious and racial out-groups have been dehumanized to the point where they are regarded as chattels or beasts to be controlled by physical force.

The dehumanizing process, and therefore legitimizing of violent acts against people, appears to be not always successful at the psychological level. That is to say, although revolutionists and others may have little trouble, in terms of their conscience, when carrying out their collective acts of violence against property, they sometimes appear to experience ambiguity about the legitimacy of acts of violence against other human beings which may result in death or injury. The practice of giving warning when a building is to be bombed, as with the Irish Republican Army (I.R.A.) in Northern Ireland and England, may be regarded as an attempt to resolve the ambiguity of legitimacy of their violence. As a psychiatrist in Algeria, Fanon treated many French police officers suffering from the psychological effects of their treatment (e.g., beating, torturing and killing) of Algerians.

The psychological aspect of the phenomenon of the legitimacy of violence in revolutionary activity also enables the perpetrators of violence to change the boundaries of what and against whom violence is considered legitimate. That is, groups defined as friendly, useful, understanding and generally nonthreatening at one point in time, may not be so defined at a different point in time. If friendly, helpful or useful groups are suddenly seen as threatening in some way, they can become objects of attack. They become dehumanized and thus legitimately to be destroyed. So, while changes in boundaries of legitimacy of violence can occur as a result of objective changes of social conditions, they may also result from *perceived* changes (i.e., subjective changes in conditions). As Palestinian refugees, American blacks, students and French Canadian separatists perceived a growing ineffectiveness in obtaining their demands they began to expand and extend their definitions of the legitimacy of violence to include destruction of property, and later the political kidnapping and assassination of those formerly not considered legitimate objects for such attacks.

There are, of course, justifications for violence other than those dictated by dehumanization. Revolutionists convinced of and committed to their cause justify the means by the end. Although they may regret the nature of the means, which often include the most terrifying and brutal kinds of force, the means are believed to justify the end because the end result promises to determine the permanent fate of mankind, to release the great masses of oppressed humanity from their otherwise everlasting condition of slavery. Under these circumstances, the most savage means of treatment of fellow humans are justified. For the peasants or other insurgents who do the actual killing, burning and pillaging, who pull the trigger or thrust in the knife, duty and obedience to the leaders for the cause provide the justification. While such acts would ordinarily be unthinkable, a deep sense of duty and obedience propels them to commit acts of indescribable horror.

Closely related to duty and obedience, and means that justify the end, is the justification of extenuating circumstances. It is argued that the situation is abnormal, unique and extreme. Whatever is necessary must be done. Never before, for example, has oppression been so crushing, demoralizing, degrading and cruel. Whether in fact these things are true is not as important as whether people *believe* them to be true. Consequently, the skill of the leadership is a critical factor in determining the willing dedication of the followers and, therefore, eventually the success of the revolution. The rationalizations and explanations which typically characterize the confrontations and conflict relations between ethnic and racial groups in the U.S. and other countries provide numerous examples of the various legitimizing techniques.

Another approach to utilizing violence and carrying on conflict is essentially a technique, intentional or not, of controlling the conflict in a way that creates demoralization among the opposition. It is essentially the process of "non-recognition." That is, in a conflict situation, one group simply refuses to give any recognition to its opposition. In effect, they (the opposition) are treated as if they do not exist—are nonentities, and are therefore not worthy of human consideration. This produces an attitude similar to that held when dehumanization occurs as previously discussed. The opposition is rendered contemptible, completely and totally inferior. Beyond the very practical limitations this places on the non-recognized group is the tremendous emotional effect such treatment is bound to have. Che Guevara's failure in Bolivia (see Chapter 17) illustrates this explicitly. The peasants, those from whom he needed support, refused to recognize the validity of his movement in any appreciable or significant way. His band quickly became demoralized and disheartened. At the same time they were pursued as if they were common criminals to be eliminated.

Finally, with regard to violence in a revolutionary situation, the extent of the organization on each side can influence the degree of success. Where a group is well organized, the ability of the leadership to communicate with its followers is greatly facilitated. A feeling of confidence in the leadership is enhanced when followers are kept informed of major actions and goals. The uncertainty which results from lack of knowledge, is extremely detrimental to morale and the general functioning of the group. The uncertainty which results from a lack of information is sometimes the cause of panic or other forms of collective, chaotic behavior.

Other factors influence the extent to which violence will characterize revolutionary activity. If there is total failure to obtain redress of grievances by any other means, violence will inevitably occur. Authorities may initiate violence by firing upon demonstrators in an attempt to maintain control. The kind of weaponry available, such as access to firearms, can increase violence and its destructiveness. Violence may be sustained by focal points, which provide centers for planning, direction and encouragement for individuals and groups operating in outlying areas and smaller centers. In some cases, if social control is relaxed, instead of being interpreted as a sign of good faith and a more sympathetic approach toward the protesting groups, the latter may simply seize upon it as an opportunity to expand their plan of operation and publicize it as an indication of weakness of the authorities. The presence of communication networks, which typically exists among population groups who protest actions in one location, can spread to other seemingly uninvolved centers and groups. The speed of diffusion of social disturbances and also counter-mobilization by authorities is much more rapid today due to the sophisticated means of communication available to almost anyone.

Thus, it can be said that the role of violence is intimately associated with the revolutionary process. Today, perhaps more than previously, violence is systematically employed in revolutionary and protest activities. But even today, violence can, and often does, erupt in a spontaneous and uncontrolled manner. Or, where violence begins as a systematically applied attempt to gain a specific goal or end, it often mushrooms into a conflagration and runs completely out of control.

II

Closely related to violence, in any consideration of revolution, are the topics of leadership and strategy. While it may be possible to discern some changes from the 19th to the 20th century, most of the principles involving leadership and strategy tend to remain essentially similar from one period to another. Of course, there are exceptions to this general rule with some revolutionary tactics being more characteristic of the 20th century than the 19th. Many of the activities of the colorful agitators of the 1960's and even the 1970's will not be found in revolutionary activities of the previous century. The bizarre antics of Abbie Hoffman or Jerry Rubin, for example, must surely be confined to the most recent period of the 20th century. Their tactics of ceremonial profanations seem unique. The use of four-letter words, public fornication, incivility and the disruption of dialogue are efforts to shock and disrupt ceremonial formality, thereby bringing it into disdain and disrespect.

There is a second exception to the general rule that leadership and strategy of revolutions remain essentially the same from one period to the next. The refinement and sophistication of technology has permitted some new developments in strategies used by revolutionary leaders. Rapid communication and transportation, as well as the ability to reach the emotions and gain the support of the public at large via the mass media are readily available. Modern 20th century transportation has vastly increased the potential for destruction of property and mutilation of human beings—each of which can be accomplished at a distance. In this respect, it is far more impersonal, less personally disturbing, and more easily accomplished without the burden of humanitarian considerations. While these factors distinguish the 20th century, the basic characteristics, styles, goals and tactics of revolutionists remain essentially the same as in the 19th. Technology has merely enhanced some of these methods.

What follows is a consideration of some of the principles of leadership and strategy in revolution. We are fully aware that for every generalization made in this respect, exceptions are easily found. But generalizations are useful if they reveal some *pattern* of events or phenomena, in spite of the fact that exceptions exist.

The term "strategy" will be employed at a very general level. Using the concept this way we shall then attribute to it various sub-components; including leadership, ideology, organization and the use of terror and violence. At this general level, and applied to political revolution, strategy can be defined as the overall plan for the operation, implementation, direction and control of those factors which can be manipulated during a political revolution. All actions, policies, instruments and apparatus necessary for mounting a revolutionary attack can be considered strategy.

The essential nature of revolutionary leadership is made up of a corps or group of competent leaders supplemented by one charismatic leader. Many attempts have been made to define the concept of "charisma". Probably the classic meaning of the concept comes from the sociologist and political economist Max Weber. By charisma Weber appears to mean a special spiritual power or personal quality that gives an individual influence or authority over large numbers of people. The charismatic leader of a revolution is thus an individual with seemingly superhuman qualities and an ability to command a hypnotic hold over his followers. The charismatic leader of a revolution has the unique ability to communicate to his followers a sense of continuity between, on the one hand, himself and his mission and, on the other, their legendary heroes and missions.

Charisma is classified into two types. In one instance it is presumably a gift inherent in a person as a natural endowment. Work, training and study are not necessary for this type. In fact, it cannot be obtained by any of these means. The other type of charisma may be acquired by means which Weber calls artificial or extraordinary. Apparently it requires some unusual effort or unique training that is surrounded by special circumstances. However, even in the case of persons of the second type it can be developed only where the potential already exists, and will remain dormant unless some special effort is made or event takes place.

The charisma of a revolutionary leader is bound up with and, indeed, may even depend upon his becoming assimilated in the thought and feelings of a people and with their sacred figures, divine beings and heroes. So while it is commonly believed that leaders, particularly charismatic leaders, are unique, they are at the same time very much a part of the people. The differences appear in their having a clearer understanding of the factors involved regarding the expectations that people have. Having such an understanding, the leader is able to utilize it to advantage in meeting precisely the demands of his followers since he knows more clearly what they want and expect. At the same time, his knowledge of them enables him to introduce new ideas and thoughts that will be accepted and will not be offensive. In other words, he is able to mold, change and create different patterns of behavior that would not be possible for someone not keenly aware of the personal, social and cultural make-up of those he wishes to lead.

Interestingly, the charismatic leader need not himself always conform to the behavior patterns of his followers since, again, he understands more clearly those things he can do without being offensive. In fact, things he does which are not permitted the average person may sometimes enhance his leadership position. It is typical for people to admire and even glorify a revolutionary leader's eccentricities. But they must be "accepted" eccentricities. Followers would be repulsed and offended by the "wrong" eccentric behavior of a leader. The acceptance of a leader and his eccentricities calls for a special kind of strategy. That is, the leader manipulates a situation to give proper impressions and to create a particular image even though much of his skill in this respect is intuitive and subconscious.

In a revolution, charismatic leadership is particularly evident during its early stages. But as the revolution progresses, leadership tends to move in another direction. Organization, careful planning, deliberative action and systematization reduce or restrict the likelihood or utility of charismatic leadership. According to Weber charismatic authority may be said to exist only at the beginning of a revolutionary process. It cannot remain stable, but becomes either traditionalized or rationalized, or a combination of both. As soon as the position of authority is well established and, above all, as soon as control over large masses of people exists, it gives way to the forces of everyday routine.

Nevertheless, charisma is not completely eradicated or eliminated by the strictures of formalization and organization. Consider some of the presidents of the United States, or other world leaders who, while demonstrating statesmanship and/or administrative skill, have shown leadership of a charismatic quality. A recent example in the United States presidency, according to some, was President John F. Kennedy. Other world leaders who have exhibited charismatic leadership would include Gandhi, Hitler, Churchill, Roosevelt and DeGaulle. Howevever, there is little doubt that charisma is less characteristic of leadership in formal, structured positions. Fewer individual decisions are called for. Satisfactory leadership is much more a function of knowing the rules and regulations of the organization, or the system, and of merely seeing to it that these are carried out.

III

Essentially, then, the spontaneity and charismatic leadership in the early stages of revolution change progressively to the deliberative, planned action of other types of leaders typical of the later stages of the institutionalization and rigidification of a movement. These

changes, as well as the different characteristics of leadership at each
stage, can be illustrated by examining the customary progression of
revolution. Before the actual outbreak of revolution there is a preliminary stage in which the leader is typically an "agitator". He can also
be described as a "man of words." He may not be a great orator but
he is able to persuade people and cause them to think. It is he who
undermines existing institutions, familiarizes the masses with the idea
of radical change, and creates a receptivity to new ideas. The agitator,
or man of words, may be a priest, scribe, prophet, writer, artist, profes-
sor, student or intellectual. Under the influence of the agitator, people
stimulate each other to increasing action, although their action lacks
direction. They are susceptible to milling, a kind of circular interaction. At this point, a second stage is begun calling for a new type of
leader.

Without the arrival of the second type of revolutionary leader, the
disaffection engendered by the man of words would remain undirected
and the resulting disorders would be easily repressed. The leader at
this stage is best described as a "prophet" or a "fanatic." Such a
person feels set apart or called to leadership, endowed with a special
knowledge regarding the causes of unrest or discontent, causes which
the agitator, or man of words, has already brought to the attention of
the people. When the old order begins to crack, the fanatic attacks with
all his might and a reckless abandon in an attempt to blow the whole
hated present out of existence. By his words and actions he is able to
shove aside the man of words. But again, once the victory at this stage
has been won and the new order begins to crystallize, the fanatic
becomes an element of strain and disruption as he keeps groping for
extremes.

When the above stage has reached its apex a third or formal stage
of revolutionary development is ready to begin with the leadership in
the hands of a "practical man of action" or "reformer." The man of
action saves a movement from the dissention and recklessness of the
fanatic. The interaction typically takes the form of discussion and
deliberation. The efforts of the revolutionary leader are in the direction of consolidating the gains made during the violent phase. Leadership requires statesmanship. In other words, the leader is one who is
able to formulate policies that can be put into practice. He must be
skilled in estimating and evaluating social forces, in understanding and
championing beliefs and convictions of the people, and in proposing
workable programs to resolve the problems of the "new" society.

The appearance of the practical man of action usually marks the end of the most dynamic phase as the revolutionary movement crystallizes. Signs of organization, legalization and administration appear when the practical man of action takes control. In other words, this type of leader, reasonable and cool-headed, tends to institutionalize and sanctify the revolution. (By "institutionalize" is meant the creation of standards or norms for behavior. Patterns of action and routines become fixed. Traditions are established and adhered to. The spontaneity characteristic of the earlier phases of the revolution and its leadership has dwindled or receded. Spontaneity is suspect and duty is prized above devotion.) Instead of the general attacks and vague aims of the fanatic, the practical man attacks specific evils and develops a clearly defined program of action.

As the institutional or final stage advances in the direction of further legalization and organization of the revolutionary groups, there is increasing reliance on discussion and deliberation as the means for fixing policies and determining action. At this point the *new* society has been consummated. The collective excitement and charismatic leadership with which the movement began slips into the background. Eventually the leadership advances from the statesman to become the "administrator-executive" type. The policies formulated by the statesman must be carried out. It is in this respect that the last type of leadership plays its role. If the new society is to function satisfactorily there must be an effective administration of the programs and policies of the statesman.

Finally, a consideration of social class and educational background reveals another interesting facet of revolutionary leadership. Leaders are generally well educated, many having done at least some college work. Leadership or revolutionary movements come often from the intelligentsia. With respect to their class background, as distinct from their educational attainments, revolutionary leaders tend to be in the middle class, and this includes communist leaders. Both the lower and upper classes are generally underrepresented as leaders in political revolutions.

IV

Turning to those who are the followers of revolutionary leaders, we find similarities to the latter in backgrounds and ideas. For example, major support for Castro's revolution came from middle class Cubans who opposed Batista. Likewise, Che Guevara's men in Bolivia were generally not from worker or peasant backgrounds. Nonetheless, revolutionists may not be typical of the middle class. Unemployment and underemployment were exceptionally high among the anti-Batista rebels. Consequently, a great deal of rootlessness was characteristic among them and provided an important common denominator in bringing them together. Recruited from the underemployed and unemployed of the cities and countryside, as well as from university and high school students and from intellectuals, they had only their rootlessness to lose and a world to conquer.

In general, followers in times of revolution tend to be young, sometimes only in their early teens, more often in the late teens and early 20's. Young people are more willing and able to participate in revolutionary activity than people in their 30's and 40's. Young people have not developed ties of family responsibilities. Their decisions are less affected by having to consider anyone other than themselves. Their responsibilities on the whole are less than they are for the middle-aged. Followers appear to be younger than leaders who have been typically between the ages of 30 and 50. The greater age of some of the leaders can be accounted for if we can assume they were revolutionists while they were younger but, instead of dropping out at that time, as many do, they retained deep and lasting grievances against the system. Often they have maintained an independent life style which tends to nourish and sustain, over the years, their feelings of resentment and bitterness against the system. And, of course, the experience that goes with older age increases the likelihood of their becoming leaders if they have continued their revolutionary interests and activities.

The role of youth in revolutions as distinguished from that of older revolutionists is shown if we make a distinction between *originative* aspects of revolution, where the youth appear to play a predominate role, and *eliminative* aspects, where older revolutionists may predominate. The former can be defined as those which require social imagination to fashion new and novel institutions. The latter, on the other hand, are those which are confined to an eradication of institutions, or at least those features of institutions judged oppressive or exploitive. Thus, even in revolution, the conservatism of age *tends* to exert itself in terms of the type of revolution in which older followers are more likely to participate. Those aspects of revolution which require originality, creativeness and new ideas are not the areas in which the older revolutionists are prominent. Such aspects are characterized by youthful participants. Generally, the old revolutionists find their revolutionary ardor diminishing as they pass from youth to middle age. Older revolutionists are more interested in remodeling or renovating the already existing system, returning it to an earlier condition which existed before it became corrupted by injustice, inequality and decay. Young revolutionists, on the other hand, with little or no commitment to the present system prefer to follow leaders who wish to fashion a completly new and, hopefully, better one.

Why some middle class youth are serious enough about revolution to commit years of time and risk their lives has not been satisfactorily explained. There have been many reasons suggested to account for the revolutionary activity: the idealism of youth; an absence of serious and challenging demands in middle class environment; professors and teachers who are cynical and critical of the status quo; faulty or inadequate socialization. Unquestionably, the importance of the socialization process in creating revolutionists has not been fully explored, especially in terms of unfulfilled personality needs. Student revolutionists, though, have quite often described their parents as having withdrawn from them when needed the most or having simply been unavailable. Obviously, many other students have had similar emotional and socialization experiences without becoming revolutionists. But one cannot avoid being impressed by this evidence which indicates a pervasive impact from parental emotional abandonment on the lives of at least some revolutionary students. Perhaps a reasonable conclusion is that while faulty socialization would not necessarily cause someone to become a revolutionist, it might create a personality susceptible to a revolutionary appeal.

Our reference to the personality problems of these student revolutionists, and the indications that their socialization was faulty to some degree, might imply that revolutionists are emotionally unbalanced, neurotic and mentally disturbed. But this does not appear to be the case at all. Let us consider, for example, the influential role of students in the Chinese Revolution of 1911. The revolutionary ideas of the students appear to have developed as a result of their exposure to Western education, technology and ways of life. A series of edicts beginning in 1901 had commanded local governors to select capable men to go abroad and study in foreign universities. Most of them went to Japan, which had already made great progress toward modernization and industrialization. The students' foreign exposure and learning fired them with enthusiasm and ideas for their own country. When they returned home they brought their revolutionary ideas with them and formed the vanguard in the Revolution of 1911. The point is that these young people were not necessarily neurotic or emotionally disturbed. Furthermore, they were clearly not the dregs of society nor those given to crime and delinquency. On the contrary, they were the more promising of their country's young people. Consequently, despite the possibility that some revolutionists may have experienced inadequate or faulty socialization, they apparently made a reasonable adjustment to life, but would appear to have developed a propensity toward involvement in revolutionary movements and activity.

Various authors on the subject have also emphasized this same theme regarding the composition of revolutionary groups. The crowds in the French Revolution, for example, were recruited from the ordinary run of Parisian citizenry. They were not from the marginal levels of society. They appeared rather to be a representative cross section of the youth and adult males who had specific grievances. They were aggravated by a lack of adequate channels for their expression.

The involvement of ordinary citizens in the French Revolution also suggests that all revolutionists are not necessarily individuals with deep and profound ideological commitments. Even more than this, the ideas and slogans of revolutionary crowds often have little to do with lofty ideals, the rights of man, socialist ideas or novel and radical revolutionary doctrines. They tend to be drawn from the traditional culture of patriotism, anti-foreign sentiments and conservative antipathy toward the unregulated law of supply and demand that adversely affects wages and prices.

V

Turning more specifically to the role of ideology in revolution, the above is not to suggest in any way that an ideology is unimportant for revolution. Ideology may have very profound effects, directing people's behavior, changing their attitudes and beliefs. An ideology to which people are commited with great intensity can undermine confidence and morale in the existing social system and regime if its contents denounce existing ideas and institutions and articulate social ills, real and imagined. At the same time an ideology offers an alternative set of values and beliefs. That is, the role of ideology does not end with destroying old beliefs and values and substituting new ones. It can provide revolutionists with a sense of unity, solidarity, cohesion, zeal, commitment and devotion to revolutionary principles, including a willingness to make extreme sacrifices without the slightest hesitation. It serves, consequently, as an instrument to moblize the populace to mass action. It can even provide a cover for personal motives and ambitions that exist among revolutionary leaders.

Perhaps second to an ideology's function of undermining old ideas and providing alternatives is that of *justifying* and *rationalizing* the demands and actions of the revolutionists. Superficially, the role of justification may not seem of great significance. After all, are revolutionary leaders and their followers, who are bent upon destroying a system, really concerned about justifying to others what they are doing? It would appear that the social psychology of justification would play a rather unimportant role for men who have already determined with great commitment the goal they must achieve. We would argue that the contrary is true, that men are willing to engage in the most extreme acts of goodness, or evil, if psychologically they feel justified in doing so. By the same token, if they are not fully convinced of the absolute necessity of their actions, their commitment to and participation in the revolution, whether as a follower or as a leader, will be at best half-hearted. Intense feelings of guilt are bound to develop if one does not feel ones acts of violence and terror are fully necessary. In fact, the formerly enthusiastic revolutionist may become repelled by his own actions and thoughts under these circumstances. He may abandon the revolution completely, or even turn against it and eventually champion the other side.

Generally, those revolutions which are successful in overthrowing a regime and creating the more permanent changes in the structure of a society are those which have been guided by a clear, forceful and systematic ideology. They have been guided by a ideology which has grown from the thoughtful attention of a commited and creative person. The communist ideology of Marx and Lenin applied in both the Russian and Chinese Revolutions would be an example. However, the leadership of the Mexican, Bolivian and Cuban Revolutions has been described as lacking a carefully articulated doctrine compared to the Russian and Chinese cases. This absence is particularly apparent in the Mexican and Cuban Revolutions. Castro's pre-revolutionary statements can even be described as demonstrating doctrinal imprecision. Obviously, particularly in the case of Cuba, the lack of a carefully articulated doctrine, or ideology, did not prevent a successful revolution.

If ideology functions as we have outlined above, then how are the successes of the Mexican, Bolivian and Cuban Revolutions to be explained? There are three possible explanations. First, substitutes for the function of a comprehensive and systematic ideology may be provided by short-term goals and beliefs which are adequate to motivate and sustain a successful revolution, but which are disconnected and perhaps even inconsistent in terms of providing an overall framework for the building of a new, viable and coherent society. Second, although an ideology of revolution was not publicly articulated, the leaders, consciously or subconsciously, adhered to some basic principles and ideals for the revolution. In this case, although it may appear that the leader is merely following short-term goals and ideals, in fact, he is not. Instead, a long-term plan is guiding his behavior. This would appear to be particularly true in the case of the Cuban Revolution. Third, the singular presence of a dynamic charismatic leader can provide a partial substitute for a coherent ideology. Instead of commitment to an ideology as a coherent framework for action, there exists intense devotion to an individual charismatic leader. His wishes, expectations and demands are given complete and whole hearted obedience. All three of the possibilities may be valid explanations for success, one being characteristic of one revolutionary situation, the others being true in other revolutions.

Incidently, an element of strategy which logically follows the development of an ideology in revolution is the creation of sound organization for purposes of directing and *systematizing* it. Organization channels the energies of the populace toward a more effective realization of revolutionary objectives. Organization welds millions of *individual* efforts into concerted, purposeful action. Unless the revolutionists develop a strong organization, their efforts will soon be dissipated in a series of disconnected actions that have no coherence.

VI

We have suggested earlier in this chapter that commonly associated with revolution is terror and violence. It is probably true that the average person thinks of these phenomena either as effects of revolution rather than as deliberately contrived strategy or as techniques of revolutionary strategists to create particular effects or accomplish specific ends in order to enhance the possibility of success. But, the leaders may be able, through collective violence, to publicize and advertize the revolution, to make it known as widely as possible. This brings the movement to the attention of others who are discontented, alienated and resentful of the current regime; such people could potentially be a sizable proportion of the population and therefore crucial to the conduct and progress of a revolutionary movement. Even the knowledge that others share similar feelings of discontent, alienation and resentment encourages those not yet involved to act in a rebellious and belligerent fashion, and to promote more openly the new doctrine, and thus the revolution.

Violence can also be utilized to crystallize various factions in the conflict because it tends to polarize and create clear-cut issues and, consequently, to line up sides. The likelihood of confrontation is therefore greatly increased and, of course, a confrontation between sides is necessary if a revolution is to occur. At the same time, terror and violence can be employed to build morale and confidence among the revolutionary leadership and the inner core of followers. Its effects demonstrate that the newly emerging revolutionists can be a potent force, a significant threat, and that they can gain a kind of recognition, out of fear to be sure, but recognition nevertheless. As discussed above, the gaining of recognition acts as a powerful force toward encouragement of any previously unrecognized group.

The fear and anxiety created by the violence of the revolutionists, in addition to providing recognition for them, puts them in a psychologically advantageous position. Resistance by the uncommitted as well as those people favorable to the old regime is considerably reduced or even entirely eliminated. Generally, people wish to avoid confrontation; and fear of the aggressor encourages this tendency especially in those who have families. For the revolutionist, creating fear among those who have not committed themselves to the revolutionary cause provides a sense of power, domination, mastery and control which is an encouragement to commit further acts of aggression and violence.

The violent acts of the revolutionists will sooner or later bring reprisals from government controlled forces. If the revolutionary aggressors can manage to escape or avoid serious casualties and other losses, the attacks by government forces may actually benefit the revolutionists. Governmental terror provoked by the rebels tends to be indiscriminate and repressive, or if nothing else, is usually interpreted that way. If government forces are not able effectively to control the rebels by counter-violence, in spite of the obviously repressive measures used, and if the rebels are able to continue their selective violence, people will begin to lose faith and confidence in the government's ability to control the situation. At this point, people will begin to turn away from the government and repressive measures will encourage sympathy for the rebel forces. Additionally, the government's tactics will have begun to make it appear ludicrous and clumsy. Thus, the strategy of creating violence and terror among the people can provide conditions which will gain revolutionary forces further support.

The degree to which revolutionary leaders can depend upon support from sources outside their own country is also an important strategy consideration. Knowledgeable leaders will often attempt to gain favorable support from these sources. Outside sources may represent countries and interests on an international scale, or may be simply one other country which has an interest in the struggle of the revolutionary forces. Of course, it is not only the insurgents, but the incumbents as well, who are competing for international support in one form or another, including moral support, funds, supplies, advisement and possibly a foreign base of operation. Inherent in international relations is a climate of world opinion which may or may not help either insurgents or incumbents, For example, international opinion may simply seek conciliation between the two sides without a commitment to either one. If international opinion is on the side of the protagonists, the help outside countries may give to the side being favored can come in several forms. These countries may provide not only men and material, but very crucial emotional encouragement and support in the form of favorable propaganda.

Important to the success of any attempt at revolution is a leadership capable of making the most effective use of the various areas of strategy. Some leaders may be very successful in manipulating the international situation to their advantage, but are very ineffective in directing the use of violence and terror, or in developing sound organization, or adhering to a consistent, well-developed ideology. Consequently, when there is available leadership capable of meeting all the various strategy needs, the probability of a successful revolution is much higher. Numerous other contingent factors still play an important role as determinants of revolutionary success. Some of these factors and their role in revolution are considered elsewhere in this volume.

3

Social Institutions and Revolution

I

Some of the most fundamental effects associated with revolutionary activity are those that act upon the major institutions of society. Some have argued that the resulting changes in institutions tend, in the long run, to be minor or temporary, and that under a new revolutionary regime old institutions and forms reappear in new guises, not always easily recognized but performing essentially the same functions as before. For example, revolutionists have sometimes attacked or attempted to eliminate the family. Communism has proposed such an elimination, including all the associated bourgeois trappings, but it appears that the family has remained or returned, in Russia at least, as robust as ever. The family has probably changed more as a result of gradual, evolutionary processes than revolution. Nonetheless, no one would deny that massive alterations have resulted in major institutions as a result of the great revolutions of both the 19th and 20th centuries.

Still, the major institutions of a society are remarkable for their stability. There are undoubtedly a number of factors that account for this in the midst of a good deal of social discontent by sizeable proportions of the population. (Unquestionably, when the discontent is sufficiently high among enough of the population, institutional stability is in jeopardy.) Part of the explanation of institutional stability, or perhaps inertia, is related to the role of psychological and sociological factors associated with the social phenomenon of "ritual." Ritual is an important social process which aids social life in a strong strain toward humanizing power and dampening extreme oscillations of change. Ritual action is a redressive, reconciling means of reaffirming loyalties. It tests and changes loyalties, or offers new ones to replace the old. But these are expressed in a kind of:

> muted symbolic display with a symbolic response which changes attitudes and values without major and unlimited conflict, and without the necessity for total and simultaneous involvement in the new value systems by old members of the society. The potential for disruptive revolutionary change by escalated violence and internal warfare is always present, unpredictable in its outcome, costly in its logistics, dangerous in the secondary conflicts which may be engendered; ritual controls and moderates these undesirable tendencies.[1]

Ritual, then, performs two important sociological and psychological roles. Sociologically, it helps protect the existing social system from extreme, violent upheavals, such as revolutions that may disrupt it so completely as to destroy it. Psychologically, ritual acts to reaffirm the individual's old loyalties or provide new ones and to permit changes in attitudes and values without major personal crises. Many of the tactics of present day extremists are in the nature of ritual or ceremonial profanations, as in the use of four-letter words, public fornication, incivility and the disruption of dialogue. Their behavior has been ritualized into a highly conventionalized performance. In other words, the numerous examples of rebellious and revolutionary activity, especially by youth during the decade of the 1960's may have represented, to a considerable extent, ritualistic behavior rather than exclusively an outright revolutionary attack against the society's institutions. As ritualistic behavior it may, therefore, have provided the important social function, as we have suggested in the previous chapter, of actually protecting the social system from much more violent upheavals of a revolutionary nature. Activity of this sort permits, and even forces social change; but it is the kind of change which is gradual or moderate enough not to be excessively disruptive either to the society as a whole or to its members as individuals. A moderate rate of change may in fact act to strengthen society by providing both a sense of progress and an incentive for society's members to introspect and evaluate themselves and their society.

Nevertheless, ritual of the sort we have been describing can lead individuals into inappropriate and self-destructive behavior in which ritual and real action are confused. For example, young radicals used a rhetoric of provocation and violence, at times of the most extreme kind. When the acts that implemented rhetoric led to real confrontations with the police, involving tear gas, split heads and arrests, the radicals experienced and expressed a sense of having been betrayed. People were not supposed to have taken their actions and rhetoric so seriously; they were not supposed to have responded with violence. The ritual was performed as a kind of metaphor and symbolic warning. The impression conveyed was that the treatment they received was grossly unfair; specifically, they objected to the tendency of the police to take them literally and respond to their provocations with terror and violence. The uses of ritual are thus ambiguous, performing a number of needful social functions, but they are also subject to abuse, dysfunction and excess.

A second important factor in the stability of institutions in the midst of social instability, and even revolutionary violence, is the extent to which the state system is able to integrate into the power structure at least those who are self-conscious, organized, interested and capable of exercising power. To a significant degree, this happened to the youth cult in America. It was co-opted in the sense that many people came to wear long hair, sideburns, beards and "mod" clothing. Even corporation executives and housewives of suburbia adopted styles formerly the exclusive garb of hippies and flower children. Abbie Hoffman franchised a shirt manufacturer to produce his American flag shirt. Jerry Rubin granted a sweatshirt manufacturer the right to use the title of his book, *(Do it!)*.

Other factors affected the youth movement. It was not in any significant sense a unified constituency. Irrational forms of extremism, counterproductive, unpolitical, and self-destructive tactics were evident. After two years of success the Students for a Democratic Society (SDS) dissolved into a melange of factionalism and futility. The aroused giant of American college youth fell into disarray. Guerrilla tactics, bombing, vandalism and hit-and-run methods often alienated uncommitted youth, and in the end provided little toward the realization of concrete revolutionary-type goals. All these actions became, to a large extent, merely cathartic experiences for the participants. In other words, the potentially powerful youth movement in the United States became incorporated within the system, its revolutionary potential incapacitated by the integrating forces of the larger society. While such an observation may be called a failure of the youth movement, it also may demonstrate the virility and viability of the larger American culture and its institutions. That is, they are flexible enough to incorporate and to integrate diverse and contradictory elements within the whole, the institutions remaining relatively unaffected.

II

In the U.S. and a number of other nations, a grave, eternally explosive and potentially violent situation which has haunted society is the problem associated with racial and ethnic minorities. If one factor stands out, providing a potential for the development of a major upheaval it would appear to be the discontent experienced and expressed among minority groups. While some integration in America has taken place, the racial question still stands clearly polarized, with white society poised on one side and minority society on the other. Although American institutions, including the educational and economic sectors, have formally changed their stance against discrimination, there exists within the informal structure of white society a massive unwillingness, or at least ambivalence toward full and equal acceptance of minority Americans. Within minority groups there exists a deep reservoir of anger, hatred and emotional complexes of inferiority. For example, the attempts of blacks to succeed personally and socially in the white man's world are often interpreted merely as attempts to overcome inferiority feelings and to prove to themselves and to others that they are as good as the white world. When blacks move into white neighborhoods, whites still move out. The race problem thus appears to be the Achilles heel in the stability of institutions of modern America and other nations struggling with a similar crisis.

In general, what happens where racial differences exist is an increasing unwillingness by the minority group to accept an inferior status and the resulting disadvantages. Although racial differences per se have no intrinsic significance, where racial consciousness becomes acute racial identity becomes the basis for political organization and, potentially at least, a source of revolution. Interestingly enough, however, the major theoretical ideas on revolution are based mostly upon factors of economics and social class. Insufficient attention has been paid to race and ethnic differences as variables in the revolutionary process. Part of the reason for this is undoubtedly the extreme difficulty of trying to establish the significance of the race variable in revolutions.

Most contemporary theories of revolution in the West and even in places in the Third World have been derived from an analysis of conflict between social classes in *racially homogeneous* societies and probably would not apply to situations of revolutionary struggle between groups of differing races. (For an exception—of sorts—see Chapter 19.) However,

> If racial divisions and class divisions coincided, so that, for example, the whites in a particular society were all members of the bourgeoisie and the blacks were all members of the proletariat or peasants, some insight into the relative significance of race or class could no doubt be derived from a comparison of revolutions in such societies with revolutionary struggle between social classes in racially homogeneous societies.[2]

The problem, of course, is that race and class are not distinct entities in any society, but always overlap each other.

III

Looking beyond these considerations to other factors with revolutionary significance and directly related to massive changes in the basic institutional structure of a society, let us consider a few psychological factors. The full import of the latter has not yet been determined in terms of their significance for revolutionary behavior and, consequently, their relationship to the stability of a society's basic institutions. But one may ask, for example, what psychological factors motivate a person to become an agitator in a revolutionary movement? What is it psychologically that moves individuals to participate in activity which has the potential to transform so profoundly the entire social and institutional structure of their own society? It is not necessarily the case that a person so motivated, is only and primarily concerned with ideological principles, nor even that he has lost all faith in the basic institutions of society to meet people's needs. The psychological needs of the agitator's own personality could be a powerful motivating force for him to play such a role. In other words, the personal satisfaction gained by the agitator may, in some instances, be a principal reason, or at least an important reason for why he agitates. Writers on social movements, such as Eric Hoffer, have described in detail a variety of psychological needs believed to be fulfilled by active involvement in a social movement (e.g., desire for attention, release of frustrations, expression of aggression).

That filling some inner psychological need is important for some revolutionary leaders is supported by the nature of the response of the successful agitator. It is generally not the type of emotional involvement where he is swept into the action of the crowd and loses control. Agitators, as a rule, do not reach the scene and act immediately on the first impulse they feel. Nor are they merely swept along by the actions and emotions of others in the crowd. Rather, they appraise the situation, weighing the facts with potential gains and losses, before deciding what to do.

Further, we would suggest that one function for the agitator is the provision of a cathartic experience. That is, tensions, feelings of hostility and frustration, for example, can be relieved by some form of active and physically aggressive behavioral expression. If this is true, then expressions of revolutionary violence could provide many with a fulfilling psychological experience and, consequently, a powerful motivating force for participation in violent activity.

But consider for a moment, a contrasting point of view regarding the function of expressive behavior. That is, expressive, aggressive activity may actually increase rather than relieve an individual's tensions, hostility and frustration. The implication of such a result would simply be that violence begets more violence. A reconciliation of the two views is conceivable if we consider the possibility that two people may experience similar emotional satisfaction while expressing themselves in very different, even opposite ways. In any case, there are important implications in attributing to psychological variables the role of a motivating force so great it will cause an individual not only to abandon, but actually attack the very foundations of his own society. A whole dimension in the study of revolutionary action and ideals remains almost totally unexplored. One implication for the development of revolutionary ideas is the need to incorporate within economic and class explanations of revolutions, important socio-psychological factors; this work has yet to be done.

The desire to destroy and recreate one's own society in revolutionary activity, as related to psychological variables, can be examined from another point of view. Many people in society grow up developing severe personality problems and unusual needs. Consider, for example, the psychological damage that results from social and psychological deprivation to people who are members of various subcultural groups, such as prisoners, refugees, ethnic and racial minorities, and those who live in extreme poverty. Their discontent, bitterness, feelings of defeat, futility and other unhealthy attitudes toward life are bound to have serious consequences. Their feelings can be expected to lead to such things as rejection of society's structure, mores and values, or to violent acts against society, including attempts to alter it by revolution.

In other words, psychological disability or pathology is promoted and sustained by the very nature of the society's often racist and rigidly stratified institutional structure. In cultures where the conditions described above exist to an extreme degree, the stability of the institutions themselves will sooner or later be affected, providing further potential for revolutionary action. The psychological deprivation and pathology of individuals may be a minor factor in creating revolution, but if other problems exist within a society and its institutions, the combination of factors will be sufficient to cause serious problems. Unfortunately, societies tend to be very complacent regarding this problem. Usually, of course, there would be many signs long before the final hour arrived. But people have a great propensity to ignore such things if they contribute to their personal disadvantage and discomfort.

Another factor which involves psychological considerations and the stability of a society and its institutions is that of "legitimacy." Within any social group large or small there is an underlying question: to what extent or degree are the customs, norms and mores (i.e., its institutions) perceived as legitimate? Speaking of political systems, for example, the more legitimate they are perceived to be the less likely citizens are willing to attack them via revolution or rebellion. While the above reference is specifically to political systems, we believe the point can be generalized to other basic institutions as well. Essentially we are arguing that people are unlikely to rise in revolutionary violence against the social system under which they live if they perceive it as legitimate, and not imposed upon them from outside. Even if significant rigidity, corruption and injustice are evident, revolution may not occur. To illustrate how important it is to "believe in" or "perceive" social processes and structures as legitimate consider the following. Philanthropic organizations or altruistic nations often fail to understand why their generosity to deprived groups or nations is not appreciated. We suggest the reason is that the legitimacy of many such efforts is not accepted. The legitimacy factor is especially important when the elements are imposed, rather than simply being made available with no strings attached. The latter is very seldom the case when a government is the source of the philanthropy. In other words, it is not true philanthropy.

Another example where legitimacy is a particular issue occurs where one culture attempts to force upon another, weaker one, a life style (e.g., family) very different from that traditionally characteristic of the latter. A similar effect has resulted where leaders of the power structure of a group have attempted to impose some basic institutional change upon their followers that has not originated among the latter or is perceived as being imposed upon them. The psychological-sociological dimension of legitimacy of the institutional structure, then, is a key variable in the degree to which people accept the system under which they live. The degree to which they accept the system as legitimate will directly affect the stability of the society's institutions and the likelihood that internal resistance and revolutionary conflict will sometime result in the society.

Closely related to the problem of legitimacy is that of "relative deprivation." The relative deprivation hypothesis holds that when improvement of the social conditions for one group is slower than improvement for other groups, dissatisfaction is created. In either case, (i.e., legitimacy or deprivation) the lack of confidence in the society's institutions results in dissatisfaction and disillusionment with those institutions. Eventually, as dissatisfaction increases, open resistance and rebellion against the institutional structures and the personnel identified with those structures may begin. The reasons for the lack of confidence in the institutions are quite different for the legitimacy problem than for relative deprivation. The legitimacy problem is often a cause of lack of confidence because some institutional structure has been imposed from outside, as when one nation invades and conquers another. The conquerors are very likely to be either ill-informed or uncaring regarding the conquered people's needs and wants. In the case of relative deprivation the source of lack of confidence is different. People may no longer be content with what satisfied them in the past. In this case, they now compare themselves with other groups, societies, peoples, nations. And if, relatively speaking, they are less well off than their comparison group, dissatisfaction can become intense.

We believe there is enough evidence regarding relative deprivation to suggest that the process leading to revolutions is in many instances very much aggravated by, or is a function of this social-psychological phenomenon. Ordinarily, people do accept their lot in life with reasonable equanimity even though great inequities exist between classes. However, when people begin to see or believe themselves to be greatly disadvantaged compared with others who belong to a similar social and economic class (i.e., the development of a class consciousness), intense dissatisfaction and hostility toward those they feel are responsible begins to arise. It appears that passive toleration even in the most unhappy circumstances is typical, unless some group with whom the disadvantaged can compare themselves is available. In other words, toleration of an inferior position becomes impossible for people to accept without some violent action against it, when they see others of their class better off than themselves. It should be borne in mind that the comparison group is not always the obvious one.

The newly emerging Third World nations are now being presented with many comparison groups, such as the new nations which have already attained statehood and independence. An important function of the comparison group for the disadvantaged is to provide new goals, aspirations, needs and desires, all of which may be partially or entirely unattainable under their present system. It is the discrepancies that they perceive between the new goals and aspirations, and the prospect for attaining them, that create the feeling of intense dissatisfaction.

The availability of meaningful comparison groups is probably a more significant factor as a source of dissatisfaction and, consequently, serves as a greater source of revolt and revolution in the present century than at any time in the past; mostly because modern-day communication and transportation systems make accessible for comparison all sorts of other groups both distant and near. Therefore, the institutions of a society may suddenly appear to its citizens as less than adequate, clearly inferior and even degenerative in various ways, when instead the people are now in a position to compare their own situation with another which is obviously superior economically, politically, technologically, as well as in other ways.

NOTES

[1] H. L. Nieburg, "Agonistics: Rituals of Conflict," in James F. Short, Jr., and Marvin E. Wolfgang (eds.), *Collective Violence* (Chicago, 1972), pp. 86f.

[2] Leo Kuper, "Theories of Revolution and Race Relations," *Comparative Studies in Society and History,* 13, 1 (January 1971), p. 90.

4

Social-Psychological Factors
in Explanations of Revolution

I

Attempts to identify one variable as the factor which creates instability, and eventually, revolution is unrealistic and denies abundant evidence to the contrary. Even theories of revolution which attempt to identify more than a single variable, perhaps as many as two or three major ingredients, simply cannot provide an adequate explanation of this awesome phenomenon. It seems obvious that many factors are involved and, typically, not the same ones in each revolution. That is, revolutions differ from each other and, therefore, the factors involved differ as well. It is possible that a few factors can be consistently found in *all* revolutions, but no one as yet has been able to demonstrate this satisfactorily. Partly, of course, this problem is a result of the fact that revolution itself is variously defined. Put another way, differing cataclysmic events are labeled with the single concept, "revolution" (see Chapter 1).

Beyond the Marxian dialectical scheme and its attribution of revolution to materialistic factors (i.e., the absence of control of the means of production by the proletariat and the class struggle resulting therefrom) numerous other factors have been suggested to explain revolution. Most important among these are the views associated with socio-psychological factors.

The inclusion of socio-psychological variables as casual elements in theoretical discussions on revolution is an emphasis associated more with the 20th century than with the 19th century. Moreover, the preconditions, those factors which precede revolution, can also be analyzed in socio-psychological terms. For example, preconditions of revolution exist when the basic institutional and organizational structure of society develops serious instabilities and when there is a decline in consensus between the government and the governed. A stable society, by contrast, is one in which consensus or understanding does exist, engendered by a homogeneous political culture. Not only is there a consensus between the government and the governed concerning the broad goals of society, but there exists as well a consensus among groups within the governed. Available also are the means to implement the attainment of the consensus. Put differently, there exists in a stable society uncoerced adherence to a mutually accepted set of procedures to implement decision-making. These procedures are deemed necessary and appropriate by both the government and the governed for order, progress and general well-being, for the resolution of issues and conflicts arising out of problems concerning the public at large, and for the elicitation and promotion of societal goals.

Where people are economically depressed, the ability to implement by action the decisions about goals is strictly limited by the economic, social and psychological means available. In such a situation there needs to be a further understanding between the government and the governed if the stability of society is to be maintained. Otherwise consensus declines, and what will likely happen is the development of tensions. Tension indicates insecurity and deterioration in the relationships between the government and the governed, and the development of a state of political instability. Such a state may progress to a serious precondition for revolution. This explanation of conditions preceding revolution explicitly includes socio-psychological elements, specifically the conditions of "tension," "consensus," and "stability."

One cannot help but be impressed, or perhaps distressed by the apparent contradictions among the various ideas about revolution.

With Tocqueville and Marx, for example, we can choose between two differing views as to when and why revolution is likely to occur: the former saw social and economic progress as the key, while for the latter it was social and economic regression. In this instance, however, rather than reject either point of view we may juxtapose them in a particular time sequence. Thus, revolutions would be most likely to occur when a prolonged period of objective economic and social development is followed by a short period of sharp reversal. From a socio-psychological perspective the implication is that previously learned behavior can be extinguished by non-reward or by frustrating learned expectations —thus encouraging people's hopes for the future and then dashing them. Those who have never had future hopes and aspirations are probably able to accept psychologically the state of non-reward more easily than those whose hopes have received some stimulation, some encouragement, but were then denied. Consequently, in nations where poverty, subjugation and discrimination are endemic, and where hope for improvement is extremely remote, revolutionary ideas among the people tend to be dormant, or just do not occur at all. And the view that violence and/or revolution is an expression of dissatisfactions felt by populations experiencing hardship after periods of relative well-being cannot account for every instance of revolution. Often, collective violence and revolution are simply the result of struggles for power. This would be particularly true in revolutions from the top, where two factions, the government and a contending elite, meet in confrontation.

In other instances, a revolution may begin when previously acquiescent citizens are faced with strictly incompatible demands from the government and some other authority, such as a revolutionary force. In this particular situation, people are likely to experience intense role conflict, which will be extremely uncomfortable, and even traumatic if the conflicting expectations of the two authorities continue unabated and no reasonable solution is available to them. In order to alleviate the discomfort, or dissonance, people may be forced to take sides and the struggle continues until only one authority remains. Although a determination of what factors are responsible for the choice of one authority over the other goes beyond the purview of this book, they would include the following: the relative power of the two contending authorities and the legitimacy, justice and persuasiveness of their demands.

Socio-psychological factors can also be seen in an explanation of the

formation of sectarian groups and organizations that are of a revolutionary nature. People who share intense feelings of dissatisfaction and
alienation are likely to unite in an unfocused quest for groups whose
codes are responsive to their particular needs. These are people in
social positions where they feel effectively shut off from the legitimate
expression of their needs. Often they show an inclination to achieve
recognition in sectarian associations. For example, the improverished
and those of the lowest social status or class are susceptible to mem-
bership in small and exclusive utopian sects, some of which are, or
become, revolutionary in nature. People with an ethnic minority status
will also have an impetus for sectarian associations. Other people of
marginal status, such as "alienated" intellectuals, may lack the audience they crave and thus seek sectarian associations. When the attention of some of these sectarian groups turns toward political concerns,
they become the catalysts for revolution.

Thus, four categories of people most prone to seek sectarian and
radical solutions in opposition to conventional and traditional mores
are: (1) socially inferior classes severely deprived of goods valued by
society; (2) pre-adolescents and adolescents whose developing interests go unrecognized in conventional adult society; (3) minority
groups and other "marginals" who are not fully accepted; and (4) the
rootless intelligentsia frustrated in their creative aspirations.

In another instance a psychoanalytic principle is implicit in an explanation of the occurrence of *underground* revolutionary movements.
The principle holds that some kind of expression of people's needs will
inevitably take place, but if open expression of those needs is denied,
a clandestine expression will result. To begin with, at a general level,
the ingredients conducive to subversive formations of a revolutionary
nature appear to be the existence of despotic regimes where there
exists a rigid class structure and extreme conventionality. Tocqueville
asserted in *L'Ancien Regime* that revolutions are less apt to occur in
free societies than in despotisms. He felt that communication among
groups was a significant factor in either avoiding major subversive
movements or making their detection by the current regime easier.

Since despotic regimes tend to be repressive, groups of a sectarian
nature may be able only to form and operate underground. An underground operation can be a potent force toward creating a climate of
revolutionary fervor among the population at large. Such groups gain
sympathy because of the oppression and discrimination they experience at the hands of the regime, and their total dedication to their

cause challenges others. Furthermore, because of its secrecy, the now clandestine association enjoys a measure of license. There develops quickly an understanding or agreement among the members of the acceptability of transgressing normal conventions if they are reasonably assured they will not be detected. Thus, a consensus within the group to carry on subversive activities easily develops. Since "free societies" permit greater freedom of communication they are in a better position to avoid the problems of alienation and the formation of subversive groups.

Three means by which a clandestine sectarian group can encourage efforts toward radical, revolutionary social reconstruction are the following: (1) They may offer psychological support for the formation of doctrines or ideologies of a political nature and for the encouragement of practices which violate rigid and unpopular norms or laws. (2) Ideologies and doctrines may be nurtured in the shelter of the group to the point where they will, sooner or later, be presented openly. (3) Through agitation and proselytizing the message may eventually spread to a larger following from which may develop social movements that challenge the current political regime.

II

Closely related to the above ideas and explanations of revolutionary phenomena is the use of descriptive *typologies* of revolution which also employ socio-psychological elements, and which provide an explanatory aspect to the concept of revolution. In some cases typologies take revolutions in their entirety and classify them as belonging to one or another of several distinct types. In other cases the typologies simply analyze a revolution into various stages or parts. As in the explanatory expositions which were discussed above, the differences in and among the typologies and their various categories and criteria were numerous. Furthermore, any particular revolution will not fit perfectly into any one typology and each in turn has been critized for inaccuracies, contradictions and other limitations. Nevertheless, typologies have proven helpful in making comparisons of revolutions and in making the examination of various stages of revolution a more objective process.

Typologies dealing with the process of revolution have been created by a variety of theorists including Crane Brinton, Lyford P. Edwards, Rex Hopper and Pitirm Sorokin. The natural history model provides an illustration of one typology which analyzes and categorizes the various stages of revolution. But having discussed in Chapter 2 aspects of the stages of a natural history model in some detail, only a brief outline of it is presented here for a reference. The natural history model would generally show a building up to a climax of violence, and then a systematic decrescendo or homeostatic return to an earlier equilibrium. Four stages of the revolutionary process are identified by Rex Hopper. First occurs the preliminary stage of mass (individual) excitement and unrest when people engage in "milling" or circular interaction similar to the milling of a herd of cattle before a storm or as a result of some other disturbance or excitement. Second is the popular stage of crowd (collective) excitement and unrest. During this stage excitement, unrest and various negative reactions toward the current system spread rapidly. The allegiance of the intellectuals shifts to the revolutionary forces as a result of loss of faith in the leaders of the government. The third, or formal stage, is marked by the formulation of issues and formation of publics. There is discussion, deliberation of issues and formulation of policies to deal with the issues as they are perceived by the revolutionary leadership. This begins a stage of reduced spontaneity and collective excitement with the begining of formal organization and structured policies. The fourth stage is labeled the institutional stage of legalization and societal organization in which there is increasing reliance on discussion and deliberation as a means of fixing policies and determining action.

What has thus been summarized is the entire revolutionary process by which mass behavior, originating in unrest and discontent, generated by institutional inadequacies, inefficiencies and corruption, develops into a revolutionary movement and ends in a new society with its own institutional rigidities and inflexibilities. Socio-psychological elements in the typology are readily seen in the references to "mass excitement," "milling," "crowd excitement," "negative reactions," "deliberation of issues," and so on. These terms, and the principles associated with them, are theoretically associated with the social-psychology of collective behavior. The implications for revolutionary action are that man, under certain social and emotional conditions, tends to respond in a particular way. When faced with an unstructured social problem, people's responses tend to be undirected, diffuse and unthinking. They are moved by the general climate of emotional excitement. But gradually intellectual equilibrium returns and people's rational processes begin to structure, organize and formalize the previously spontaneous elements of the revolutionary situation. As the revolutionary movement ends, habits and traditions reassert themselves and gradually take over.

The natural history model of revolution is subject to criticism as a description of the revolutionary process. For example, a revolution, as is true of most other social events, is more accurately described as a process rather than a series of stages. One can also question the logic in deriving the stages, their slight vulnerability to proof, and their limited fruitfulness for further investigation. There is also a supposition, in the natural history model, of a single state of mind or shared tension being experienced by more or less the entire population. But in the Paris Revolution of 1830, a coalition of groups with differing objectives was at work in the early days of the revolution and only a small segment of the French populace participated. The "single state of mind" is contradicted by the continuous shifting of the form, focus and intensity of conflicts as the struggle for power proceeds.

Another typology is the six-fold one of Chalmers Johnson. (1) The "jacquerie" aims at the restoration of legitimate government within a regime rather than at engineering new structural changes in the social system. A jacquerie is usually carried out in the name of an idealized leader or ruling body against the unworthy or illegitimate ruler. A sense of community or nationalism and a commitment to the system are not challenged. It is questionable whether jacqueries are actual revolutions and not mere rebellions. (2) Another questionable type of revolution is one Johnson calls "millenarian rebellions." Their ideology identifies its followers as the beneficiaries of an imminent, even supernatural, complete transformation of the social order that will ring out the old status quo and ring in the new, the faithful, in a veritable paradise. Millenarian movements, as we discuss in Chapter 6, should not be dismissed as merely utopian since they seek an immediate change in the system. (3) "Anarchistic rebellions" occur in response to conditions in society created when major changes have already been made in order to relieve societal problems. Anarchists do not support the changes but wish to reverse them. They revolt for a future that derives from an idealized past. Not only do 19th century European anarchistic attempts at revolution fit into this category, but so does the American Civil War. (4) What Johnson classifies as "jacobin communist revolutions" are those attempts at the replacement of an old order with a new one that is more "enlightened" and "democratic," one that will, for example, transform "subjects" into "citizens" or "comrades."

The French Revolution, the Mexican Revolution and the Russian Revolution all come under this heading. (5) "Conspiratorial coups d'etat" are elitist and tutelary. They are usually undertaken in the name of the people or the nation, but with no mass participation. Palace revolutions and Latin American and Middle Eastern coups are examples of this type. (6) Finally, there is the "militarized mass insurrection" which is made by the masses under the guidance of a conspiratorial or revolutionary leadership. Nationalism is central to its ideology as the major appeal that is sufficiently general and vital to produce the mass support required for success. Major examples are the revolutions in China, Ireland, Viet Nam, and Algeria.

Other models have not dealt with the stages or categories within any single revolution, but attempt to categorize or classify whole revolutions as being a certain type. Tocqueville, for example, delineated three types of revolution (i.e., political revolution, social revolution and religious revolution), though he considered the possibility that one comprehensive revolution could combine all three. The comprehensive revolution would be the most difficult to control, and termination would be a much greater problem than if only one type were involved. Violence is likely to be extensive in the combined type and there tends to develop a low estimate of, or even contempt for laws and legal procedures. Individuals and minorities may experience great discrimination against their claims which receive little consideration in view of the overriding purpose of society. Even if stable government in this type of revolutionary situation is eventually established, the violent origins tend to be perpetuated in its patterns of administration and in the mores of the ruling class.

A narrower and more specialized focus on a typology for classifying revolutions is one which identifies four types of *political* revolution. The criterion that determines into which of the four types a particular revolution should be classified is the "target" or aim of the revolution; that is, a revolution is generally fomented with a specific purpose in mind and it can be classified according to that purpose. First, there is civil revolution where the target is an internal one (i.e., the goal of the revolutionists is to overthrow or eliminate the existing government or controlling authorities). Second, there is national revolution where the aim is a mass violent overthrow of a foreign (external) power and the termination of its rule. Examples would be the Algerian, American and Vietnamese Revolutions. The third type is counterrevolution. It should have only provisional status as a revolution since it occurs during or after another revolution. It is a confrontation where mass violence is designed to return to power a political group or regime that has been removed by a revolutionary movement. An example would be the Vendee movement of 1793-96 in France. Finally, a fourth type also deserving only provisional status is a revolution where the goal, or aim, has been aborted. Essentially, the revolution has failed and an unintended result has occurred.

Thus, the concept of "target" provides a distinctive criterion for categorizing revolutions in a systematic manner while it also has definite socio-psychological implications. The specific target of the revolution can be said to give coherence and meaning to the actions of the revolutionists. In this respect the target or aim is viewed as a source of motivation or a driving force that can be employed to overcome the normal inhibitions and uncertainties that people have regarding a revolutionary way of life.

The importance of objective and materialistic conditions, such as oppression, poverty and injustice, as causes of revolution should not be minimized. But, if the socio-psychological dimension is also included, greater weight and completeness is added to the explanations of why revolutions occur. The key element in socio-psychological explanations is the concept of "definition of the situation." In other words, social and economic inequity and injustice have been tolerated in the past and are still tolerated today. They become major issues in the creation of unrest, disturbance, violence and, eventually, a full blown revolution when they are *defined* or *perceived* as inequitable, unjust and intolerable. The means by which this recognition and definition occur could be the actions and words of an agitator, the pronouncements of the mass media, the results from travel abroad by members of a society, or any number of other means. But it is this knowledge that creates discontent and dissatisfaction and that provides for a definition of the situation that calls for revolutionary action.

It has not been possible in this consideration of variations and trends in ideas about revolution to be comprehensive or even representative of all the possibilities available. But, as we have demonstrated, for a more adequate understanding of revolutionary phenomena, single factor explanations of revolution are inadequate. Multifactor or multivariable explanations are necessary to account adequately for human behavior in revolution, and one important dimension to the multivariable approach is the inclusion of socio-psychological variables.

5

Urbanization and Revolution

In examining the concept of revolution in the 19th and 20th centuries, urbanization is a phenomenon of major importance. The massive concentrations of humanity that exist in today's urban centers around the world are potentially the greatest single factor of influence on the destiny of mankind. Whether that destiny will be peaceful and secure or continue to be fraught with revolutionary and other types of violence will depend upon the extent to which the urban dweller can successfully resolve some of the significant problems of the urban way of life. After considering some general characteristics associated with the urban process and urban living, this discussion will examine problems which appear to have serious potential for massive or revolutionary disruptions and upheavals, particularly among the newly developing and urbanizing countries.

I

Cities as centers for government, commerce, the arts, crafts, intellectual life and ritual have existed for many centuries. In some respects the modern metropolitan community is comparable with the city-state of ancient and Renaissance times. In other ways urban developments of today are the unprecedented offspring of modern transportation, communication and rural urban migration.

For thousands of years the form and function of the city remained more or less static in a relationship in which city dwellers lived in close dependence upon the majority population who were rural dwellers engaged in agriculture. The dramatic changes which have occurred in the city are a result of the industrialism which sprang up in Western Europe and America during the 19th and 20th centuries. The technological changes which followed not only stimulated the growth of urban centers, but created a potential for social revolution. Since revolutions are the primary concern of this book we shall examine aspects of the city which tend to create them. These aspects include strains and stresses which were absent from traditional (rural oriented) society, but appeared as new and unforeseen problems of urban development arose: the modern slum, ethnic diversity, immigration, conflicts of interest and new features of the ancient problem of disease.

In some respects the city can be compared with a delicate mechanism, or system, that can be thrown out of gear or into a state of imbalance at many points, and from a variety of possible causes. The fact is that city life is hazardous to a considerable degree. This is evident if one considers the potential loss in human life every time there is some particularly dramatic calamity, such as a great storm, earthquake or flood, or some other catastrophic event, such as a war, riot, strike or revolution. The act, or failure to act, of a single individual can sometimes create havoc in the lives of urban dwellers.

But it is the purported freedom and choice available that are attractive to many who live an urban existence—the choice to live anonymously, even to live outside the system and its norms, or in opposition to the normative structure, and with less danger of exposure. Those who wish to plot and foment subversive activities typically find in the city an environment conducive to their ideas and ideals.

While cities are characteristically thought to provide great economic freedom there is an important sense in which massive regimentation prevails among populations of industrial cities. According to Walter Lippman:

> To have economic independence [freedom] a man must be in a position
> to leave one job and go to another; he must have enough savings of some
> kind to exist for a considerable time without accepting the first job of-
> fered. . . . the industrial worker who has a choice between working in one
> factory and not working at all, the white collar intellectuals who compete
> savagely for the relatively few private positions and for posts in the bu-
> reaucracy—these are the people who live too precariously to exercise
> their liberties or to defend them. They have no savings. They have only
> their labor to sell, and there are very few buyers of their labor. Therefore
> they have only the choice of truckling to the powerful or of perishing
> heroically but miserably.[1]

Some do choose to perish heroically, to struggle for ideals, or to
struggle simply because they are bitter, distraught, disillusioned, and
feel they are unjustly oppressed. For whatever reason (there need not
be a coherent one), these are the people whose interests and imagina-
tions can be captured by the promises and challenges of a charismatic
revolutionary leader.

Peasant societies, in contrast to urban settings, carry on their politics, religion and economics most often as a function of family, kinship,
sex and age. Since in such societies there is usually little or no distinction of labor and since knowledge is limited, each man is able to
participate more directly in the totality of social and cultural life. Thus,
to a great extent, all men share more or less the same assumptions and
expectations, as well as an understanding of the role of the individual.
In a rapidly changing heterogeneous urban milieu there is seldom
found the consensus common to small traditional (rural) communities.
In the city there is a much greater responsibility upon the individual
for his own behavior; this is not found in the extended kinship unit of
rural oriented society. The individual in the city must often consciously
judge conflicting evidence regarding the motives of those with whom
he must deal. Moreover, government authority in cities is not above
suspicion either, since it also is freer from community control and
much more subject to temptations of corruption than in peasant communities.

The competition for space and special advantage within the urban
environment encourages innovation, rationalistic calculation and individualism—all of which stimulate unsettled social, economic and
political conditions, and which open the way for sudden, radical
change. These unsettling processes are particularly evident in the urban milieu of the newly urbanizing and industrializing cities around
the world. Dramatic adjustments of behavior and thought are required

for new standards of consumption, new relationships between the sexes and members of families, new positions of the several age groups, new circumstances affecting health, and in new causes of death. Among the urban peoples of developing nations the social scientist is provided with a living laboratory for the study of revolutionary dynamics associated with modernization and urbanization, including the influence of massive migration to the city. The subsequent process of acculturation reveals the turmoil facing those struggling with new life styles of contemporary urban existence.

Africa provides a current example of a developing and urbanizing continent experiencing the trauma of wrenching social change. In Central and West Africa civilization has been dominated by primitive tribal life which, until very recently, was completely rural in character. They remain, even today, regions dominated by rurality and by a people getting their subsistence mainly from hoeing, herding, or hunting and fishing. The cities, particularly those of rapid and recent growth, are predominantly male in terms of sex distribution. They are young cities, with the bulk of the population between the ages of fifteen and forty-five. The expansion of African towns and cities is a result mostly of massive migration, even though natural growth is also a significant factor. The migrants are mixed, unstable and made up of people from several linguistic groups. Usually they are completely unskilled. Few of them bring their families. Competition for work, mostly casual labor, is intense because of limited job opportunities. Furthermore, indications are that those recruited for jobs offered by government agencies tend to be in disproportionate numbers from families who have been long residents in the city. Consequently, the immigrants tend to remain unemployed. Language difficulties are considerable. Family organization and group life tend to depart from traditional patterns and, therefore, a weakening of social control occurs. A wide social and economic gap between different social categories exists, adding to the factors creating and heightening discontent and frustration to the point where social and political unrest reach revolutionary potential.

II

A factor of major significance as a determinant of political, social and economic instability is the rapidity with which urbanization occurs in the developing nations. In other words, the potential for social upheaval is greatly enhanced because of the spectacular rate of urban growth in these countries

Africa again may be taken as an example. Although still the least urbanized of the world's major regions, its urban growth is among the most rapid. According to the United Nations' revised estimates between 1950 and 1960 the urban population of Africa increased by 69% compared to Latin America's 67%, which is also a dramatic increase. While death rates in Africa remain high, they have shown some tendency to decrease; however, the birth rates have remained high, thus accelerating the actual growth rate.[2] If the recent trend in urban growth continues, African cities, many already teeming with social discontent and political unrest, would have to accommodate about six times their present population by the year 2000. An increase of poverty and pathology can be expected along with an expansion of the slums and shanty towns with their human turmoil and misery. Such conditions provide the material for deep resentment and dissatisfaction among the newly arriving inhabitants who, when confronted by a revolutionary agitator, respond readily in the hope that he can provide immediate relief from their intolerable condition. If he calls for revolution they would appear to have little to lose, and perhaps they would gain a new world.

In the Middle East the growth of population is also in the urban areas. Rural-to-urban and town-to-city migration have accounted for about a fifth of the total urban growth in the Syrian cities of Damascus and Aleppo, about one-third of the urban growth in Iraq, and up to half of the urbanization of Jordan. Additional migration has come from other countries to the oil-rich ones, compounding problems of unrest among the latter. Palestine refugees make up a further percentage of migration. As a result, the Middle East has been described as having a "rapidly emerging population problem" of major proportions. Although reliable demographic data for the area are by no means adequate, indications are that Iraq, Jordan, Kuwait, Lebanon, Saudi Arabia and Yemen, which had a relatively modest total population of about 30 million in 1963 were expected by 1980 to increase to 46 million persons. If this projection holds true it would be an increase of more than 50 per cent, with most of it in the urban centers.[3] The significance of this skyrocketing growth for the social and political future of these countries and those around them is revealed by the repeated incidents of domestic turmoil and inter-nation strife. The explosions of outright war between Israel and the Arab nations illustrate the point. While the conflict with Israel is motivated by many deeper resentments, these are undoubtedly aggravated by the population problem.

The urban population of Asia has also been growing at an unprecedented rate during the last four or five decades (approximately four per cent a year, with a little more than half of it being from in-migration from rural areas). The major impulse for urban expansion in much of Asia has come mostly from rural population pressure and a stagnant rural economy, rather than from the rise of manufacturing in urban centers as was the case in 19th century Europe. One significance of this type of growth is that people are being *pushed* away from the rural areas to the cities. By contrast, 19th century European cities *pulled* people to them because of attractive opportunities for economic and social advancement created by newly developing manufacturing industry. Consequently, a general attitude of hopelessness and despair is prevalent among Asians migrating to the cities. As in other countries where migrating people are overcome by despair, the pronouncements and appeals of agitators create hope for a better way of life and a willingness to attack and destroy the society which gives them nothing but misery. The extended conflicts in Viet Nam, Cambodia and other Asian countries provide ample evidence of the deep determination of these desperate people.

Similar in many ways to Asia is Latin America's rapid urban growth and relatively slow increase in industrial employment. The problems attendant upon such growth are also similar in many respects to those of Asia: a profound despair of the future and discontent with the present. The attitudes and life experience of the urban masses of Latin America are violently expressed in revolutionary activity with a regularity found nowhere else in the world.

III

The problems associated with the urbanizing process of developing countries which can and do lead to protest, disruption and other forms of activity of a revolutionary nature so far have been spoken of generally. Reference has been made to evident sources and kinds of strains, tensions and fears which face the newly urbanizing peasant as well as the long-time city dweller. Greater specification of the serious and potentially explosive ills facing rapidly urbanizing societies will provide a better understanding of the possibilities for violent revolution.

Basically, the problems of the developing nations tend to be similar to each other, stemming most often from both the dramatic social changes occurring in the cities and from the radical adjustments necessary to a new and uncertain way of life. The rural migrant populations face problems of housing, family breakdown, destitution, malnutrition, poor health and the absence of adequate schooling. Typically, these problems are being attacked on only an ad hoc basis. The migrants' sheer numbers, in the cities already struggling with problems of government services, organization, decay, sanitation and uncontrolled and unplanned growth simply multiply an already extremely unsatisfactory situation. Moreover, although the migrants as a whole do exist in abject despair, there often occurs a rising of hopes and expectations which are usually, sooner or later, dashed by the hopelessness of their situation.

A reasonable and planned geographic distribution of population could alleviate the deteriorating conditions of the developing cities. So far extremely few successful programs for accomplishing this exist. China, and to some extent Russia, have had some success in the redistribution of population. China, using rather drastic measures, has attempted to preserve some balance between rural and urban population distribution. "Excess" urban population has been transferred en masse to the countryside. The Soviet Union, through the use of public appeals, especially to younger people, has been successful in moving large numbers of workers to undeveloped regions. Several hundreds of thousands of young people went to work virgin lands in Kazakhstan, and an even larger number took up employment in Siberia and in the northern and far eastern regions of the country. The actions by Russia particularly have provided a most important population pressure relief valve. China's method of population distribution can be questioned as a solution to population pressures in that forced migration can build its own resentments and hatreds.

A disruptive condition associated particularly with urban centers of developed countries is the presence of minority people, sometimes in large numbers. While the presence of minorities is not in and of itself a social problem, the attitudes and beliefs the majority members have toward minorities may create serious social, political and economic difficulties for the urban society. In some respects this situation is similar to that of the presence of migrants in the cities of the developing nations. Quite characteristic are feelings of anxiety and resentment on the part of the majority toward the presence of minorities, especially if the latter tend to be very conspicuous and display a tendency toward aggressiveness. Often these anxieties are excessive and based more on myth than reality, but the fact that they are *believed* to be real causes majority members to act in a negative manner. The authorities are encouraged and even pressured to take aggressive actions and repressive measures to force or induce a more submissive posture on the part of minority people. Characteristically, this forces the minorities into greater self-protective isolation and intensifies attitudes of hostility toward the authorities and the larger society they represent.

Two other prominent types of problems are commonly associated with the presence of significantly large minority groups in "older" cities. First, as a result of long-term discriminatory policies against minorities there is usually a serious lack of suitable social services available to them. There exists a desperate need to provide these services in order to help them cope with overcrowded, deteriorated living conditions and other attendant problems, not the least of which is a growing resentment toward the majority society and the worsening of relationships between the two. Second, an inherently political problem is the need to provide or create an atmosphere in which minorities feel a part of, and a desire to participate in the larger polity. It is essential, if a society is to continue as an integrated whole, to incorporate within its structure dissident minority groups. The latter could readily become revolutionary if they see themselves as permanently cut off from the mainstream of the society in which they must make their destiny.

But modern industrialized nations are faced with other seriously disruptive social problems in spite of a long history of urban experience. In other words, the presence of minorities is only one of the problems faced by the developed urban countries. In many respects the problems of the cities in the developed countries are very similar to those in the underdeveloped and developing nations. True, city government is usually more stable in the developed nations. Services are more adequate and reliable, including medical, social and sanitation services. Communication and transportation facilities are reasonably efficient. But residential and commercial development often presents a problem in urban centers of both developed and developing countries. In the cities of both North and South America, for example, ugly shadows are cast by areas of residential and commercial blight. It ranges from small intensive slums to the more extensive drabness where structures may be reasonably sound, but where further deterioration will occur unless some public action is undertaken. As has often been noted, it is in these areas, vacated by middle and upper income families who have moved to the suburbs, that the rural-urban migrants, the poor and minority groups predominate, and with them, urban social ills and health problems.

Comprehensive planning, particularly in the area of housing is believed by many authorities to be a basic requirement to relieve the building up of social and psychological tensions. While declarations concerning the need for comprehensive planning abound in Latin America, for instance, and, in a few cases, while planning agencies or consultants have presented concrete proposals on the problem of housing, overall there is little evidence of progress toward the application of planning. Economic and physical planners continue to go their separate ways. The programs aimed at universal housing shortages are embarked upon, once irresistible pressures have built up, but without reference to either economic or physical planning criteria. Urban housing programs are beset by financial, personnel, administrative and technical difficulties, and have not yet come near meeting the growing needs of the cities.

Part of the urbanization in Latin America is taking place in peripheral settlements, where more youthful migrants with growing families are moving in an attempt to escape the crowded living conditions of the urban centers. These settlements, often created by public housing programs, may select occupants on the basis of family size and are therefore typically characterized by immediate overcrowding. Also characteristic of these low income urban settlements, even the better ones, is a drab, uninteresting environment, separated from the city proper and lacking in many of the attractions usually associated with city life. The educational system and social structures of the cities are largely inaccessible, providing very little opportunity for young people from the settlements to escape from their marginal and debilitating social and occupational status. As a result of these and other problems the settlements have been a source of populist movements with authoritarian, dictatorship and revolutionary-style leaders. Violent outbursts and confrontations have been experienced in several cities when the populist movements are frustrated and when the living conditions among the settlements deteriorate beyond what the people can tolerate.

In Asian countries a similar situation exists regarding the deplorable state of housing and urban planning, making the area a veritable time bomb of psychological tensions and social dissatisfactions. In addition to housing shortages there are inadequate public services, inferior health conditions, overcrowding, plus a lack of recreational opportunities and facilities. Not unexpectedly, in Africa also, redevelopment trends based on recent surveys reveal a large proportion of the urban population living in the squalor of overcrowded and unhealthy housing. In many cases indications are that the situation is worsening, intensifying the dissatisfactions which already exist.

The problems discussed to this point all have important implications, specifically in terms of various kinds of political action. But also, the political structure of the various countries presents its own sources for urban problems. Throughout history the main political leaders have been urban based. In the past, even large land holders have typically had the city as their base, and they have resided there at least part of the year. The central role of cities in the nations of the world indicates their significance for political structures. A political organization, in order to continue to exist, must have a favorable climate for development. Conversely, since they are only partial systems, which must import food and raw materials to sustain their populations, cities could not survive without support from a stable, viable, political system. To create and sustain such a system requires that cities with swelling populations, particularly among the disadvantaged or lower classes and minority groups, provide adequate channels of and incentives for political participation so that such groups may come to feel that the national policy is responsive to their needs, aspirations and anxieties. But as has been indicated previously, the political systems of newly urbanizing nations sometimes attempt to exclude the new arrivals, or at least make no effort to include them in the political process. This is an important reason why they become members of the alienated, the disillusioned and dispossessed, ripe for recruitment to the ranks of revolutionary and subversive movements aimed at overthrowing the government.

Yet, in some cases, newly urban populations rush into the political scene with little sense of or need for commitment and, consequently, tend to disrupt, without providing any positive contribution to a political process already struggling to maintain some equilibrium. Important for stable and predictable political activity is political action which carries with it a sense of responsibility. Unless there is some element of personal sacrifice, some sense of costs involved, some requirement to risk something in order to gain something else, political action tends

to degenerate and become frivolous, erratic and lacking in any consistent commitments to the goals and actions of the political process.
When it is possible for people to enter and leave the political arena
without having to calculate the personal consequences, their actions
tend to become highly unpredictable. There have been instances when
newly urban populations have suddenly withdrawn from the political
arena into which they had initially rushed with ideals and enthusiasm,
leaving behind confusion and uncertainty.

There is another aspect to the political problem facing newly urbanizing nations as they attempt to resolve their national problems
through the rational political process. Many of the needs of newly
arriving rural migrants are purely personal and private. They may have
broken with their families at home. They may be bored with the rural
existence and seek excitement and/or perhaps a family. Others have
personality problems and needs that they attempt to fulfill by involvement and participation in the newly organized political structures of
the city. It may be true that personal needs and desires can be met to
some extent by participation in the political process through: finding
a sense of identity; breaking the bonds of loneliness; discovering new,
less confining roles to play; overcoming emotional inhibition; and
learning respectable ways to express aggressiveness and hostility.
However, if these goals come to dominate political behavior, rational
policy objectives begin to break down and meaningfulness is sought
in political action per se, not in the objectives of the policy. The
effectiveness of the entire political process is weakened under these
conditions, and the entire structure of the society will eventually be
threatened with a good deal of social instability.

Contact between contrasting life styles creates another problem involving new migrants in developing cities. Characteristically, there
exists a sharp cleavage between the life styles of people in the large city
and the still primitive life styles of the more traditional village-based
people. When the two societies and their technologies come into contact as the villagers migrate in substantial numbers to the urban centers, the result upon the migrants is to create personal insecurities and
anxieties which are the effects of an atmosphere of anonymity and
impersonality in the large city. While some of the long-time urban
residents may see the new arrivals as harmless, simple souls who can
for the most part be ignored, others may see them as a threatening
force to their way of life. The migrants may be viewed as an economic
threat on the job market, for instance. They may be feared as a politi-

cally explosive and violent social force and therefore needing to be closely controlled and perhaps socially or even physically isolated from the rest of society. Finally, they may be resented as a potential source for increasing crime, delinquency and other forms of deviance.

Evidence does indicate a high incidence of deviant social behavior on the part of the newcomers and slum dwellers in the cities of developing nations. Penned in their slums, they view the established and better-off groups as antagonistic or indifferent to their plight, which thereby increases their sense of powerlessness and alienation. Victims of forces they cannot comprehend, lonely and desperate, they have moved to the cities for the purpose of improving their social and economic existence and cannot even find employment, they turn to delinquency, violence and participation in sectarian and subversive movements in an attempt to find a sense of belonging. Radical and revolutionary political movements have generally been most successful in recruiting their followers from such populations.

Related to the employment problem among the migrants to the cities of developing countries, and also a serious source of discontent, is the wide disparity that exists between the income of the different classes and groups. Sometimes an indigenous elite exists possessing vast resources of wealth and power. Even among the people who work for a living tremendous discrepancies of income are typical. For example, in the African city of Leopoldville, the annual per capita income of Africans was estimated at some 4,350 francs, the equivalent to $87.00 in U.S. funds. This placed them above the national average but far below the average for foreigners, which was estimated for Leopoldville at 250,000 francs ($5,000) per person.

Moreover, while Africanization of the civil services and a number of business concerns has provided some with an increased salary, the process has tended further to widen the gap between foreigners and the new urban wage earner. A recent survey in East Africa showed that the senior civil servant earns from ten to twelve times as much as the artisan and twenty-five times as much as laborers. The latter includes most of the urban peasants.

But, are the problems of these urbanizing countries something new and unprecedented, limited to the 20th century? That new problems have arisen as a result of industrialization and urbanization does not discount the fact that pre-industrial societies also had numerous problems. Typical were inadequate water and sewage systems which created disease epidemics. Typical also was an almost complete absence of social mobility due to status ascribed by birth and position in a kinship network. Struggles for power among the elite were common. Except for a few who were privileged by birth and had inherited an affluent standard of living, most people remained at a subsistence level. And there were numerous other problems. But the important point is that the problems of the pre-industrial era were not cast in an atmosphere of skyrocketing aspirations as is the case among the urbanizing and industrializing nations today.

Vast expectations have been aroused among the masses of migrants crowding into the cities of newly developing countries, but they are not fulfilled. Or, as was pointed out earlier, after initial fulfillment they are often dashed because of a change of economic conditions, or because, for other reasons, the new opportunities for wealth and status disappear. Consequently, there occurs not only discontent and alienation but, not infrequently, open rebellion.

> Unchecked, disregarded, left to grow and fester, there is here enough explosive material to produce in the world at large the pattern of a bitter class conflict finding to an increasing degree a racial bias, erupting in guerrilla warfare, and threatening, ultimately, the security even of the comfortable West.[5]

IV

Finally, it is important to recognize some factors which have tended to ameliorate the grim picture of discontent, imminent violence and revolutionary developments in the cities of the developing countries. In other words, although the new urban migrants would appear to be potential recruits for protest, revolution and other forms of rebellion, they have not been in every case. Despite substandard living conditions and economic privation, several forces tend to counter the trend toward violence and revolution. Often the rural-urban migrants have a deep devotion to their religion, which may be opposed to violence. Many if not most of the migrants have achieved, relatively speaking, some social and economic progress for themselves. And they are usually anxious to avoid any action that would jeopardize their progress, despite the fact that from an outside observer's point of view they would have little to lose.

As a consequence, rather than being a "misery belt of the dispossessed," waiting for the revolutionary spark to ignite them to violence and destruction of the society, the rural-urban settlers have been to some extent "social safety belts." And, if in the near future they can by some "miracle" be made to feel that they are in fact real members of society, that they are being taken into consideration, and that they can occupy a place of respect and dignity in the community, then the threat of their destructive violence may subside. The other problems of rapid urbanization could then be dealt with by administrative procedures. But, if instead of participation, increasing alienation and isolation are allowed to continue, it would seem that a holocaust of revolution in the newly developing and urbanizing nations will occur beyond those disturbances and localized revolts and movements already in progress.

NOTES

[1] Quoted in Ralph E. Turner, "The Industrial City: Center of Cultural Change" in Paul K. Hatt and Albert J. Reiss, Jr., (eds.), *Cities and Society: The Revised Reader in Urban Sociology* (Glencoe, N.Y., 1957), p. 194.

[2] "Urbanization: Development Policies and Planning," *International Social Development Review,* I (New York, 1968), p. 39.

[3] *Ibid.,* p. 63.

[4] *United Nations Economic Bulletin for Africa,* I, 2 (June 1961), pp. 50–65.

[5] Quoted in John F. C. Turner, "Uncontrolled Urban Settlement: Problems and Policies" in Gerald Breese (ed.), *The City in Newly Developing Countries: Readings on Urbanism and Urbanization* (Englewood Cliffs, 1969), p. 527.

6

On the Eve of the Modern Concept:
The Greeks to the Glorious Revolution

I

Little is known about (political) revolutions prior to the Greeks. To the early Egyptians, and the ancient world in general, the concept appears to have no form that would distinguish it from rebellion. At best revolution meant the replacing of a weak, useless ruler by a stronger one. The very process implied divine intervention whereby the gods were expressing their will by sanctioning the overthrow of the fallen ruler and his replacement by the victorious one.

It is to the Greeks that we owe the origins of our concept. Unfortunately for our precise—some would say picayune—20th century minds the Greeks had no single word for revolution. They wrote of "uprisings," "change," "transformation," as well as "revolution." These words all were applied to changes of rulers—which we would call palace revolutions—and also to the social changes involved in the rise of an aristocracy or the fall of aristocratic domination. The Greeks were students of contemporary politics and history, and as such they pointed to the relationship between political upheaval and the social disturbances that were likely to accompany it. They observed that changes in the political structure and the dissolution of states resulted in changes in social relationships among individuals.

Thucydides (c460–c400 B.C.) was an astute observer of the revolutionary process. He noted that revolutions were inevitable as long as human nature remained the same. They differed in character with every new combination of circumstances. He saw revolutions as giving birth to wickedness and being caused by a love of power. Popular slogans, such as "a fair share of political rights for the masses," were misleading, he said, because leaders always rewarded themselves at the public cost. Although Plato (427–347 B.C.) was concerned with politics, and especially military intervention in politics, he did not pay any particular attention to revolutions (i.e., he was more interested in permanence than change), and he employed the words "change" and "revolution" interchangeably.

It was left to Aristotle (384–322 B.C.) to lay the foundation for the study of the modern concept. Like his predecessors, Aristotle was inconsistent in his terminology, but his study of revolutions was empirical and analytical. In Book V of his *Politics* he evaluated the causes of revolutions in the various forms of government with which he was familiar: democracies, oligarchies, aristocracies, monarchies and tyrannies. In each case the revolution generally involved the change from one type to another, or modifications within the same type. Aristotle believed that any one of these forms was likely to exist at a given time and that without a state order was not possible. But these forms were not ideal; they rested on fallible ideas which led to dissatisfaction and upheaval, which in turn sometimes led to changes in the forms of states. For Aristotle, therefore, revolution was not an extraordinary occurrence but a necessary and useful fact of political life. Revolution was essentially a political concept, affecting authority within states, for which violence was not essential.

Aristotle distinguished between two general kinds of revolutions in governments. One affected the constitution, when a change was sought from one form to another, as from democracy to oligarchy. The other did not affect the constitution, whatever it was, but sought a change in administration. But given these differences, and differences in degree within each of the two kinds, the basic cause of revolution was inequality. "Inferiors revolt in order that they may be equal, and equals that they may be superior. Such is the state of mind which creates revolutions."[1] (Here Aristotle anticipated by some 2300 years the rather sophisticated socio-psychological view that it is the dissatisfied state of mind which produces the revolution.[2]) When Aristotle wrote about equality he was not using the term as John Locke or Thomas Jefferson did in reference to natural rights. For him equality and inequality as they relate to revolution must be understood in terms of the relative political and economic status of individuals. Simple inequality between different groups or classes is not a cause of revolution. But an inequality in which there is an incongruity or imbalance between the corresponding political, social and economic status within groups or classes is a factor which contributes to revolution. Thus, for Aristotle, wherever political and economic power were separated a revolution was possible. The concept of revolution, therefore, implied a political or constitutional change of some magnitude, with subsequent social and economic alterations; that change was a natural part of the political process and was the vehicle by which one form of government replaced another and societal imperfections were adjusted. Although he did not say explicitly that revolutions occur in a cyclical pattern (Polybius—c205-c123 B.C.—did thus referring to revolution in the sense of a slowly turning wheel of Fortune whereby societies changed naturally from one form to another until they returned to their point of origin), he implied that they did and thus gave the modern concept its useful and most easily recognizable form.

II

The more than 1000-year period of the Roman Empire and the Middle Ages saw little by way of important contributions or changes in the idea of revolution. The Romans were not unlike the Greeks in their use of a variety of words for similar revolutionary events. Actually, since the history of Rome is generally characterized by a lack of anything we might label a revolution, though there was turmoil and rebellion, it is not surprising that the Roman contribution was negligible. In a similar vein the Medieval period, which was collectively an age of obedience and rigid life-styles, witnessed little that we might term a revolution. For our purposes, therefore, these periods comprised a virtual dark age.

With the Renaissance, new life was breathed into the concept of revolution. The kind of political upheavals that had characterized Greek times returned. But tradition and the weight of history prevented the revolutionary implications of the period from being realized on any significant scale. The political structure might be altered but it simply did not enter people's minds that the existing order as a whole could be transformed radically. There would be change, but it would be more gradual than radical, and such change—or revolution—would still be a part of the divine order of things. Revolutionary activity, therefore, was generally conservative in that it was bent on maintaining a situation or restoring a former one, real or imagined. Even Machiavelli (1469–1527), who is sometimes credited with being a father to modern revolutions because of his writing on the political use of force, was more interested in gaining prestigious employment for himself than in developing a political theory. In fact, Machiavelli hardly talked about revolution at all, though he did see political violence as being above morality. Where Renaissance observers used the term (or a similar one) it was usually to describe a return to some starting point. For example, the banishment of the Medici from Florence in 1494 was a return to a more democratic regime, and the reinstatement of the Medici in 1512 was a return to the regime before 1494. This was the primary usage of the term that Italy transmitted to northern Europe: revolution as restoration.

The period of the Reformation conformed to this view but in such a way as to have important societal consequences. In at least one respect, the Reformation may justly be called the Protestant Revolution in that it produced a religious revolution by permanently dividing Christendom and a secular revolution by weakening and transforming two systems of government, the Holy Roman Empire and the Roman Catholic Church. Protestant revolutionists asserted that they were returning to a former, better order which had once existed but which had become distorted. This distinction was quite real to contemporaries, especially since it gave respectability to their movement. The religious conflict rapidly acquired social and political characteristics, and changes in religion often resulted in societal changes in the state. In Germany, the Reformation coincided with several independent social movements that complicated the revolutionary process. The Revolt of the Imperial Knights (1523), the Peasants' Revolt (1524–25) and the Kingdom of Münster (an Anabaptist revolt in northwestern Germany, 1534–35) are the most important. These all failed primarily because the social and religious beliefs directing them were too narrowly based; they appealed to a numerically insignificant group, as with the Knights, or to the lower classes, as with the other two. But the Reformation nonetheless preached a message of revolution.

Martin Luther, John Calvin and the others all wished to purify and reform the church. But by no means was that all. They sought to end the old order of the antichrist and his blind followers, to emphasize the value of the individual in the eyes of God, and to be rid of the monasteries and their useless monks. They were also interested in improving the secular world, to expand justice and to see that the law of man was in conformity with the law of God. These revolutionists of the Reformation, therefore, through their sermons, were concerned not only with the next world but with serving God in this one. Unlike the medieval man whose better world was in heaven, the men of the Reformation began to think more seriously about realizing some of that heaven on earth, and in their own life time at that. Luther's message of justification by faith alone was revolutionary in the 16th century. Calvin took Luther's message and applied it to everyday life. God's law, which to Luther was a threat that drives men to His mercy, was to Calvin a way of life as well. God's law guided Calvinists to live according to strict biblical morality; and to do so meant to change society. But it must be reemphasized that these Protestants were conservative revolutionists. Although they wished to eliminate injustice and evil and create a new age, it was to be a new age based on the old (an old order that was, no doubt, somewhat utopian) and one that did not completely destroy society. They were not trying to begin anew, but to recreate. Nevertheless, their struggle was revolutionary in that the bond between authority and tradition was dissolved. They presented a monumental challenge to law, order and the status quo that would not go unnoticed.

III

The century and a half following the Peace of Augsburg (1555)—which marked a plateau in the Reformation struggle—was characterized by a variety of revolutionary struggles: the Dutch Revolt (1568–1648), insurrections in Catalonia (Spain) and Portugal in 1640 and in Naples (Italy) and Palermo (Sicily) in 1647, the Fronde in France (1648–53), and the Puritan (1640–60) and Glorious (1688–89) Revolutions in England. Although they were all generally conservative revolutionary movements they set examples and served to pave the way for the further development of the modern conception of revolution.

These upheavals rested on beliefs that were deeply antagonistic to the existing regime or to its policies, personnel or forms of government. Yet these beliefs did not constitute a revolutionary ideal in the modern sense in that they failed to form a unified world view of the historical process. Theirs was not a comprehensive plan for complete societal reform in that there was an absence of important demands for social equality, universal political privilege, or economic egalitarianism. The men of these revolutions were limited in their aims by traditional patterns of thought. As such, their revolutions were not dominated by any idea of progress but by a return to a past golden age via renovation. Arms were taken up to defend old standards, to protect the homeland against foreign interferences, or to protect the sacred constitution from illegal encroachments by a misdirected or malevolent regime. Although the thrust of these revolutions was conservative, the ideas on which they were based effectively served as an ideal for revolution and as a focus for loyalty among the discontented. Thus, the revolutionary ideal was somewhat atavistic, but this did not entirely prevent the revolutionists from generating new conceptions of the political and social order (witness the Puritan Revolution). Yet, in each case, although the movement began as a restoration, it resulted in demands for basic changes in society.

The uprisings in Palermo and Naples were peasant revolts resulting from social distress and directed at the local ruling elite, not the government behind it. These movements lacked reform programs, adequate support, leadership and organization. And they even lacked a set of unifying beliefs that we might call a revolutionary ideal. The revolts in Catalonia and Portugal were separatist movements while the Fronde was an abortive attempt on the part of the ruling elite to gain more power for itself. The main source of discontent in all three seems to have been the centralizing tendencies of the governments in question. And yet they all failed to generate a new and comprehensive conception of the social and political order—however much the potential was there. These upheavals, then, failed to become great national revolutions like those in the Netherlands and mid-17th century England and must be classified as mere rebellions.

Neither the Dutch Revolt nor the Puritan Revolution were mere rebellions, the Dutch Revolt was the work of a highly organized minority, officered and controlled by the nobility, disciplined and united by Calvinism and supported by the business and working groups

whose hatred of the Spanish was probably greater than their loyalty to
their own government. It began as a rebellion by the Dutch provinces
against what they considered oppressive Spanish domination. That
rebellion became an early form of what the 20th century calls an
anti-colonial revolution when the Dutch came to realize that the only
alternative to domination was independence. But, at least at the start
of the revolt, Dutch nationalism was a minimal force and there was
lacking any common political ideology that could unite the revolutionists. The aristocratic rebels wished to capture the machinery of
government without drastically altering the political structure or social
order, and there was economic diversity and political particularism
among the provinces. All this, at first, gave the upheaval the character
of a series of separate local revolts.

As the revolt unfolded, the more revolutionary among the population carried it along a path of political and social revolution. The lesser
nobility, the businessmen and the artisans were, by virtue of their
social position and economic ambition, the leaders among the revolutionary forces and they succeeded in uniting the economically advanced and socially heterogeneous Dutch provinces of Holland and
Zeeland behind a program of domestic liberty, toleration and patriotism. As the local revolts merged into the Netherlands Revolution
there arose a new conception of the social and political order. The
revolutionary ideal for the Dutch was embodied in a capitalist, bourgeois republic with a marked mercantile national identity. Religion was
a binding force for the different classes and religion provided an organization and propaganda vehicle capable of creating a national,
though minority party. Although Calvinism did not advocate the overthrow of established authority it did sanction resistance to that authority to preserve and foster the true religion, so long as it was led by those
who were themselves possessors of some established authority (e.g.,
nobility). In the final analysis, the Dutch Revolt was both a revolution
of its own time as well as one which pointed to the future of the
concept. It was a constitutional struggle, separatist in character, in
which the social structure remained essentially unchanged. The United Netherlands was less united than at first hoped, and the revolutionary terminology was couched in a conservative cover. But a new,
soverign political form was established (i.e., the Estates–General) with
new men to fill it, the religious changes were complete and independence was achieved.

The Puritan or English Revolution took place within a nationally integrated political system where Parliament was an established vehicle for organized national opposition. The discontented elements were influenced by and operated out of a coherent body of widely generalized beliefs and a revolutionary ideology that had emerged during the previous century from a fusion of Puritanism, common law tradition, the values of country (as opposed to court) society, and the skepticism identified with Renaissance learning. This ideology gave direction, purpose and unity to the revolutionists in their conflict with the Stuart kings.

Of particular note is that the mid-17th century English concept of revolution originated with the exiled Puritan writers of the previous century. In abandoning Calvin's caution they proclaimed the right of resistance and thus became among the earliest to express surprisingly modern ideas about revolution. They did not develop their ideas fully nor did they probably understand the implication of their views, but they did, nevertheless, express them. For these Marian exiles, as the Puritans who left England during the reign of Mary Tudor were called, revolution was an instrument of God, granted to a minority of the godly people, or saints. The saint was a revolutionist who was acting on the basis of a new law: the king would have to be overthrown and not merely resisted, tried and not simply assassinated. Revolution was part of the eternal warfare between God and the devil; in this way the rhetoric of opposition and struggle played an important part in the evolving of the concept of revolution. From the mid-16th century to the time of Oliver Cromwell and John Milton the ideas of the Marian exiles were a powerful force in political life; Milton cited the Marian exiles in defending both the revolution, which was begun by the people themselves, and the execution of a tyrant king. Even a generation later, John Locke was still denying the idea that saints have a special role in revolution.

In the English Revolution we see the strands of revolution pulling in opposite directions; its Janus head faced both the past and the future. But the revolutionists of 1640 looked back to different pasts. On the one hand, the Puritans were seeking a return to what they imagined to have been the state of the early church before it had become distorted. And on the other, lay members of Parliament and lawyers were defending an ancient constitution against a tyrannical king and sought an earlier time when kings, courtiers and the church were all guided by the common law. All wanted to recover freedom rather than establish it anew. Thus, an important difference between the 17th century English ideal of revolution and the late 18th century French ideal was in the former's attempt to restore freedom that once was, not to establish it for the first time. While the conservative element is clear in the English Revolution its progressive face, like the dark side of the moon, is there to see, but only if we probe deeply. Although these revolutionists did not as a rule use the word "revolution" and spoke primarily of restoration and reform, implicit in their terminology was the modern notion of improvement and change for the better. For a short time, but probably for the first time, the revolution produced men who fought and called for complete liberty and not just liberties, for equality and not just privilege, and for brotherhood and not just deference.

The English Revolution was indeed a revolution. In overthrowing a king the Puritans committed judicial murder, not assassination; the very trial of the king was an examination of the nature of monarchy and not a mere personal attack on a poor king or his evil advisors. The revolution witnessed the appearance of a truly national army, the New Model Army, of men who knew for what they were fighting, and a written constitution which attempted to establish a new political order. This was a revolution that showed that real change was possible and that change could remake society. Although the revolution failed the ideas it brought forth survived: ideas about toleration, limited monarchy and a policy based on the consent of a broad spectrum of society. This helps to mark the English Revolution as perhaps the first "great" revolution in history.

Interestingly, the English Revolution was followed a generation later by another, though different kind of revolution which also made a contribution to the development of the concept while at the same time it served to strengthen the conservative characteristic of revolutions. The Glorious Revolution—unequivocally labeled a revolution by contemporaries—was not a revolution which resulted in a new order; in fact, while it struck a crucial blow to the restorationist concept of revolution, it resulted in laws which strengthened much of the old order. Basically, the English rejected one king as unfit to rule and summoned another one as they instituted a limited monarchy. It was an aristocratic revolution engineered by the ruling classes for themselves, and not for the common people who supported them. The most important theorist for the revolution was John Locke (1632–1704). His use of the word "revolution" in his *Two Treatises of Government* was, in part, to describe a completed dynastic change, a return to a previous constitutional point, but not a reversal or restoration. When a monarch betrays his trust, Locke said, the people have the right to rebel in order to return society to its proper point in the constitutional cycle; the completed cycle is the revolution. But it is important to note that Locke was providing a justification for revolution. Whereas people did not normally change kings at will, in 1688 an English Parliament made the choice and assumed a power it previously did not necessarily have by confirming a new state of affairs. Locke asserted that the right of revolution belongs to the people. The people are a community even after the dissolution of government, and thus it is the people who decide when a revolution is necessary. Locke conceived and wrote most of his work before the revolution actually took place and as such it opened the possibility for a revolution to be brought about; it was not a mere rationalization for one just completed.

IV

A somewhat different approach to revolution was millenarianism. Although not limited to the period under discuscussion and not unrelated to other movements to be discussed later, it seems fitting to allude to it here. Millenarianism is the rejection of the present, evil world and the hope of a complete and radical change which will be reflected in the millennium; it foresees a world without faults and deficiencies, promising terrestrial and collective salvation. A heaven on earth will be realized by the actions of a "chosen people." Revolution for millenarians will be different from other conflicts and result in a world completely transformed and redeemed. (This characteristic of early modern European millenarian movements makes them somewhat similar to the early revolutionary stages of communist and fascist movements in this century.) The ideology of these early movements was religious and chiliastic, but as revolutionary movements they involved no organization, strategy or tactics. The revolution, it seems, would make itself, but the millenarian would have to prepare himself spiritually beforehand.

V

On the eve of the age of the democratic revolution the very word "revolution" was finally being accepted universally in Europe, but its use was predominated by the astronomical meaning. The importance of the word for 16th and 17th century science (Nicholas Copernicus' monumental *On the Revolutions of the Heavenly Spheres* was published in 1543) helped to make it popular and eased the way for its introduction into the language of politics. But a 1611 English dictionary, reissued in new editions several times during this century, still defined revolution as "a full compassing; rounding, turning backe to its first place or point, the accomplishment of a circular course;"[3] no non-scientific definition was offered. Even a number of 17th century political theorists, such as Thomas Hobbes and Frances Bacon, did not readily adopt the word in their political tracts. In spite of this resistance, it seemed only natural for politics to borrow from astronomy since the connection between worldly changes and the motion of the heavens was always accepted. "The revolutions of the globe we inhabit give rise to the mishaps and accidents of human existence,"[4] is a dictum attributed to Galileo. Clearly then, the astronomical conception of revolution implied that it was possible to place political upheavals into an acceptable scheme. Change was circular, like the motion of the stars. Revolution was a return to earlier, better days, a turn away from disorder and a restoration of order.

But the concept of revolution which astronomy popularized did not remain limited to restorative usage only. Revolution was also becoming synonymous with reversal and alteration in general. Events in mid-17th century Italy and England began to generate a more modern connotation. The 1647 revolt in Naples, for example, was dubbed *revolutioni.* At least one English writer, the scientific-minded Matthew Wren, distinguished between earlier events as "revolts" and the Puritan "Revolution" by appealing to the heavens and using "revolution" to convey the notion of a completed political cycle. But then the restoration of Charles II in 1660 was also referred to as a revolution in that it terminated a complete political movement in which there was a return to an earlier state.

Thus, by the time Locke wrote his *Two Treatises* prior to the Glorious Revolution the word "revolution" possessed a variety of meanings, but to all it meant rather sudden change, completed in a circular movement. The concept was compatible with the cyclical interpretation of history of Plato, Aristotle, Polybius and Machiavelli. Yet there were real underlying differences: revolution meant change in the form of government; it meant dynastic change within the existing form of monarchy; it meant dynastic restoration; and it meant social, economic and administrative change. Yet, as we have seen, in 1688-89, the word was applied to a permanent political change, not just a restoration or reversal. The Glorious Revolution was important less for what actually transpired than for the change that came over the concept. *Revolution* was now a non-evaluative term for great political transformations.

NOTES

[1] Aristotle, *Politics,* in Paynton and Blackey, *Why Revolution?,* p. 11.

[2] See James C. Davies, "Toward a Theory of Revolution," in *ibid.,* pp. 177–198.

[3] Quoted in Vernon F. Snow, "The Concept of Revolution in Seventeenth-Century England," *The Historical Journal,* V, 2 (1962), 168.

[4] Quoted in Karl Griewank, "Emergence of the Concept of Revolution," in Paynton and Blackey, *Why Revolution?,* p. 17.

7

Age of the Democratic Revolution

The last four decades of the 18th century were characterized by a series of revolutions and movements for political change, the best known and most important of which were the American and French Revolutions. Although each of these events was distinctive in its own way, all seemed to reflect somewhat similar ideas, antagonisms and needs, all of which launched the concept of revolution into the forefront of socio-political terminology and provided both a backdrop and point of reference for the 19th century. These revolutions may be seen as a series of challenges to the authority and social structure of the 18th century world; undoubtedly contagion played a role (i.e., the news of revolution in one country encouraged it in another), but these challenges were real and arose independently throughout the western world. Collectively they marked the appearance of the belief—some would say myth—that revolution would solve the problems of the world. They were democratic in a general sense in that the idea of a greater equality, vis-á-vis the older form of social ranking and stratification, based upon birth and heritage, was present. They were also democratic in that they were a challenge to political power limited to privileged classes and in that they advocated the delegation of authority and the removability of those in power.

I

What was the nature of revolution for the people of 1776? In fact, was the American Revolution really a revolution or was it instead an aristocratic struggle between ruling elites, cleverly camouflaged as a popular mass movement? These and similar questions have plagued historians throughout this century as they have attempted to come to grips with America's past. The American Revolution has been glorified and venerated, vilified and denigrated. It has been praised as the first modern revolution and damned as a great lie. The truth, it seems, lies somewhere in between. For example, one important feature of the American Revolution was that the revolutionary principle of "consent of the governed" was vital to good government. However, this consent was not sought from Indians, slaves, unpropertied persons and women; liberty was not intended for everyone and the institution of private property was still held sacred. But since the 18th century mind did not think this way it is questionable whether such criticism is historical. Therefore, although the radical at the time, in perspective the revolution appears moderate or even conservative.

The fundamental goal of the American Revolution was neither the overthrow nor the radical alteration of the existing social structure but the preservation of the sacred political liberty of Englishmen—and Americans—which was threatened by the alleged corruption of English officials. Unlike the French and Russian Revolutions, the American Revolution did not attempt to establish new foundations for society. In fact, that foundation had already been altered in America from the 17th century; European institutions, ideas and habits had been modified by the colonial experience. But it was not until the conflicts of the 1760's and 1770's that these changes were used to justify the political change that resulted in the American Revolution. From the 1760's the colonists came to believe that English policies were violating the principles of freedom and liberty both in England and America; the oppression in America, viewed by many as part of a plan for enslaving the colonies, was only the most visible part. Once this view became popular it acted as an accelerator to the movement of opposition and propelled America into revolution. Thus, at the heart of the American

Revolution was not the disruption of the social order, but the realization and fulfillment of the inheritance of liberty and of what was taken
to be America's destiny in the world. In this sense, revolution for
America was a rebirth, a coming of age, a fulfillment of promise, a
maturation. As John Adams wrote in 1765: "America was designed by
Providence for the theatre on which man was to make his true figure,
on which science, virtue, liberty, happiness, and glory were to exist in
peace."[1] Revolution would create the "American" as a "new man."
Revolution would change the spirit of man and the fabric of society,
which was more essential than merely changing the political structure.
To be sure, the revolution was composed of pluralistic factors which
do not always fit neatly into opposing camps. It was diverse and not
necessarily new in its parts. The revolution was a product of compromise, modification and even improvisation. But, from its combined
English and colonial heritage it chose and discarded until it produced
something new and different.

The views of American revolutionists were based, in part, on English
ideas, especially on the works of Milton and Locke. The people, it was
believed, had the right to rise up against their rulers if the latter failed
to promote the public welfare. The people could do this through
limited resistance to nullify specific acts or through revolution if it was
believed the government should be terminated completely. However,
by the mid-18th century this view had been modified. The right of
revolution was still valid, but limitations of violence and resistance
were emphasized to act as a restraint. Thus, the American Revolution
was faced with the problem of reconciling the right of revolution with
the injunction to restraint. Revolution was never to be employed initially. Milton had advised that "all due means of redress" were to be
tried before force. Locke had written that where injury may be relieved
and damages repaired by the use of law, there could be "no pretence
for force." In other words, implicit in the concept of revolution for
Americans, as well as for Englishmen, was that they were justified as
defense mechanisms only. Governments could be overthrown only
when "the Mischief be grown general," and the tyranny or "Designs
of the Rulers become notorious;" not just a few individuals, but the
"Body of the People" had to feel concerned.[2] This was the framework
within which American revolutionists labored and which formed the
basis for their concept of revolution. Actions of government would
have to be assessed to determine their utility for the public good. If
the English government was found seriously wanting in this respect a

revolution could be started. But American revolutionists still had to gain broad popular support and they would have to be careful so as to avoid anarchy and effect an orderly revolution.

But revolution did not mean national independence at the outset. Independence became the aim only after other possibilities had been exhausted and after Americans realized that they could not find more acceptable solutions to their grievances. Prior to 1776 an attempt was—and had to be—made to alter the distribution of power *within* the constitution and to accept a de facto change in the relationship between the colonies and the mother country. In other words, before 1776 the revolutionists were seeking not an American revolution but a British-style revolution. In fact, where the Declaration of Independence laid the responsibiltiy for unconstitutional acts directly on the king, and not his "evil" ministers, it was conforming to English revolutionary tradition. Nevertheless, American pride in being British faded in the 1760's and significantly disappeared in the 1770's thus making independence and revolution possible. The revolution, to quote John Adams again, "was effected before the war commenced. The revolution was in the minds and hearts of the people; . . . *This radical change in the principles, opinions, sentiments, and affections of the people was the real American Revolution."³*

Unlike the French Revolution, which rejected the past, the American Revolution, in some measure, fulfilled the past. Having no feudal structure to overthrow, much of the American Revolution was a reform of existing institutions. When Thomas Jefferson wrote about equality, it was equality before the law, not social and economic equality— and this was what Locke had meant by equality. Men should have a share in the political power equal to their function or stake in society.

But more importantly and fundamentally the American Revolution was an ideological, constitutional and political struggle. The intimate relationship between revolutionary thought and the conditions of life in America endowed the revolution with a unique force and made it a profoundly transforming and influential event. The revolution saw the re-conception and re-formulation of the basis of government and of the people's relationship with government with the aim being the preservation of liberty: the legislature should reflect the society and act on behalf of the people; human rights should be above the law and be the gauge of the law's validity; absolute sovereignty in government should not merely be the monopoly of a single, powerful body but the common possession of several bodies, each limited by the checks and balances of the others. Most importantly, the ultimate source of sovereignty should lie with the people themselves.

The American Revolution was not a social revolution. No significant reordering of society was intended. Yet, American society was transformed significantly. It may have been unintended, but ultimately the American Revolution undermined a basic premise of 18th century society—and thus its legitimacy—that the existence of rich and poor, socially superior and inferior were part of the natural order of the universe. Perhaps, it was thus suggested, politics was more of a factor in determining such a situation. In this way, the revolution intensified the sense of a new era which had become manifest during the age of the Enlightenment.

In the final analysis, revolution for America was the means to build a better world than any that had ever been known. Such a world could be built because authority was supposed to be under constant surveillance, because the position of men was supposed to be based upon achievements, not birth, and because the use of power over individual lives was supposed to be restricted. The revolution would establish such a society with institutions that would express human aspirations, not destroy them. The revolutionists were at one and the same time political conservatives and radical visionaries; they wished to preserve the best of the English constitution while they created a life on earth that would be blessed with abundance rather than damned by scarcity.

To protect their liberty Americans began one of the earliest modern anti-colonial wars for independendence. This move towards independence was a rejection of previously established relationships out of which emerged an ideology and a form of government called "republicanism." It was, therefore, this republicanism, as a separate form of government, different from England's, which transformed a rebellion within the British Empire into a revolution and a symbol for liberation everywhere. In this sense the events in America helped inaugurate the age of the democratic revolution.

II

If the American Revolution was one of the first revolutions of this period certainly the French Revolution, which was ignited in 1789, became the most famous—or infamous. There were other upheavals that comprised the age: the Irish and Dutch rose in defiance against their governments in the 1770's; in Geneva there was a small-scale revolt in 1763; in Belgium there was a conflict in 1789; and there was one in Poland in 1788. But the French Revolution epitomized the democratic revolution. As we have seen, the word "revolution" was used by the English in 1688, and by others occasionally as well. But in 1789 "revolution" became virtually institutionalized. The revolutionist was no longer an insurgent but one who, with reason, stood on the side of revolution. *Revolution* came to replace the "state," the "church," and even "God." The French Revolution quickly absorbed and exceeded the influence of the American Revolution. Although most of the other democratic revolutions had been defeated by 1792, the disaffected in those countries were receptive to events in France and many of their movements were revived with the international wars that began in the 1790's.

In 1789 revolution once and for all came to be viewed as a finite process, no longer a supernatural phenomenon controlled by forces beyond human influence. Revolution was to be a man-made action aimed at creating a new order founded on liberty, freedom and reason. Mankind, it had come to be believed in the 18th century, was perfectible and revolution was a means for achieving perfectibility—and a superior means at that since its results would be visible quickly. In the process, revolution would do away with outmoded institutions and become the means by which the original rights of man would be restored, rights which had been stolen from the beginnings of history. It was this rather grandiose ideal which gave the French Revolution its tremendous force and its international significance. Without it, 1789 would have been a mere rebellion of little more than local importance, and it would not be possible to call this an age of revolution that attempted to change the world. Until the success of the Russian Revolution more than a century and a quarter later the French Revolution was *the* great precedent and example of a true revolution.

Wendell Phillips, the American abolitionist, once said that "a revolution is as natural a growth as an oak. It comes out of the past. Its foundations are far back." The extent to which the cultural phenomenon of the 18th century known as the Enlightenment was a cause of the French Revolution has been a subject for debate among historians for generations. Although we do not wish to enter this debate it is our contention that it takes more than just ideas—but ideas based on concrete political, social and economic grievances—to cause a revolution. However, this is not to say that the relationship between the Enlightenment and the French Revolution is tenuous. The Enlightenment affected the course and feeling of the revolution, and it provided the ideals for which the revolution was fought, at least in its early stages. From the Enlightenment came the expectation, not of revolution per se, but of a civilization of the future, of the reachable future that would be more rational, progressive, efficient and equitable than then existed. The revolution began as the fruition of the Enlightenment: liberty and toleration, the rights of man, and the religion of humanity.

The French Revolution started as an aristocratic attempt to recapture control of the state in order to defend French laws and protect the French nation; it was this group which pressured the crown into calling the Estates General. But their attempt failed because it minimized the economic and social crises facing the nation and it underestimated the independent attitude of the Third Estate. (Interestingly, the middle class, or bourgeoisie, in their desire for prosperity, law and order, is usually a conservative force. But because the inefficiency and selfishness of the aristocracy prevented the middle class from achieving their goals in France they became the revolutionists of 1789.) The revolution was neither led nor made by any party in the modern sense of the word. The initial revolt of the aristocracy taught the Third Estate, which was dominated by the middle class, the language, methods and glory of opposition. Although the revolution grew by itself, unplanned, what was prevalent among its main figures and their supporters was a common set of ideas which had been expressed throughout the century. It was these ideas and the ideal of revolution thus established which helped to make the French Revolution seek not only a readjustment in society but the destruction of the old order and the construction of a new one.

The summoning of the Estates General raised the hope of Frenchmen that the government would do something about their problems. These raised expectations and hopes were shattered by the events at Versailles in June and July, 1789. Hostility towards the aristocracy and advisers of the king was intensified by the growing popularity of a revolutionary pamphlet which had appeared earlier in the year. The chief message of *What Is The Third Estate?* by the Abbé Siéyès was that the nation was sovereign and that the Third Estate was virtually identical with the nation. The Third Estate, he wrote, did most of the work in the country, but received none of the lucrative and respected positions, which were reserved for the privileged. The aristocracy was a small and useless minority that could be eliminated without a loss, and its elimination would make the nation even greater.

In the days that followed there was much disorder and violence, but Frenchmen looked forward to a new, fair and equitable order. On August 26 the "Declaration of the Rights of Man and the Citizen" was issued. Despite all that happpened between 1789 and 1815 this document—a product of the Enlightenment—became the embodiment of the revolution, the symbol of the new society and the chief pronouncement of the 18th century revolution. To be sure, the idea of commiting these rights to paper and appending them to a written constitution came from the American example. But unquestionably it was the French document which was carried eleswhere to provide a revolutionary incentive in other countries. Because of its importance in summing up what revolution meant to the French—and Europeans in general in the 19th century—it would be useful to highlight the key points: "Men are born and remain free and equal in rights," it stated. "Social distinctions can be founded only on common utility." The basic rights of man are "liberty, property, security and resistance to oppression." Liberty is the right to do anything that is not harmful to others, which in turn is to be established by law. Law should be the expression of the general will and must be uniform for all. Citizens have the right, "personally or by their representatives," to take part in the formulation of the law. Law must be obeyed by all and all must be subject to the law. Innocence is presumed until guilt is proven; where punishments are necessary they are to be just. Opinions and the press are to be free, subject only to the needs of public order. Taxes and an armed forces are necessary, but for the benefit of all and under the control of society as a whole. Property is a basic right but could be expropriated, with compensation, for the public good. All government officials are to be held accountable for their actions, with ability determining place. And finally, sovereignty resides in the nation.

If the Declaration of Rights was the embodiment of the French Revolution then the personification of the revolution, in its early and extreme stage, was an attorney named Maximilien Robespierre (1758-94). A member of the National Convention and its Committee of Public Safety he was incorruptible and had a fundamental faith in the Revolution. He and his fellow Jacobins believed in a collective, civilian, revolutionary dictatorship, not dissimilar to the kind some 20th century revolutionists would later advocate. He viewed such a body as a temporary but powerful guardian of the nation, acting on behalf of the people, until the new society could be firmly established. He believed in Terror and Virtue: "Virtue without which Terror is evil, Terror

without which Virtue is helpless." Virtue was characteristic only of a
minority and, coupled with Terror, was necessary during revolution.
Robespierre wanted a democracy for France, but only a representative
democracy.

Our major concern here is not with all the events of the Revolution,
with the role played by Napoleon or with deciding a terminal date.
What remains now in this discussion of the French Revolution is to
determine its contribution to the development of the concept of revolution. There are, to be sure, aspects of the French Revolution that tie
it to earlier revolutions; it was, after all, in part a return to the past,
and it was begun with a program to renovate the ancient constitution.
But more importantly and, for all intents and purposes, for the first
time revolution came to mean an attempt to create a new historical
future. Revolution ran counter to the flow of history as it sought to
advance history to a higher level. Revolution became the process of
beginning anew! As Thomas Paine (1737-1809), the English-born
American revolutionist and friend of France, said: "We have it in our
power to begin the world over again." When the French cut off the
head of Louis XVI and proclaimed a republic, beginning it in the Year
One, they were coupling the experience of a new beginning with the
idea of freedom and liberty. It was Condorcet (1743-94), a nobleman
and *philosophe* executed by the Revolution, who expressed the view
that "the word *revolutionary* can be applied only to revolutions which
have liberty as their object." Even though the Terror of the Jacobins,
the reaction of Thermidor and the dictatorship of Napoleon broke the
spell that liberty and freedom naturally resulted from revolution, the
ideal of revolution as it relates to the extension of liberty and freedom
became a part of European revolutionary tradition.

Of equal significance is the fact that with the French Revolution—
and later to be reenforced by the Russian Revolution—, revolution
came to be a phenomenon that extended beyond mere national boundaries and was part of a world-wide movement for the liberation of all
peoples from tyranny. The revolutionists of 1789 believed passionate-
ly that their principles were not only life-giving but true, and therefore
must be adopted by all the world. Napoleon claimed to share at least
this latter view. Only by a global victory could the new order lead to
the establishment of a universal society in which all people would be
at last free from oppression and want. But the French Revolution
spread as much by design as by the fact that much of Europe had
similar institutions, ideas and social conditions; a ready-made audience

for the Revolution existed in most countries. Since the old order was responsible for wars and injustices it was only right and just, even obligatory for the Revolution to be extended. The National Convention, in April, 1792, proclaimed: "The French Nation . . . engages not to subscribe to any treaty and not to lay down its arms until the sovereignty and independence of the people whose territory the troops of the Republic shall have entered shall be established, and until the people shall have adopted the principles of equality and founded a free and democratic government."[4] In this way the French Revolution believed it represented the masses of poor in all countries. (Here the French Revolution anticipated the revolutionary views of Russia, China, Cuba and Algeria as well as, perhaps, the alleged view of the United States in the role of policeman of the world.) As Tocqueville wrote: "By seeming to tend rather to the regeneration of the human race than to reform France alone, it roused passions such as the most violent political revolutions have been incapable of awakening."[5] Although France failed to impose itself on the rest of the globe French ideas succeeded in transforming the world. Other revolutions preceded and even contributed to causing the French Revolution; the American Revolution specifically provided a constitutional model for France, as well as for Latin America. But it was the French Revolution which sent shock waves throughout the planet.

The French Revolution is proof, if proof is needed, that ideas matter in history. The French Revolution was the embodiment of a great idea: sovereignty of the people or the nation. It was an idea that transformed a domestic conflict into a monumental war of ideas. Popular sovereignty means that the people who rule are the same as those over whom power is exercised; the people, in other words, rule themselves and popular sovereignty is freedom. The Englishman Edmund Burke saw the danger in this principle in that popular sovereignty could be fatal to liberty. That is, whatever government has the power to do it has the right to do and thus any act is permissible; anything done in the name of the people is not a crime, and this could justify tyranny and aggression. A people must, it seems to us, beware of self-proclaimed saints, whether the emerge from the political right or left, or anywhere in between. The test of true popular sovereignty is whether a people, if they are dissatisfied with their rulers, can freely and peacefully cause their government to change its policies, or themselves change their government.

The age of the democratic revolution had no single spokesman, but

Thomas Paine's *The Rights of Man* (1791) goes some way to provide the keynote for the period as well as for the concept of revolution in the 19th century before Marx. He wrote: "What we formerly called Revolutions, were little more than a change of persons, or an alteration of local circumstances. They rose and fell like things of course, and had nothing in their existence or their fate that could influence beyond the spot that produced them. But what we now see in the world, from the Revolutions of America and France, are a renovation of the natural order of things, a system of principles as universal as truth and the existence of man, and combining moral with political happiness and national prosperity."[6]

NOTES

[1] Quoted in Bernard Bailyn, *The Ideological Origins of the American Revolution* (Cambridge, Mass., 1967), p. 20.

[2] Quoted in Pauline Maier, *From Resistance to Revolution: Colonial Radicals and the Development of American Opposition to Britain, 1765-1776* (New York, 1972), p. 35.

[3] John Adams to H. Niles, 13 February 1818, in C. F. Adams (ed.), *The Works of John Adams* (Boston, 1850–56), X, 282.

[4] Quoted in Carlton J. H. Hayes, *The Historical Evolution of Modern Nationalism* (New York, 1931), pp. 39f.

[5] Alexis de Tocqueville, *The Old Regime and The Revolution* (New York, 1856), p.27.

[6] Thomas Paine, *The Rights of Man* (New York, 1951), pp. 135f.

8

Revolution
in the 19th Century

The French Revolution (1789) was a guidepost for most 19th century
revolutions. A sense of national identity had developed fully and was
expressed in such words as *citoyen* (citizen) and *patrie* (homeland).
Subsequent revolutions attempted to create a similar sense of nationalism. Although the 19th century witnessed revolutionary activity, the
idea of revolution persisted more than actual revolution itself. The
men of the period planned, wrote and theorized about revolution as
never before. For many 1789 was only a beginning which had aroused
hopes that they might attempt to fulfill. It was generally believed,
especially in the first half of the century, that revolution would give
birth to a secular state with civil liberties and guarantees for private
enterprise, and a representative, liberal, bourgeois government of tax-
payers and property owners. The 19th century was also the age of the
so-called Industrial Revolution. The changes it brought about helped
to metamorphose revolutionary activity to become more egalitarian

oriented and preoccupied with violence. Industrialization made the nature and structure of economy and society a primary subject for revolutionists. No longer would political concerns alone be central to revolution. Rather, all aspects of society were interrelated with revolution. This development reached a climax with Marx, who will be discussed in the next chapter.

I

Joining the ranks of Aristotle, Milton, Locke and Paine as a truly great theorist of revolution was Alexis de Tocqueville (1805-59) whose life bridged the gap between the French Revolution and Marx. Tocqueville's primary concern was with understanding the factors necessary for a free, stable and democratic society. This, in turn, led him to investigate revolutions. Tocqueville rarely treated revolution separate from the specific societies and events he analyzed so that it is from these works that we must determine his contribution. Revolution, he wrote, was not the work of conspiracy but was due "to the natural emergence of emotions long felt." He analyzed three broad types of revolutions: political, social and religious. A political revolution he saw as a change in the quality of the government. Social revolution resulted in the replacement of one class of leaders for another, of the substitution of one system of property control for another. A religious revolution witnessed the elimination of one set of principles concerning the nature and destiny of man and the adoption of another set. Any revolution that was all three at once was likely to be very violent, not only at its inception but also after stable government had been reestablished. Such was the price of revolution. Tocqueville was also a pioneer in demonstrating the relationship between the economic and political aspects of revolution. Revolutions, he wrote, "are not always brought about by a gradual decline from bad to worse. Nations that have endured patiently and almost unconsciously the most overwhelming of oppression, often burst into rebellion against the yoke the moment it begins to grow lighter. The regime which is destroyed by a revolution is almost always an improvement on its immediate predecessor, and experience teaches that the most critical moment for bad governments is the one which witnesses their first steps toward reform."[1] Revolution is what will challenge a government when it no longer fulfills the function that once made it legitimate.

Tocqueville was born too late to feel a personal involvement in the

French Revolution. Yet, he was an inside observer to the revolutions that swept France and Europe in 1830 and 1848. Those of 1830 need not detain us for more than a moment. Suffice it to say that the principles and ideals of 1789 had been challenged by aristocratic elements only to be defeated in 1830. The Revolutions of 1830 marked the beginning of the triumph of bourgeois power in Western Europe; the ruling classes now began to be the bankers, industrialists and civil servants.

The Revolutions of 1848 were the most important to confront Europe between 1789 and 1917 because they were, in part, an attempt to complete the work and fulfill the aspirations created by the age of the democratic revolution and because they provided something of a basis for the writings of Marx, the spiritual father of the Russian Revolution. Yet, 1848 was considerably different from the two great historical revolutions between which it is seemingly wedged. The Revolutions of 1848 were led by men who had grievances, aims and ideals, but little destructive fury; there was little extreme violence that characterized these revolutions. The leaders were moderates and intellectuals who did not direct any highly organized or dynamic groups. The revolutionists were not prepared to transform society in totality; in fact, there was considerable respect for authority and property.

After 1830 the various groups and classes in Western Europe became acutely aware of the conflicts within society. Aristocratic privilege and oppression were at the heart of these conflicts, which were rendered more complicated by confusion and fear resulting from a rapidly changing world. Most of these groups and classes participated in the 1848 revolutions, but for a variety of reasons. In this sense the Revolutions of 1848 were disjointed. Yet, there was at least one goal that was common to all: each of the groups wanted to participate in society far more than they already did (if they did at all) so that their interests and rights would be respected. In this sense it is proper to speak of 1848 as a unified set of revolutions. Perhaps the notion of contagion may help to lend further credence to 1848 as a composite revolution. To be sure, Germans, for example, did not revolt merely because Frenchmen did. But the Europeans who made and joined these revolutions shared a number of common convictions; that their world needed to be reordered significantly resulted in feelings that went beyond local issues and provided a common identity among the disaffected. Despite differences in social and political structure, language, race and economic levels Europe responded to 1848 with considerable uniformity. The course of the revolutions was generally the same. Each began with a popular uprising which compelled the governments to yield quickly. The exuberance of victory was deflated by a cognizance of division among the victors. These divisions were not healed and thus time was given to the conservatives to take the offensive. Finally came successful counterrevolts and a resurrection of the old establishment. This was the outline followed in France, Germany, Italy, Austria and Hungary. Unlike many other revolutions, those of 1848 were not the results of war; rather, they came after three decades of a peace based on conservatism and reaction. They were as much revolutions of hope as they were of despair.

The Revolutions of 1848, with economic and social discontent providing a common background, were ignited by the workers, participated in by the masses, and controlled by the middle classes. The middle classes particularly wanted to participate in their governments and reform them along national lines. In this regard, 1848 was a conflict between national self-determination on the one hand and dynastic and aristocratic interests on the other. The latter stood for arbitrary rule and autocracy, the former for the rights of man and self-government; dynastic interests related to land whereas national self-determination related to men as individuals apart from the land. With rapid industrialization and urbanization it is clear that European society was changing less quickly than the ideas and hopes of those who were affected. There is, to be sure, always a discrepancy between things as they are and things as they ought to be. But to the revolutionists of 1848 the gulf between the ideal (of freedom, humanity and reason) and the reality was great enough to warrant action to readjust the balance. Here lies the key to the origins and thus the idea of revolution for 1848. For the businessmen, merchants, artisans and workers there developed an awareness of the need for rapid change in their conditions.

Space does not allow for an examination of each of the 1848 revolutions so we will turn to Germany for further evaluation. Unlike the 1789 French Revolution the German Revolution of 1848 did not begin as a result of a financial crisis that the old regime could not resolve. Instead, it was a delayed reaction to hard times, a protest against conditions that were already improving, but not fast enough. The aristocracy lost its domination of politics as the upheaval of peasants and artisans gained initial success. The peasants and artisans turned to the middle class for guidance and leadership. These liberal leaders were dreaming of a parliamentary government and an economically strong Germany. For them 1848 was a first step towards the reorganization of society and the creation of a new order based on talent and wealth. "Behind their blueprints for federal union and individual freedom rose the vision of a land of factories, banks, railroads, and steamships in which political and economic liberty were one."[2] But these middle class liberals knew that they possessed neither the strength nor authority to impose their views on the nation. They needed the assistance of the workers and peasants to defeat the aristocracy and maintain themselves in power. Unfortunately for the revolution an uprising in the spring of 1849 by workers was suppressed thoroughly enough to destroy the revolutionary spirit of the rank and file. The middle class liberals were isolated and their victory was to be short-lived. The liberals failed to reflect the interests of the German people; they tried to govern on the basis of bourgeois ethics and thus lost sight of the masses whom they had used to gain and needed to maintain power. The policies of the liberals neglected the workers' immediate needs— needs which had inaugurated the revolution—and thus lost their necessary support. When their common enemy (i.e., conservatism and aristocracy) was initially defeated the common purpose evaporated and the victory was fragmented.

To each of its main participants revolution meant something different. To the middle class liberals it was a chance to establish parliamentary government and material prosperity. To the workers it was a chance to gain control over industrial production and improve their lot. To the peasants it was an opportunity to abolish manorialism and redistribute land. But each group fought for its own goals so that concerted action was unlikely after their initial collective victory. With victory each group came into conflict with the others, which made the eventual victory of reaction possible. The German Revolution of 1848, therefore, was really several simultaneous revolutions, each with its own aims and ideals. After overthrowing a government they all considered oppressive the liberal middle class revolution came to dominate. It achieved some successes (e.g., the Frankfurt Parliament, the Fundamental Rights of the German People, and the Constitution of March 28, 1849) but they were made possible only by the other revolutions. The peasants and workers were willing to accept liberal leadership, but only so long as their material needs were satisfied. The many revolutionists were successful only in condemning the past. Too many conflicts and problems meant liberalism would not work. A new order acceptable to all was impossible to build.

A similar fate met the other 1848 revolutions. They were all in one way or another unsuccessful attempts at a radical transformation of society. In fact, many people lost faith in the concept of freedom, and the belief that popular based revolutions were a useful means of change was undermined. If nationalism and demands for popular sovereignty contributed to the coming of these revolutions, then they also contributed to their failure. The revolutionists of 1848 worked to make a world where men could feel a greater degree of equality and to make nations within which this feeling could operate. They failed because they misjudged their obstacles and were reluctant to trust the people.

After 1848 the ideal of revolution was slowly but significantly altered by a variety of forces, the three most important of which were Anarchism, Syndicalism and Marxism. Before turning to them, however, we will digress for the space of a couple of sections to consider two other significant 19th century upheavals, the American Civil War and the Paris Commune. The former, while having important consequences for the history of the United States, involved the concept of revolution in a regressive departure from its generally accepted mid-century status. The latter was an event that, though it was short-lived and achieved little, exercised a profound influence upon the course of French history, revolutionary theorizing and the subsequent international history of revolution.

II

The American Civil War (1861-65) was a revolution of sorts. It was not an attempt to change the political, economic or social system and replace it with another. It was not a revolution in the sense of a popular uprising against oppression. Nor was it a revolution where the concept is associated with freedom and its advancement (although the victory of the established government—the North—did result in constitutional amendments which theoretically, at least, aimed at improving the lot of former slaves). The Civil War was, however, a conservative and secessionist revolution against a changing society and the established government and in defense of something old (i.e., the Southern way of life). As with anti-colonial revolutions, home rule, independence and the overthrow of the existing political structure were sought, but unlike them, revolution was begun for the purpose of conserving something old, not creating something new. In this way, the Civil War saw revolutionary methods used to gain conservative ends. In another sense the Civil War provides a theoretical link between the pre-18th century concept (i.e., revolution as restoration) and the 20th century Fascist or Nazi concept (i.e., regressive and racist—see chapter 12). This is not necessarily to condemn Southern revolutionists as fascists or to imply that Hitler, Mussolini and company modeled themselves after Jefferson Davis, Robert E. Lee and company. But there is, we believe, at least this one common strand among these movements insofar as the nature of the concept of revolution is concerned.

III

The Paris Commune, or French Revolution of 1871, came in the wake of French defeat at the hands of the Germans during which time the Second Empire of Napoleon III fell. This was followed by a four-month German siege of Paris, a sharp conflict between supporters of republicanism and monarchy, and the infusion of socialist ideas and aspirations.

There were elements of class revolution in the Commune. Whereas French history had been characterized by a severe gap between the rich and poor, during the Second Empire republicanism, to the rich, had meant disorder and unrest, while to the poor it had meant social reform. The siege of Paris accentuated the differences between the essentially rich and poor, and set the stage for the violent outbreak of class hostility in the Commune (which was elected to govern Paris). After the siege the country might have returned to a more normal condition, at least insofar as class relations were concerned, but matters had gone too far; class divisions had widened and violence was an accepted part of life.

On the eve of the revolution the lower middle class and the workers were drawn closer together when the new, monarchist-dominated National Assembly declared that all debts were to be payable immediately. The Assembly also transferred its meeting place (from Bordeaux) to Versailles, instead of Paris, which was interpreted as a first step in the re-establishment of the monarchy. This was followed by the suppression of several newspapers—thus jeopardizing freedom of the press—and the removal of the cannons which the Paris National Guard had mounted in strategic parts of the city. The tension and emotions of Paris erupted in March, 1871.

The Commune was not communistic—as the name may sound—but rather a belief in a type of government that had its roots in French history—many communards believed that they were simply continuing and promoting previous French revolutions. Although they were ideologically disunited, they all seemed to identify with some aspect of French revolutionary tradition. Whereas there were some socialist and Marxist members of the Commune who viewed it as the beginning of a future pattern for revolutions, it is probably more accurate to regard the Commune as the climax of an egalitarian and even utopian revolutionary past. The idea of the Commune connoted glory and victory (i.e., the 1793 Commune of Paris had helped to defeat the invaders of France) and this was especially meaningful considering the proximity of the Germans.

The Commune was a reaction against an overcentralized government that had existed under the monarchy and empire. It was a demand for the decentralization of authority and a federalized state wherein small, self-governing sections would be the chief characteristic. In this way the Commune was a move for local autonomy and an attempt to reduce society to more human needs and dimensions. Another, and not unrelated aspect of the Commune was its patriotic overtones—in this way it was a revolution against those who had capitulated. The revolutionists, whatever their ideological convictions, were almost all chauvinists who deplored the weakness and incapacity of those who had led France in her disastrous conflict with Germany.

The Commune ended in late May, a brief two months after it had been founded, in a bloody civil war with government troops. Marx, and later Lenin, hailed the Commune as the first real proletarian revolution and a part of the movement for social reform all over Europe and the world. To be sure, there were ideas of a new society present among many of the communards, but mostly only as part of the larger ideal of the republic; only where that ideal contained the germ for social reform can we speak of the Commune as a social revolution. The class grievances that existed were not based upon inequities in the social order per se, but upon the hostility against the way the war had been fought and the peace settled. The class that made the revolution did so more for patriotic reasons than socialist reasons. The French proletariat did not identify with international socialism or Marxian ideology, but with the republican and social theories of 19th century French theorists, such as Louis Blanqui. The revolution was essentially a spontaneous uprising, sparked by unrest and patriotism.

In the final analysis, the Commune, or Revolution of 1871, may be interpreted as an attempt to resolve old grievances for local autonomy from an anti-republican Assembly while it came to symbolize resistance to a foreign foe, especially since Parisians felt that they had been betrayed into defeat. The poor of Paris—who believed in the old, revolutionary idea of a republic—became revolutionists after being humiliated by the war, the peace and the Assembly. Revolution, to most of the communards, despite socialists, Marxists and anarchists among them, was not a new beginning per se, but a renewed beginning of an old hope, plucked from the not too distant revolutionary past. In this sense it was an amorphous idea that attracted the disenchanted of Paris following the end of a siege that had failed. The Commune had no universally recognized leaders and no single, generally agreed upon ideology. But perhaps this was the cause of its strength; it was something different to all its participants. The Commune has been glorified in this century as a symbol of modern revolution but this, it seems, is unhistorical.

The ideology of the Commune, as has just been shown, was in part a product of anarchism, Marxism and socialism. Anarchism will be dealt with in the next section and Marxism in the next chapter. Socialism, in 1871, was perhaps best personified in the ideas of Louis Auguste Blanqui (1805-81). Blanquism contributed a great deal to the consolidation of the spontaneous rising that gave birth to the Commune, although Blanquists hardly comprised anything like an organized party. Blanqui himself was an advocate of immediate political revolution—which alienated him from Marx. He was a middle class intellectual whose political disappointments led him to identify progress with the proletariat. Although he was a utopian in that he believed that the perfectibility of mankind could be advanced through the actions of a few enlightened men, mostly Blanqui was a man of action.

Blanqui was an important link between the Jacobins of the French Revolution and modern revolutionary socialism. He believed in the necessity of a tightly-knit, disciplined, insurrectionist organization, an enlightened elite not unlike Lenin's communist elite which would act as the vanguard of the proletariat. To Blanqui revolution was both an idea and a will to carry it out. Translated into action this meant that the elite would have to cut itself off from the masses—to be certain of the discipline, secrecy and resolution needed for the revolution—and, in their name, destroy the political system of capitalist oppression. For a revolution to result in socialism it had to be begun by socialists. The elite might utilize the assistance of the proletariat, but it had to begin and lead the revolution to guarantee the masses the power that had so often yielded to the bourgeoisie. In other words, Blanqui's revolution would virtually force the people to be free. Here perhaps, in his acceptance of the special revolutionary role of a conspiracy of the elite, is the crux of Blanqui's revolutionary ideal. The elite, coming from the déclassé elements of society (mostly bourgeois intellectuals and enlightened workers), knew the causes of oppression but did not wish to profit from it. Since the masses were too ignorant to free themselves the elite would lead the way. And since the elite could not always count on mass support (because of the limitations imposed by the legal system and lack of mass consciousness) it could best serve the masses by cutting itself off from them so as to organize safely a secret force which would destroy capitalism.

Like Marx, Blanqui believed in a vague communist millenium. But he qualified this belief with a conviction that the success of such a society depends upon the quality of the mass mind. Thus, full enlightenment will be necessary for the establishment of communism. In fact, enlightenment was the precondition for a successful revolution and for the good society it would create. Communism was a consequence of enlightenment, and not the other way around. "The material causes of poverty," he wrote, "such as capitalism and all other forms of exploitation only exist because of the ignorance of the masses." For Marx, the opposite was true: "It is not the consciousness of men that determines their being, but, on the contrary, their social existence that determines their consciousness."[3]

Blanqui's interest in revolution included some sort of egalitarian and collectivist economic system. But he apparently lacked the theoretical equipment to enunciate his socialism with any precision. Moreover, he was not interested in analyzing the social order in any more detail than would include a definition of injustices, an attack upon the status quo and a prediction of destruction. Nevertheless, the influence of Blanqui on subsequent generations of European socialists in general and the French left in particular has been great.

IV

As much as anything else modern Anarchism has been a product of the industrial revolution of the 19th century. Although it had its historical roots in earlier revolutionary utopian and millenarian movements, as well as in the 18th century Enlightenment, it evolved out of the ideal of revolution of 1789. Yet, it was precisely the failure of subsequent 19th century revolutions and reforms to satisfy economic and social needs which led the anarchists to challenge both their society and other revolutionists.

Anarchism, as a creed for political action, has stood, in the words of one of its own, for "destruction, terrible, complete, universal, and merciless."[4] While the methods of anarchism have often been violent the movement has been generated as a result of rapid social change by destroying as much of the state as possible and restoring a simpler, pre-national, pre-industrial life which would emphasize cooperation instead of authority. Voluntary associations, not governmental restraints, are the indispensable conditions for total political, social and economic liberty. Revolution is the process by which the grip of authority is loosened or removed, so that the functions of life can regulate themselves. Revolution for anarchists is a sudden, rapid, major change in the political form of the state, followed quickly by fundamental economic and social changes. But these important changes are most likely to take place after the elimination of goverment, and not its replacement with another. In other words, the people themselves, as opposed to their representatives or a government, should change society. Anarchists see the revolution as a present, not future phenomenon. The revolution would not be merely political since there have been many political revolutions which have only replaced one regime with another or one class with another. Revolution for anarchists—and they have never made a successful one—is social in that society and the economic structure must be changed along with the destruction of the state. The aim of revolution is not to transfer power but to abolish the institutions of authority and the social system upon which it rests.

As with most political doctrines anarchism has had a number of important advocates, not all of whom have always been in agreement. Three of its most influential 19th century founders were the Frenchman Pierre-Joseph Proudhon (1809-65) and the Russians Mikhail Bakunin (1814-76) and Prince Peter Kropotkin (1842-1921).

For Proudhon revolution and progress are identical in that future progress would not be possible without a revolutionary change in the social and political order. The revolution, to be effective, must be contagious and eventually universal. But the revolution must do more than overturn the old order. It must also lead mankind towards greater rationality and sociability. Proudhon feared that his contemporary revolutionists would fail to provide such leadership, and that revolution would then result in a new tyranny. Still, revolution is inevitable and its purpose "is to straighten society up again, as a young tree is straightened with the aid of a support, to make it take a different direction." It is "an act of sovereign justice . . . springing out of the necessity of things, and [is] . . . its own justification."[5]

Bakunin was an advocate of the complete overthrow of the existing order and he was responsible for the organized anarchist movement in parts of Europe. Revolution would be directed against institutions, not human beings. The power of the masses should be unleashed, but because they are incapable of building a new society Bakunin moved anarchist theory from Proudhon's abstract speculation on the use and abuse of political power to a theory of practical political action. Like Proudhon's, Bakunin's revolution would be universal and not confined to a single people. But the revolution cannot be improvised; circumstances will bring it about although some organization will be necessary, temporarily, to direct it for the people. But the initiative, which is spontaneous, belongs to the people; thus the revolution, unlike Blanqui's is to come from below. Social revolution must accompany political revolution, because the latter alone will only be bourgeois revolution which "will neccessarily end in new exploitation of the proletariat by the bourgeoisie—exploitation perhaps more skillful and hypocritical, but certainly no less oppressive."[6]

Neither as precise as Bakunin nor as theoretical as Proudhon, Kropotkin shared their indignation against the existing order. For him the anarchist revolution would be a prelude to moral rehabilitation as it fought against law, religion, authority and all forms of inequality. Revolution means "the rapid transformation of received ideas about morality. . . . It is not a simple change of governors [but] the taking possession by the people of all social wealth [and] the abolition of all the forces which have so long hampered the development of humanity . . . . [The people must] act according to their own will, and march without waiting for orders from anyone."[7]

The role of violence to revolutionists is always crucial. While there have been a minority of anarchists who were pacifists, revolutionary violence has characterized the mainstream of anarchist theory. Proudhon (and later Kropotkin) pondered the possibility of revolution without violence, and while he would have preferred it he concluded that a peaceful revolution was "too ideal for our bellicose nature," though the existence of anarchy per se is the antithesis of force. Bakunin wrote that "the urge of destruction is at the same time a creative urge," thus anticipating the defense of violence by countless revolutionists and glorifying it more than most. He did not hesitate to call forth "the bad passions of men" in order to destroy the old order completely. Unlike Bakunin (and his follower Sergei Nacheyev), most anarchists have not wanted bloodshed; but all have wanted change and have been willing to meet "legal" violence with their own violence when necessary. In line with this comes a word of caution from Emma Goldman, an American anarchist, who noted that the means influence and modify the end, and may even become identical with the end. Still, the anarchist should accept nothing less than complete freedom as an aim and his struggle must be constant. Direct action is necessary to prepare for the revolution and to make certain that once it has begun it proceeds properly. Anarchists may differ over tactics but they generally agree that all action should be based on free will. Revolution is thus a spontaneous rising of the people, but with "the people" seen, not in a Marxist collectivist sense, but as a grouping of sovereign individuals, each of whom must make his own decision to act. In this regard anarchists believe in the creative power of the people which is released in the revolution. Bakunin's faith in the masses was most complete, with destruction liberating their latent creative power. Revolution instigated by the masses, to Proudhon, would be revolution based on liberty.

History for anarchists, unlike for Marxists, does not proceed along the inevitable road of dialectical necessity. Rather, it emerges out of struggle, and human struggle is the result of man's free will. It is an awareness of this need for struggle to liberate society that brings anarchism to revolution. Government and property are forms of slavery which bring out the worst in man. The state must not be taken over but abolished, and with it must go all forms of compulsion. The revolution must result, not in the dictatorship of the proletariat, but in the abolition of all classes. Bakunin believed that you could not make the state wither away with a Marxian-type dictatorship since that would only result in a dictatorship *over* the proletariat in the name of mankind; instead, the people should represent themselves. To Proudhon the fundamental idea of revolution is "no more authority! That means something we have never seen, something we have never understood; the harmony of the interest of one with the interest of all."[8] Communism was not desirable because of its utopian nature and its denial of experience, destruction of the individual, and compulsion of everyone to surrender to the state.

As with most revolutionists, the anarchists we have been discussing held stronger ideas regarding the destruction of society than they did about its reconstruction. If only in a general sense, they recognized that life in an anarchist society would be decentralized, debureaucratized, simplified and inclusive. The ultimate goal of revolution, said Bakunin, is an international union of humanity, with each person fully able to develop his own potential. Society would be organized to guarantee that exploitation of labor was impossible and that the enjoyment of social wealth was shared by all insofar as everyone contributed toward the production of that wealth. Society would be composed of a network of balancing interests, based on the "natural" urge of mutual aid. Proudhon, who has been called the "father of modern anarchism," said that the ultimate triumph of the revolution would be the establishment of "justice." Justice is not only a law, but a "power of the soul and an attitude of mind." With it will come what is common to virtually all revolutionary ideals: a new humanity and a new man.

Revolutionary anarchism, it may be said by way of a postscript, marks a transition between the democratic revolution of the late 18th and early 19th centuries, on the one hand, and the socialist revolutions of the subsequent period.

V

Syndicalism was a late 19th and early 20th century French form of trade unionism which aimed, initially, at possessing the means of production and distribution, and ultimately, at overthrowing the state and controlling society. An amalgam of the theories of anarchism (especially Proudhon), socialism and Marxism, revolutionary syndicalism's primary goal was in the moral rehabilitation of man, which would be achieved in the struggle to destroy the state. As a vehicle for human transformation the class struggle would give birth to a sense of unification and a spirit of cooperation among the workers. Syndicalism, it was thus believed, would involve a psychological as well as an economic and political change which would be capable of remaking the world. "It leads the workers to battle, calls them to action, and shows itself as the power capable of regenerating the world."[9] The new order created by the spirit and action need not be pre-planned, which would only tend to make it utopian. The only pressing concern is action, for it alone is creative. This is an important point because in revolutionary syndicalism, most clearly and definitively, the creative value of direct action is underlined. Direct action is crucial not only for the ends in mind, but also for the psychological effect that such action has upon the actors themselves. The classical expression of revolutionary syndicalism is to be found in the writing of Georges Sorel (1847-1922).

An ex-Marxist, Sorel sought a new road to salvation for the workers and for society. Contemporary capitalist society, he said, lacked proper ethics and was suffering from moral disintegration. The middle classes were incapable of maintaining a decent society based upon cooperation and unselfishness. Sorel did not create revolutionary syndicalism, but he did express and elaborate upon the ideas which were a part of the movement. The new morality Sorel sought would emerge, not so much after the revolution as from the very struggle itself; the new morality would be the product of the workers' revolution. "It is to violence that Socialism owes those high ethical values by means of which it brings salvation to the modern world."[10]

Sorel discounted intellectual theorizing and traditional political activity as being useless diversions; only direct action could save the proletariat. No great movement, he said, especially one that hoped to gain the support of the masses, could succeed without a "myth." A myth is something which has the power to clutch the imagination of the people and inspire them to action. It is the belief in an imminent event which will transform the world. A myth should not be confused with a utopia, which is merely a description of things. Sorel opposed utopias because they directed men towards reforms which only patch up the existing system. Instead, a myth is a determination to act. The myth should be kept vague and not clearly defined in order to maintain its potency; but it is a glorious event which justifies full participation. The myth of the working class, according to Sorel, is the "general strike" (or mass strike), out of which the new society would emerge. Strikes bring out the best in the proletariat; "the general strike groups them all in a coordinated picture, and by bringing them together gives to each one of them its maximum intensity."[11]

Where syndicalism provided labor unions with a dominating role in revolution it was not without its utopian side. It dismissed the problems of the centralizing tendencies of modern industrial society by merely believing in decentralization. It claimed to solve the problem of a state by proclaiming that there would be none; the labor unions would govern without being a government. And it failed to explain how the general strike would be the panacea for modern man.

But none of this is to minimize the value of syndicalism in the development of the modern concept of revolution. Most importantly, revolutionary syndicalism espoused the doctrine of direct action. Direct action is the workers' helping and educating themselves in preparation for final emancipation. Direct action need not be violent, though it often is. But violent or not, it is the manifestation of the soul and the spirit of the workers themselves, without the intervention of others.

NOTES

[1] Alexis de Tocqueville, *The Old Regime and The Revolution* (New York, 1856), p. 214.

[2] Theodore S. Hamerow, *Restoration, Revolution, Reaction; Economics and Politics in Germany, 1815–1871* (Princeton, 1958), p. 101.

[3] Both quotes in Alan B. Spitzer, *The Revolutionary Theories of Louis Auguste Blanqui* (New York, 1957), p. 46.

[4] Mikhail Bakunin, *The Catechism of the Revolutionist* in Max Nomad, *Apostles of Revolution* (New York, 1961), p. 235.

[5] P.-J. Proudhon, *General Idea of the Revolution in the Nineteenth Century* (London, 1923), pp. 76, 40.

[6] *The Political Philosophy of Bakunin,* ed. by G. P. Maximoff (New York, 1953), p. 372.

[7] Peter Kropotkin, "Revolutionary Change" (c. 1880) in *Kropotkin's Revolutionary Pamphlets,* ed. by Roger N. Baldwin (New York, 1970), pp. 238, 247f.

[8] Proudhon, *General Idea,* p. 292.

[9] Quoted in Rev. James J. Maguire, *The Philosophy of Modern Revolution* (Washington, 1943), p. 60.

[10] Georges Sorel, *Reflections on Violence* (New York, 1912), p. 295.

[11] *Ibid.,* p. 137.

9

Revolution According
to Karl Marx

I

No 19th century figure has had as direct, determined and profound an influence upon the history of the world as Karl Marx (1818-83). A German born political philosopher and socialist, Marx lived less than a satisfying personal life; three of his six children failed to survive childhood and most of his adult years were spent in poverty. Although he wrote a great deal and was a renowned thinker in his own lifetime, he was hardly an immediate success in any material fashion; he was not even a political leader of any consequence. But he was a giant intellect and he was a revolutionist. (For the sake of convenience we are using Marx's name alone here although it would be just and proper to use his associate's, Friedrich Engels—1820-95—simultaneously in discussing most of Marxism and revolution.) His method of study was based not on observation and scientific deduction but upon an *a priori* conceptual scheme supplemented by a wealth of documentary material. For Marx ideas were useful only insofar as they influenced events. To his way of thinking his was the only method and the only cause. Marx's ideas on revolution provide the cornerstone for the edifice known as Marxism; in essence Marxism is a theory and a program for revolution, and Marxism (at least it was for Marx and Engels) is inseparable from the concept of revolution.

Marx learned about revolutions from his study of history, his peripheral involvement in the events of 1848, and his examination of the Paris Commune. He considered himself a scientific socialist—to distinguish himself from contemporary utopian socialists, such as Proudhon —and a determinist (i.e., he had Hegelian training). He believed that capitalism would be destroyed as a result of the inevitable operation of historical and economic laws, and that society would move towards the predetermined goal of socialism (a term he frequently used interchangeably with communism). Yet, the inevitable historical process could be accelerated, and that should be the task of socialists.

That there have been varying interpretations of Marx is obvious from just a glance at late 19th and 20th century history. His followers have spelled out his ideas differently—each of course in the name of Marx—and there have been many alternate roads taken along the path to socialism. For example, that revolutions by violence and non-violence have counted Marx as their inspiration was (and is) due to Marx's own ambiguities, rhetoric and lack of clearly defining key terms. But it has been a source of universal appeal and has made his collected works a revolutionist's bible.

Marx believed that the revolutionary future lay with the industrial workers in the cities of the West. As such, he was a product of 19th century history and thought, and Marxism forms a part of the legacy of the Industrial Revolution. Marxism was a protest against the inhumanity suffered by the workers. Humanitarianism could not exist under capitalism. Equality and freedom were impossible in a society dominated by a privileged few and where the majority were paid subsistence wages. Although the advance of capitalism was part of the order of history, so was its defeat. The Industrial Revolution had led theorists to think in terms of the divergent interests of different social classes. The middle and working classes of the cities could best be counted upon to initiate revolutions. The peasants in the countryside, however, were mostly ignored; at best, the peasantry would form an auxiliary force in the coming struggle. Peasants were geographically scattered and thus harder to gather and discipline; moreover, their aims were limited, they had not experienced the intensification of labor that characterized capitalism, and they tended to become a conservative force. Experience taught Marx to mistrust the religiously superstitious, backward rural population. As a consequence, the future of revolution would rest with the workers of the industrialized nations. Marx claimed to know more about the suffering of the workers than anyone else and more about the method for their emancipation.

II

Like Hegel, Marx conceptualized the idea of revolution as part of the forces of irresistible change, as history seeking its own fulfillment. But he also envisioned the active involvement of the individual as a necessity made possible by the evolution of society. "Men make their own history, but they do not make it as they please; they do not make it under self-selected circumstances, but under circumstances existing already, given and transmitted from the past."[1] In this way Marxism becomes a theory of the possibilities of revolution. Marxism combines facts with ideals. Although Marx would have denied it, his theory is utopian in that it foresees the appearance of a new and perfect order of human existence. But it is otherwise anti-utopian in that it is neither content merely to wait for that new order nor is it blindly optimistic. The new order would come out all right, but only through revolution; this revolution is a precondition for the appearance of socialism.

Marx saw history as proceeding from epoch to epoch, with each epoch being characterized by a different mode of production (i.e., slavery, feudalism, capitalism, socialism), and the mode of production determining the entire character of society. Revolutions, which Marx saw as the "locomotives of history," mark the transition from one epoch to the next. The change in the mode of production is the social revolution which, in turn, is the heart of the revolutionary process. Political revolution—which involves the destruction of the state and the assumption of power by the revolutionists—accompanies, and in fact initiates the social revolution, but it is not of supreme importance or as fundamental to the concept as the social revolution. Revolution is like birth: the social revolution is the entire physiological process, from conception, by which a new order is born; the political revolution is only the most obvious and sudden climax of the process. (We may note that Lenin, as we shall see in the next chapter, placed somewhat greater emphasis on the political aspects of revolution.) Still, the proletariat will not be able to change the social foundations without first destroying the old political system entirely, since every part of the state apparatus is contaminated with bourgeois ideology. Therefore, social revolutions must be preceded by political revolutions.

Many critical studies have revealed that the great success of Marxism has been based less on its logic and common sense or its claim to being scientific than on an appeal that is emotional, moral and even religious. Marx, of course, claimed that by studying history scientifically he was able to determine its course, present and future. But the truth is that much of Marxism rests upon a rather unscientific assertion of faith—a faith that the perfect society is both desirable and inevitable. Earlier in this chapter we made a passing comparison between the doctrines of Marxism and the Bible. This was no idle remark. The belief in and hope for the redemption of the human race is the faith that sustains Marxists. In fact, by twisting a Marxian aphorism, it may be said that in the 20th century Marxism has become the opium of millions of people.

III

Marx's works fill volumes and he wrote on a variety of subjects. He began to publish his ideas in the decade of the 1840's, reaching a plateau in 1848 with the *Communist Manifesto* (written, as with most of his works, with Engels). In it his idea of the proletarian revolution that will terminate the present history of man and initiate a true history became prominent. Although the *Manifesto* was primarily propaganda and political rhetoric it has been (and is?) a tremendously effective work.

In the *Manifesto* Marx acknowledged the revolutionary role in history of the bourgeoisie. That class was responsible for bringing the world to its present (i.e., 19th century) level, which was no minor achievement. All nations, in time, must adopt bourgeois methods of production or they will perish. But, cautioned Marx, the greatness and grandeur of the bourgeoisie is transitory. These middle classes must and will be succeeded, and their achievements inherited by the proletariat, who only begin to exist with the start of their struggle against the bourgeoisie. That struggle, the revolution, will begin slowly; there will be defeats as well as victories. But eventually the workers will organize as a class and a party. With increasing success they will be joined by intellectuals and even rulers, just as earlier in history members of the nobility—in the early stages of the French Revolution, for example—joined forces with the bourgeoisie. It is the bourgeois intellectuals (like Marx) who have come to understand the historical process, who educate the proletariat regarding the nature of the class struggle and the historical process, and who provide the intellectual leadership as organizers of a communist party. The party is not a separate party; it has "no interest separate and apart from those of the proletariat as a whole." From this emerges the principle of the party as the vanguard of the proletariat because the party has "over the great mass of the proletariat the advantage of clearly understanding the line of march, the conditions, and the ultimate general results of the proletariat movement."[2]

Neither communism nor the communist party, said Marx, is trying to interfere with established society. Rather, that society is coming to an end, as it must historically; the communists are fully aware of this, as they are of the new society that will emerge from the ruins of the old. Communists thus are the executors of the laws of history. (Humankind's move toward freedom, as viewed by Marx, has at least some of its origins in the Enlightenment and the French Revolution.) Since history does not always proceed automatically, the communists help it along. One of their primary roles is to increase class consciousness which is necessary for the coming revolution. Communism (or socialism) will be the end result of the revolution, but the struggle will be a prolonged one. The first step in the successful revolution will be a transitional period characterized by a dictatorship of the proletariat. During this phase class differences will disappear, production will be concentrated in the hands of a vast association of the whole nation, public power will lose its political character because it will no longer be an instrument of class rule, and the old bourgeois order, with its class antagonisms, will be replaced by "an association in which the free development of each is the condition for the free development of all."[3] The *Manifesto* ends with its famous call for the workers of the world to unite, since they have only their chains to lose, but the world to win.

In sum, the *Communist Manifesto* does not attempt to portray revolution as merely desirable, but as inevitable. It is not so much a plea for revolution as it is a virtual prediction about the way in which the revolution will eventually occur.

IV

In his earlier, as well as later works Marx elaborated upon his conception of revolution. He would probably not have agreed with Lenin that "without a revolutionary theory there can be no revolutionary movement." Marx believed that revolutionary movements were the result of conditions which the masses found intolerable. Such movements did not depend upon theory for their formation. Yet, Marx did hold that a proper revolutionary theory would aid a revolutionary movement by providing it with a *raison d'etre* and by educating and directing the masses to the correct ends and means of the revolution.

In his evaluation of the possiblities for revolution Marx opposed the endeavors of those who sought to ripen conditions for revolution through direct confrontations with authority. He critized Blanqui, for example, who thought that revolutionary activity could be initiated by elite intellectuals who, through the use of terrorism, would coerce the state to become more repressive. This, said Marx, merely revealed a contempt for the masses; such revolutionists were frustrated elitists who were more interested in themselves than in the proletariat. A conspiratorial organization was the only condition these elites deemed necessary. But such a situation was artificial and would achieve nothing significant. Meaningful revolution can occur only when the necessary pre-conditions have appeared, the most important of which are the full development of capitalism and intense class consciousness.

Marx was not a romantic. He did not believe that the pre-capitalist world or any pure state of nature was superior to capitalist society. In fact, the reverse was true. Compared to earlier societies capitalism was progressive and the bourgeois revolution was an important step toward complete human freedom.

Modern revolution for Marx would develop in two phases. In the first, the bourgeoisie would seek to assert itself. It was the duty of the workers to support themselves and await the second phase when they would make their own bid for power. It was unlikely (though Lenin later would not wait) that these two phases would be accomplished in a single revolution. Marx had no faith in the bourgeoisie, the peasants or the lumpenproletariat (i.e., submerged working class). The bourgeoisie would use the other classes to further its own ends and perpetuate its own state. But capitalism inevitably created contradictions in society that reforms would not solve. This would show the workers that their only hope lay in revolution. Thus, the class struggle and victory of the proletariat were both crucial and inevitable. Just as revolutions are the locomotives of history, Marx said, so class struggles are the locomotives of revolution. The proletariat has within itself the power to effect a transformation of society which will emerge out of the conflict between itself and the bourgeoisie. The salvation of society, in other words, would come about through the activity of a force already existing within it.

The proletarian revolution would destroy the bourgeois state and change economic relationships so that land, machinery and capital would be expropriated by the masses in the name of everyone. Since all divisions of labor in society would be abolished no new class will need to appear. Without realizing it the bourgeoisie make it possible for the proletariat to take over since they train the workers in the ways and means of production. The conflict against capitalism prepares the proletariat, first to organize for revolution and subsequently to rule. Then, "between capitalist and communist society lies the period of the revolutionary transformation of the one into the other. Corresponding to this is also a political transition period in which the state can be nothing but *the revolutionary dictatorship of the proletariat.*"[4] Marx went into little detail on this stage, so that the exact nature of the future dictatorship of the proletariat is uncertain. (This helps to account for the post-1917 split among Marxists, especially over whether Lenin and the Bolsheviks were true Marxists when they established the Soviet single party state, which they called a "dictatorship of the proletariat.") But the "dictatorship" was the final stage before society became stateless. As a means to this end the dictatorship was necessary, although as a form of state itself it was not. The dictatorship would be less evil than all past states, but since it was a state it would be evil nonetheless and therefore temporary. In the end all classes and class antagonisms would be abolished because the communist revolution would be carried out by that class which no longer counted and was itself the expression of the dissolution of all classes and nations within the present society.

V

One of the best ways to appreciate the diversity of opinion concerning Marx and revolution is to look at his views on violence and the possibility of revolution in one or more countries. In some of his early works (i.e., mid-1840's) Marx expressed the view that violence was necessary, not only in order to overcome resistance and overthrow society but to effect a psychological alteration of man himself. Only when the working class overthrows the ruling class can "a revolution succeed in ridding itself of all the muck of the ages and become fitted to found society anew."[5] In 1849 Marx went to live in London under a functioning parliamentary democracy where reform was a real possibility. He then moderated his views about the inevitability and necessity of violent political change. In addition, the failure of 1848 revolutions, during which there was only a minimum of concerted activity on the part of the proletariat, taught Marx to be more patient; revolution was not going to be achieved too quickly. The class struggle and the proletarian revolution were still inevitable, but now Marx began to take a broader and deeper view. In the 1850's he came to realize that the advances of science and technology were creating new conditions and a new world in which both industrialization and the size of the proletariat would grow. Time and organization would be necessary to instruct the workers in their mission. This is why the First International was created in 1864. To this body Marx said in his inaugural address: "To conquer political power has therefore become the great duty of the working classes. . . . One element of success they possess—numbers; but numbers weigh only in the balance, if united by combination and led by knowledge."[6] Marx later acknowledged that the revolutionary transformation of the world would take different forms; in countries where workers had political rights and could use them effectively violence might be avoided. There are countries, such as England and America, he said, "where the workers can attain their goal by peacful means."[7]

For Marx the final revolution would be a universal phenomenon. It might begin on a national level at first, but it would overflow national boundaries to become world-wide; national revolutions would be partial manifestations of the larger process. Yet, in 1847, Engels wrote that since the connections among the nations of the world were so close and since social developments in the Western countries were so similar revolution will not be merely national, but will take place simultaneously in at least those "civilized countries" and thus become a universal revolution. In 1850 Marx expressed the view that bourgeois revolutions must not be terminated, but instead, be made

> permanent, until all more or less possessing classes have been forced out of their position of dominance, until the proletariat has conquered state power, and the association of proletarians, not only in one country but in all the dominant countries of the world, has advanced so far that competition among the proletarians of these countries has ceased and that at least

the decisive productive forces are concentrated in the hands of the proletarians. For us the issue cannot be the alteration of private property but only its annihilation, not the smoothing over of class antagonisms but the abolition of classes, not the improvement of existing society but the foundation of a new one.[8]

Both Marx and Engels expected the revolution to begin first in England before it turned into a world revolution. England was the most advanced industrial country and possessed the largest working class; she also dominated the world market so that revolution in England would naturally make her the leader of the world into revolution. While they never abandoned hope for this role of England, in the late 1840's (especially with the failure of the Chartists to control the workers) Marx and Engles turned to France where they thought the workers, with the traditions of 1789 and 1830 behind them, would start the revolution. But when these expectations failed to materialize the two theorists looked to Central and Eastern Europe. However, here there were other problems: a small conscious working class, capitalism that was not advanced, a weak middle class, a strong landed class, and socialist leaders whom they viewed as utopians. At best, the proletariat would have to join the bourgeoisie in destroying feudal society before the workers' revolution could proceed.

Thus, a definitive position on the universality, permanence, nature and country of origin for the revolution was lacking.

VI

For Marx revolution was a complete and total—social, political, economic and ideological—process, or it was nothing at all. It was a natural phenomenon, part of the evolution of man, by which man was and will be radically transformed. The aim of the final revolution, therefore, was to humanize society in effect, to modernize society, so that man will be able to fulfill his true nature and reintegrate himself with his natural world.

Marx saw man as being essentially a producer, and history as the development of production and the relationship between the actual producers (i.e., slaves, serfs, wage laborers) and the owners of the means of production (i.e., slaveowners, landowning feudal nobles, capitalists). This socioeconomic division of society into a majority of non-owning workers and a minority of non-working owners has been a characteristic of the history of humankind. Therefore, concluded

Marx, it has been the division of labor which has kept the classes divided.

As Marx analyzed his own times he deduced that modern machine industry would not be compatible with the system of wage labor for very long. This would result in a communist revolution which would destroy wage labor as a mode of production and the bourgeois state as a form of society. Revolution would resolve the conflict and contradiction between the productive powers and the social relations of production. The purpose of the communist revolution is not to gain wealth and material satisfaction but to change the mode of production. According to Marx's analysis of the nature of man, revolutions are made by man as the unfilled producer, not the hungry consumer. Man as a producer has the need to develop freely and express the many aspects of his productive activity. The effect of the revolution will be to eliminate a set of social relations of production that has become a restraint upon the productive powers of man, and thus to free those powers.

Marx went further on this point although, like Bakunin, he was aware of the pitfalls of elaborating upon his vision of the future. Communism was not simply institutional reform; it was instead, a change in the nature of man and a solution to the conflict between men and nature. Revolution was not meant just to free men from the oppression of others, but to liberate the life processes of society from the shackles of scarcity so that there could be abundance. In the new society created by the revolution the need for profit would disappear and production would be for use only, not competition. Under capitalism the machinery of production and the institutions of society dominate people, but under communism institutions and machinery would be at the service of humankind. The goal of all social revolutions, for Marx, is freedom, but with freedom meaning the liberation of human creativity from which abundance would result and human needs would be met.

In the true communist society humanity would leap from the realm of necessity to the realm of freedom. Abundance and affluence would eliminate necessity and make freedom—that is, man's creative and artistic nature—possible. With humankind free from material need and greed there would be the opportunity, for the very first time, for everyone to pursue any and all interests, to become universal, "to do one thing today and another tomorrow, to hunt in the morning, to fish in the afternoon, rear cattle in the evening, criticise after dinner, just as I have a mind, without ever becoming a hunter, fisherman, shepherd or critic."9 Division of labor is an evil and an enemy to human freedom. Fundamental to Marxism is the proposition that all forms of occupational specialization (even intellectual activity) are slavery and should be eliminated. To be limited or restricted to a particular kind of occupation is to be less than free. Such limitations constrict human nature, which seeks to develop in all possible ways. In the new society alienation, supression and exploitation would cease because there would be no foundation for them. States would disappear since it was class struggles that were responsible for political power struggles. Society would be collectivist with all participating and all needs attended to. All human potential could be developed. Marx did not believe that his vision of the pure communist society was utopian. Since he based it on what he considered a realistic analysis of history and society it was, on the contrary, scientific and therefore inevitable.

The revolution of communism, as with the earlier social revolutions, would involve a change in the mode of production. In this sense, it would be both destructive—by eliminating the old, capitalist mode of production—and constructive—by establishing a new, socialist one. But there is an important way in which the revolution of communism would be different from previous revolutions. Whereas earlier revolutions witnessed the replacement of one form of productive activity with another within the division of labor (e.g., serf to wage labor), the communist revolution would abolish the division of labor and thus traditional "labor" itself. In this way the communist revolution would be the last revolution because there would be no circumstances which could precipitate another one. Free creativity would be the mode of production; in it there would be no subjugation of people, but emancipation since everyone would be able to develop in all directions and labor would become a pleasure instead of a burden. Through revolution the world would be changed so that people themselves could be changed and redeemed, and humanity realized.

VII

A basic contribution of Marx to the concept of revolution was that it must reach and have meaning for *all* of society. It must be more than a violent substitution of one set of leaders for another and it must have meaning for those beyond the ruling elite. Like the anarchists Marx had no use for the existing order. If he wrote a good deal about economic change it was because he regarded economics as the fundamental factor for the determination of all the characteristics of the social order. But there is an important and basic difference between Marx and the anarchists. For the anarchists the sole object of revolution was the destruction of the state. For Marx the object was the destruction of capitalism, wage labor and classes, and the temporary establishment of a centralized economy after which the state would disappear. Although anarchists concluded that a centralized economy would render the retention of the state a necessity, Marx's belief that it would not was founded on his theory that the revolution would radically change human nature which, in turn, would make the state superfluous.

Marx has been dead for a century now. Much of what he said has proven to be wrong and much of what he expected has not yet been realized. Capitalism in the advanced industrial nations has not been replaced by socialism nor have the working classes in these countries come to power (in fact, it may be that more workers support the capitalist system than oppose it). To be sure, communist movements have seized power through revolutions in industrially retarded countries (e.g., Russia and China), but these movements have been dominated more by middle class intellectuals and peasants—about whom Marx had serious reservations—than by workers.

Nevertheless, Marx's inaccuracies have not prevented him from becoming the inspirational source for numerous revolutionary movements all over the world. In spite of the failure of Marxism to provide all the answers there is much in it that is appealing. That appeal, like the appeal of religion, is in large measure spiritual. Through his scientific socialism Marx wrote about "what ought to be" and "inevitability." One cannot prove or disprove what ought to be; it has to be accepted on faith. The forces of history are on the side of the believer. Marx provided a guarantee of victory that no other revolutionary theorist has ever matched.

The followers of Marx, like those of Christ, have been virtually innumerable. While Marx was clear about what revolution would bring, he was inconsistent about revolutionary strategy. In Russia the Mensheviks adopted his view that the proletarian revolution should only be initiated after the bourgeois revolution ran its course. But Marx also acknowledged the possibility that the one revolution could follow immediately after the other. This latter Marxian strategy was adopted by Lenin and the Bolsheviks.

NOTES

[1] Karl Marx, *The Eighteenth Brumaire of Louis Napoleon* (1852) in Karl Marx, *On Revolution*, ed. by S. K. Padover (New York, 1971), p. 245.

[2] Both quotes from Marx, *Communist Manifesto* (1848) in *ibid.*, p. 91.

[3] *Ibid.*,p. 98.

[4] Marx, *Marginal Notes to the Program of the German Workers' Party (critique of the Gotha Program)* (1875) in *Ibid.*, p. 503.

[5] Marx, *The German Ideology* (1845–46) in *The Marx-Engels Reader*, ed. by R. C. Tucker (New York, 1972), p. 157. See also Marx's *The Poverty of Philosophy* (1847).

[6] Marx, *Inaugural Address of the Working Men's International Association* (1864) in *ibid.*, p. 380.

[7] A Marx speech, 8 September 1872 in Padover, *op. cit.*, p. 64.

[8] Marx, *Address of the Central Committee to the Communist League* (1850) in Tucker, *op. cit.*, p. 367.

[9] *The German Ideology* in *ibid.*, p. 124.

10

Lenin's Concept
of Revolution

I

Marx, as we have seen, believed that the nature of capitalism was such that the condition of the proletariat would deteriorate as capitalism advanced. The number of workers would increase while society would divide into two hostile classes: a relatively small but wealthy bourgeoisie versus a large but impoverished proletariat. As this process was unfolding the proletariat would come to realize that its impoverishment was the result of class struggle and the nature of capitalism. The proletariat would then rise in revolution, overthrow the bourgeoisie and the capitalist system, and establish a dictatorship of the proletariat. With society no longer composed of antagonistic classes the state, itself an instrument of class oppression, would simply wither away and be replaced by a classless society composed of some kind of common or cooperative institutions. This process, according to Marx, was inevitable and did not necessarily depend upon the actions of any one individual.

But Marxism did not go unchallenged, even in its own time. A number of perplexing questions were raised. How did the proletariat "come to realize" that capitalism was evil and must be overthrown? How would the proletariat be made aware of the revolutionary role it was to play? Did this realization come automatically or were the workers instructed and guided? Also, would the proletarian revolution occur spontaneously or would it have to be planned and organized? These, among others, were the kinds of crucial and nagging questions that plagued Marxists and encouraged different interpretations of Marxism. Moreover, it also led the followers eventually to factionalize. Simply stated, those factions may be divided into adherents with two broad views, one passive, the other active. The former held that the inevitability of the proletarian revolution would be spontaneous and, therefore, little need be done but wait. The latter view held that the inevitability of the revolution required planning and, therefore, Marxism was both a summons and a guide to action.

Another problem Marxists faced was that at the end of the 19th and beginning of the 20th centuries some of Marx's expectations were not being realized. Capitalism was growing stronger instead of becoming weaker. The conditions of the workers were improving instead of becoming more miserable. Workers were getting the vote and their elected representatives were serving in governments. As states became interested in compromise, reform and representative democracy and were less and less the instruments of class hostility, the revolutionary tendencies of the workers weakened. Also, the bourgeoisie, instead of becoming a small, contracting class, was expanding, and internationalism was losing ground to nationalism. The gap between Marxian theory and reality was widening, and a proletarian revolution seemed distant and even utopian. Revisionism became the order of the day.

Revisionism, for avowed Marxists, is a loaded word although, in point of fact, most have been revisionist in one way or another—out of necessity, to be sure, though they rightly deny it because Marxism has become a dogma from which deviation is heretical. But the initial use of the word is usually applied to the work of Eduard Bernstein (1850–1932), a German theorist at the turn of the 20th century. Bernstein said that since the conditions of the workers were improving and reforms were becoming more widespread the Marxian notion of the inevitability of revolution needed to be revised. The moral and spiritu-

al aims of the revolution Marx predicted (i.e., justice, humanism, freedom) were still valid, but the theory about how to achieve them possessed weaknesses. Conditions, said Bernstein, necessitated that
Marxism become evolutionary, not revolutionary. Workers should be
educated so as to be able to vote themselves into power, legally and
constitutionally. An elite core of professional revolutionists was not
necessary. Capitalism was not developing catastrophically; the way to
arrive at a socialist society was through humanizing and socializing
capitalism instead of violently destroying it. Especially in advanced
capitalist countries having parliamentary political systems the state
would progress toward revolutionary change. "Revolution" would
become rhetoric, but the sum total of the reforms, said Bernstein,
would comprise a real revolution. To many other Marxists Bernstein's
revisionism was not only wrong but a dangerous apology for the evils
of capitalism and the docility of the workers. One such opponent of
Bernstein was a Russian named Vladimir Ilyich Ulyanov, better known
by the pseudonym Lenin (1870–1924).

II

Lenin not only rejected Bernstein's revision but he failed to see any
incongruity between reality in Russia and Marxist theory. The fact was
that Russia was experiencing significant capitalistic and industrial advance. Economic conditions, according to Lenin, were not so very
different from what they had been in Western Europe when Marx was
first writing. In Russia the workers were living and working under
intolerable conditions and there were few serious or promising efforts
for reform of any kind. Thus for Lenin, revisionism was not only
inaccurate and anti-Marxist, but it also promoted a false sense of class
harmony and prevented revolution. This, Lenin would not tolerate. It
is almost unnecessary to say, however, that Lenin's contribution to the
concept of revolution goes considerably further than a mere refutation
of Bernstein's heresy. Lenin was both a thinker and a man of action,
a revolutionary theorizer and a revolutionist; not since John Calvin has
anyone so combined the two roles.

The most fundamental contribution of Lenin was his combining the
revolutionary theory of Marx with the revolutionary tradition of Russia
while still preserving the essence of both. At first glance this would
seem to have been an impossible task; the differences in assumptions
and techniques between the two were significant. Marxism, for exam-

ple, was allegedly a scientific approach to history; it was concerned with the role of the urban, industrial worker in the inevitable revolution that would be realized in the economically advanced countries of Europe. Much of this was alien to 19th century Russian revolutionists who were living in an economically backward, politically autocratic, and largely agrarian country. Revolution was not seen as an inevitable phenomenon; moreover, it would have to involve the peasantry, who comprised the majority of the population, while a conspiratorial elite would seize power and establish a new social order from above. Lenin's distinction as a theorist of revolution was to merge and reconcile these seemingly opposing views. In the process Marxism was expanded (or changed) from an ideology suitable for advanced capitalist nations into a theory for revolution and progress in backward countries. Where Marxism was concerned with objective and inexorable economic laws, Leninism developed into a concern for the directing of economic and social processes for specific, desired ends.

When we talk about Lenin's ideas we have to distinguish between his long-range views and his short-range analysis. In the long range of historical perspective Lenin was an orthodox Marxist who believed in the inevitable breakdown of capitalism and the emergence of socialism. Lenin once even said that he was merely a popularizer of Marxism. Like Marx, Lenin sought to coordinate legal and illegal means of struggle; for destructive purposes both men were willing to join with other parties. But in his analysis of his own time and country Lenin altered Marxism; he believed in subordinating Marxian principles to the primary task of carrying out the revolution. For example, and by way of a generalization, Lenin was not convinced (as Marx was) that after the revolution events would run smoothly; that is why he concerned himself with class consciousness and its propagation. He considered ideas an important agent for revolution; only through an awareness of his own nature and that of society could the proletariat be led to act in his own interests. Hence, Lenin was concerned with revolutionary strategy and he emphasized organization as the means by which the elite would direct the masses to act appropriately. Also unlike Marx, Lenin saw revolution as fundamentally a political phenomenon (for Marx it was social). Lenin contended that the decisive factor in a revolution was the nature of the political organization and not the stage of social and economic development.

To be a Marxist, according to Lenin, one had to accept the inevitability of and work for the proletarian revolution. The seizure of power by the proletariat and their leaders was Lenin's immediate goal. It is not that these specific ideas were so new and original that makes Lenin important. But he viewed tactics as plans that must first be executed and then modified through experience. He was a man concerned with action; he presented his ideas more logically and convincingly than anyone else and he became the greatest individual force behind the Russian Revolution.

Before proceeding further let us summarize the main characteristics of Leninism: it was a particular attitude towards revolutionary strategy; it was an adaptation of Marxism to Russian conditions and in an imperialistic world; and it was a conception of the rule and organization of a revolutionary party.

III

Marx had opposed the making of a revolution through a conspiracy; those who thought and acted in terms of conspiracies would only play into the hands of reaction. However, Marx did recognize the need for a firm revolutionary base before action should be undertaken. The description and organization of such a base was a major contribution of Lenin to the idea of revolution. Lenin's idea concerned the nature and role of organization; not the organization of a nation or even a class, but of a small group of individuals who would be specialists in revolution. In 1900 Lenin and his associates began a newspaper called *Iskra* (Spark). In its first issue, in an unsigned article, Lenin set forth two ideas which were crucial for the development of his concept of revolution: (1) left to themselves and without the guidance of a "socialist vanguard," the workers would become reactionary and eventually bourgeois; (2) this "socialist vanguard" would have to be composed of people who devote to the revolution their whole lives, and not just their free time. These professional revolutionists were either self-appointed or chosen by other revolutionists from among the workers or intellectuals. The revolutionists were not to be responsible to any rank and file and they controlled and directed the masses. Lenin was here making a significant alteration in the Marx-Engels dictum that "the emancipation of the working class is the work of the working class itself." Unlike Bernstein, Lenin denied being a revisionist even though evidence indicates he was. He interpreted Marx, claimed that his was the only correct interpretation, and that even where he differed from Marx or was innovative this was only because of the differences in the conditions of Russia which permitted such deviation.

Lenin clearly had his doubts about the workers acquiring a proper class consciousness. When he wrote that "without a revolutionary theory there can be no revolutionary movement,"[1] Lenin meant that the workers must be guided in their struggle by professional revolutionists. Left to themselves workers forget the class struggle. Workers may strike but such action was simply a trade union struggle, which was reformist, not revolutionary. Workers

> were not and could not be conscious of the irreconcilable antagonism of their interests to the whole . . . political and social system. . . . [Class consciousness] could only be brought to them from without. The history of all countries shows that the working class, exclusively by its own effort, is able to develop only trade-union consciousness. . . . There is a lot of talk about spontaneity, but the *spontaneous* development of the labour movement leads to its becoming subordinated to bourgeois ideology.[2]

At best, therefore, the workers might be sympathetic to a revoltuion against capitalism, but they would not have sufficient consciousness to render them determined participants in that revolution. Lenin's solution was to express the need to organize a revolutionary elite which would guide the workers; the elite were the real agents of the revolutionary transformation to socialism and without them there could be no genuine revolution. The elite, having mastered socialist theory, would propagandize and agitate but they would not initiate a conspiratorial coup d'état. The revolution itself would be a mass affair culminating in a national armed insurrection.

Lenin later made note of another important factor that was missing from the consciousness of the proletariat; they were, he said, limited by national interests and loyalties and were consequently unable to appreciate the problems they shared with workers everywhere. Here again the professional revolutionists play a key role. They unite the interests common to all workers and they represent the interests of the movement as a whole.

Who were these professional revolutionists, this elite who would guide the masses and raise class consciousness? They were generally bourgeois intellectuals whose consciousness was the result of the dialectics of ideas and who would educate the workers in socialism. How did this elite operate? They were an organization or a party. Since theory precedes practice the organization of a party must precede the extension of the party to the workers and it must also precede the revolution. The party is the personification of class consciousness; it has a purpose and it is composed of individuals, "revolutionists by profession" (Lenin's term), whose aim is to destroy the existing order and prepare for the dictatorship of the proletariat. The task of the party is "to make the proletariat capable of fulfilling its great historical mission. . . . The party exists for the very purpose of going ahead of the masses and showing the masses the way."[3]

Lenin's concept of party was crucial and the revolution it would lead was of paramount historical importance. Russia was a tsarist state which meant that the party could not be a broad one open to all; this would only make it vulnerable to the authorities. The party would have to be able to function in a repressive society. It would therefore have to be limited to those who were active participants; it had to be small, secret, centralized and highly disciplined. In the party the virtues of democracy (e.g., elections, majority decisions, universal suffrage) had to be sacrificed to the absolute needs of central leadership and discipline; all authority rested with a small number of professional revolutionists. Lenin thus refused to be influenced by any mass opinion: "the important thing is not the number [i.e., majority], but the correct expression of the ideas and policies of the really revolutionary proletariat."[4] A party that merely reflected the spontaneous and unenlightened ideas of the proletariat masses would lose sight of the larger aims of the revolution and its socialist objectives. In the process, said Lenin, such a party would become a part of the existing order and abandon socialism. This, Lenin would not tolerate. Lenin's concept of party was so controversial that it divided the Russian Social Democratic Labor Party into two camps in 1903: the Mensheviks (minority) who were less overtly revolutionary and less conspiratorial (i.e., they had no use for a separate elite party, preferring instead a loose, democratic party of all the proletariat) and the Bolsheviks (majority) who followed Lenin.

Lenin's strategy for revolution was, in some respects, not too different from that of Blanqui (see Chapter 8). Although Lenin did not deny his debt to Blanqui, the Russian condemned the Frenchman's failure to understand the nature of power. Blanqui's elite party would seize power only to turn it over to the masses. Lenin rejected this technique of a conspiratorial minority in favor of his party which was the incarnation and organization of the will of the people. Through mass support political power would come; then the party would be able to translate consciousness into reality. Thus, for Lenin, revolution is not the responsibility of the professionals alone but must, instead, be the work of most of the people. During a revolution initiative is transferred to the masses, at least at the start, and it is the true test of the professional revolutionists to utilize the force of the masses to hurdle to power on the inertia of spontaneity. The revolutionist must guard against being overwhelmed by the masses and he must never lose sight of the party's direction or hold up the revolution. This is what guided Lenin and the Bolsheviks in 1917.

Lenin's writings on organization, class alliances, party and professional revolutionists helped to create a Marxist(-Leninist) ideal of revolution for underdeveloped and backward nations. It is based on the conviction that men make history and need not wait for the times to be ripe. Lenin remained within the framework of Marxism but, whereas the *Communist Manifesto* had referred to "the gradual, spontaneous class organization of the proletariat," Lenin believed that "spontaneity"by itself was dangerous to a genuine workers' movement. Where Marx expected consciousness to emerge only in a revolution, Lenin stated that a party of professional revolutionists was necessary to bring revolutionary consciousness to the workers. Where Marx believed that the new man would emerge from the revolution and the new society, Lenin was convinced that it was necessary to begin to mold the new man beforehand in order to be able to create the new society. Thus, the substitution of party for class as the motive force of revolution was one of Lenin's most distinctive innovations in both the theory and practice of revolution. To be sure, the *Manifesto* mentioned the need to organize the proletariat into a class and then a party, and Lenin referred to the party as the vanguard for the class. But the change in emphasis is significant and clearly points out the differences between the historical and economic laws with which Marx was concerned and the real world of power politics to which Lenin was committed.

IV

In the early years of the 20th century Lenin dealt with two other problems in his interpretation of Marxian theory. One concerned the fact that Russia had yet to experience her bourgeois revolution which would have to occur before the proletarian revolution. The other concerned the role of the peasantry. These he linked together.

After 1903 Lenin began to emphasize a possible role the Russian peasantry might come to play in the interests of revolution. The otherwise conservative peasants might be enlisted on the side of revolution by the promise of land. The Russian Revolution of 1905 showed Lenin that the peasantry had revolutionary potential. This led him to the notion that in a backward country like Russia it might be possible and necessary to create "a revolutionary-democratic dictatorship of the proletariat and the peasantry."[5] In fact, although the value of the peasants would perhaps only be temporary their support might be essential for victory. (Marx, it will be remembered, distrusted the peasants as conservative and reactionary.)

Since the bourgeois revolution in Russia might not be completed because of the backwardness of Russia's middle class, and since the Russian proletariat was very small, help was needed. A dictatorship of proletariat and peasantry, led by the party of professional revolutionists, would assist the bourgeoisie in concluding its revolution. When the bourgeois revolution was completed then the workers would take control and move Russia towards a proletarian revolution—but that was in the future and Lenin was primarily concerned with the alliance between proletariat and peasant and their joint involvement in the bourgeois revolution.

Lenin thus made three more modifications in Marxism. First, he introduced the notion of a partially developed bourgeoisie; backward countries need not wait for the middle class to develop and make its own revolution—in fact, the bourgeois revolution must be made to succeed. Second, he outlined a revolutionary role for the peasantry; it was an outline not forgotten by Mao Tse-tung and his followers. Third, he again implied, reinforcing earlier ideas, that a proletarian revolution was possible in a country that was not fully capitalistic. Marxism was coming to have greater and greater significance for developing nations and, thanks to Lenin, it would continue to do so.

V

Marxism, as we have seen, is considered by Marxists a science of revolution. The growth of capitalism has made the proletarian revolution justifiable on moral grounds because capitalism is an inhuman form of civilization which has rendered man no better than a machine. That revolution is also inevitable because capitalism, by nature, is plagued by weaknesses and contradictions that are destined to destroy it. For example, capitalism creates its own executioners in the proletariat. But capitalism in the early 20th century was not quite developing as Marx predicted and the proletarian revolution no longer seemed inevitable. Problems had emerged. Europe's economy, instead of contracting or stagnating, was growing stronger. Workers were sharing in the wealth instead of becoming more impoverished. With World War I the proletariat of Europe became increasingly patriotic instead of acting as if they were nationless; workers were not, according to Marx, supposed to be interested in wars between capitalist countries. Moreover, the consciousness of the workers was becoming reformist, not revolutionary.

Earlier, Lenin had made some adjustments in Marx's theory of revolution; in 1916 he made another. He made use of the concept of the growth of monopolies to develop his theory of imperialism. The monopolistic industries in Western Europe, at first privately and then through their governments, were exploiting and dominating Asia, Africa and Latin America (e.g., through the export of capital which employed native labor at minimal cost). These monopolies, he said, were able to create huge profits for their capitalist countries which were used not only to enrich the bourgeoisie further but also to bribe the proletariat—with, for example, higher wages and better working conditions—into a semi-satisfied state of submissiveness. Thus, Marx's predictions of falling profits in capitalist countries and the impoverishment of the workers was being delayed because of this extension of capitalism. In other words, the exploitation of colonies created imperialism. Imperialism was the highest stage of capitalism and, for Lenin, it explained why the proletariat was chauvinistic, fighting for its share of their country's hopes to gain more of the world for its own use. In this sense, Leninism may be viewed as Marxism in the age of imperialism.

But Lenin also claimed that imperialism is decaying capitalism, it is capitalism on an international level, "it is capitalism in transition, or more precisely, . . . moribund capitalism."[6] He asserted that Marx's predictions were still true, except that now their realization would be delayed. Lenin believed that imperialism, like capitalism, had inherent weaknesses and contradictions which would lead to its own destruction and the advent of revolution. As the economies of colonies developed the profits of the mother countries would be reduced. There would be some successful anti-colonial revolutions, profits would be further reduced, production would reach a limit and the imperialist stage of capitalism would come to an end. That is, falling profits would impoverish the workers and polarize the classes. But the end result would now see the exploited nations as proletarian nations and the proletarian revolution would be world-wide. All this, said Lenin, was inevitable. But where Marx had emphasized economic development as the prerequisite for revolution, Lenin stressed political awareness.

Lenin's work on imperialism, although based on the ideas of others, was a major step in altering Marxism still further into a revolutionary theory, ideal and strategy for the economically backward areas of the world. Marxists now looked not only at Europe but at the other continents where revolutionary potential was growing. As Sigmund Neumann has written, Lenin's theory of imperialism "represents an attempt at the coordination of social and colonial liberation and therewith a claim to revolutionary world leadership."[7]

VI

"Permanent revolution" was a term Marx had used to describe the necessity of continuous revolution until such time as communism was reached. However, the man with whom the term is most frequently identified was the Russian Marxist and revolutionist Lev Davidovich Bronstein, better known as Trotsky (1879–1940). Trotsky was an unusual writer and speaker, as well as a prime organizer of the Red Army; he was Lenin's close associate in the 1917 Revolution but later, in 1929, after a long conflict with Stalin, he was exiled from the U.S.S.R.

Using Marx as his foundation Trotsky developed his "theory of permanent revolution." Trotsky recognized that early 20th century Russia was not economically advanced enough for a socialist revolution. His analysis of the situation, based also on the 1905 Russian Revolution, proposed a solution. He argued that the socialist or proletarian revolution should not be consigned to the future but should be pursued even as the bourgeois revolution was progressing. Revolutionists should not stop half-way and wait for capitalism to develop but should, instead, continue full force with the dictatorship of the proletariat established even during the bourgeois revolution. Thus, both the bourgeois and proletarian revolutions should proceed simultaneously. The reason for this was that in a backward country like Russia the proletariat was too small and the bourgeois not revolutionary enough; if the revolution took the time to solve all the problems of the peasants and of the bourgeois society the revolution might be delayed and even betrayed. To prevent its own premature demise the revolution would also have to go beyond the national boundaries of Russia and initiate revolution elsewhere in Western Europe. Agreeing with Lenin that the revolution in Russia could not be continued within its bourgeois phase, Trotsky advanced the notion that the revolution could not be confined within geographical boundaries. Permanent revolution, he said, "means a revolution which makes no compromise with any form of class rule, which does not stop at the democratic stage, which goes over to socialist measures and to war against the reaction from without, that is, a revolution whose every next stage is anchored in the preceding one and which can only end in the complete liquidation of all class society."[8] Therefore, a Russian revolution would be the first step in a world revolution that would continue permanently until all the world had reached socialism. (Even in the 1920's Trotsky believed that Russia would not be able to consummate the revolution herself; Stalin only paid lip service to the idea of permanent revolution.)

Although he at first rejected Trotsky's theory of permanent revolution, by about 1915 Lenin came to accept it. Lenin amplified upon Trotsky's theory saying that just as the peasantry would be needed by the proletariat in the bourgeois revolution, the proletariat would need an ally in the proletarian revolution. For Lenin, while bourgeois revolutions were national events, the proletarian revolution would have to be international. He hoped that the bourgeois revolution in Russia would spark the beginnings of a world-wide proletarian revolution which would turn around and aid Russia to establish her own proletarian dictatorship. Although the proletarian revolution would be international in scope it would have to take the form of a series of national revolutions which would at first establish socialist regimes within national boundaries. (Marxist-Leninist strategy was not opposed to utilizing the forces of nationalism.) But this was only a preliminary.

VII

On the eve of the October Revolution, though not published until 1918, Lenin wrote *State and Revolution*. In this, perhaps his best known work, Lenin detailed the political program that should be followed by the dictatorship of the proletariat after the victorious workers' revolution. Basically there were three main points: (1) the repressive organs of the bourgeois state should be destroyed; (2) a working class democracy should be established with representatives completely subordinated to the will of the masses); (3) the job of government should be that of the masses.

Lenin followed Marx and Engels in his definition of the state as an organization founded upon and utilizing force for the suppression of some class. All states have used force to suppress one or more classes. The workers' revolution, he said, would overthrow the bourgeois state and substitute for it a state which, in the name of the masses and on their behalf, would use force against the rule of the exploiters. In previous revolutions exploitation of the many by the few remained as the revolution merely passed state power from one class to another. Usually, in bourgeois revolutions there was some compromise between the bourgeoisie and their defeated enemies. Such compromise, said Lenin, would be impossible in the proletarian revolution which "must not consist in a new class ruling, governing with the help of the *old* state machinery, but in this class *smashing* this machinery and ruling, governing by means of *new* machinery."[9]

Following Marx and Engels, Lenin said that the purpose of the revolution would be to destroy the bourgeois state and replace it with a new proletarian state which would eventually wither away. That is, where the bourgeois state can only be "put an end to" by revolution, the proletarian state can only "wither away."[10] Lenin was sensitive to charges that what he wrote might be misconstrued as utopian. He acknowledged that "to destroy officialdom immediately, everywhere, completely" is utopian. "But to *break up* at once the old bureaucratic machine and to start immediately the construction of a new one which will enable us gradually to reduce all officialdom to naught—this is *no* Utopia, . . . it is the direct and urgent task of the revolutionary proletariat."[11] The state, said Lenin, will be able to wither away when society has realized the Marxian formula for the new order: from each according to his abilities, to each according to his needs; that is, when people regularly observe the fundamental rules of social life, which have been known for centuries, and "their labour is so productive that they voluntarily work *according to their ability*. . . . there will then be no need for any exact calculation by society of the quantity of products to be distributed to each of its members; each will take freely 'according to his needs'."[12]

Marxists envision a significant change in human nature that is a prerequisite for the classless society. They believe that under socialism greed, injustice, selfishness, oppression and even laziness will disappear so that no form of social compulsion will be necessary. When this happens the dictatorship of the proletariat will be able to wither away. Only then, wrote Lenin, will it be possible *"to speak of freedom. . . . Freed from capitalist slavery, from the untold horrors, savagery, absurdities and infamies of capitalist exploitation, people will gradually become accustomed* to the observance of the elementary rules of social life . . . ; they will become accustomed to observing them without force, without compulsion, without subordination, without the *special apparatus* which is called the state."[13]

Lenin foresaw under socialism a time when the masses would all participate independently in every aspect of the administration of the affairs of state and not just in voting. In other words, "under Socialism, *all* will take a turn in management [i.e., governing], and will soon become accustomed to the idea of no management [i.e., government] at all."[14] Generally a pragmatist Lenin was aware that the creation of such a society would not come easily and that it would face resistance. The state organization created to overcome that resistance Lenin, following Marx, called the "dictatorship of the proletariat."

Thus, the key points which Lenin was concerned with in 1917 were his belief in the necessity of destroying the old state, replacing it with the dictatorship of the proletariat, and his own view (as opposed to Marx specifically), which he had been advocating for almost two decades of an elite—in this case, the soviets and the party—which would provide the machinery through which the dictatorship could rule.

Lenin wrote *State and Revolution* in August and September, 1917. He had intended to write at least one additional chapter to the book, but as he himself said in the last sentence of the postscript to the first edition, "it is more pleasant and useful to go through the 'experience of the revolution' than to write about it."[15] The October Revolution intervened and the book was left unfinished.

NOTES

[1] V. I. Lenin, *What Is To Be Done?* (1902) (New York, 1929), p. 28.

[2] *Ibid.,* pp. 32ff, 41.

[3] Quoted in Alfred G. Meyer, *Leninism* (New York, 1962), p. 33.

[4] Quoted in *ibid.,* p. 35.

[5] Lenin, *Two Tactics of Social-Democracy in the Democratic Revolution* (1905) (New York, 1935), *passim.*

[6] Lenin, *Imperialism; The Highest Stage of Capitalism* (1916) (New York, 1939), p. 126

[7] "The International Civil War," in Paynton and Blackey (eds.), *Why Revolution?*, p. 113.

[8] Leon Trotsky, *The Permanent Revolution* (New York, 1931), p. 22.

[9] Lenin, *State and Revolution* (1918) (New York, 1943), p. 96.

[10] *Ibid.,* p. 17.

[11] *Ibid.,* p. 42.

[12] *Ibid.,* pp. 79f.

[13] *Ibid.,* p. 73f.

[14] *Ibid.,* p. 98.

[15] *Ibid.,* p. 101.

11

The Russian Revolution

As early as 1905 Lenin wrote: "From the democratic revolution we shall begin immediately and within the measure of our strength—the strength of the consciousness and organized proletariat—to make the transition to the socialist revolution. We stand for uninterrupted revolution. We shall not stop half way."[1] This seems to sum up the activity of Lenin's life which was geared towards achieving a socialist revolution in Russia. The success he achieved and the prestige he acquired gave rapid and long lasting validity to his ideas.

Prior to the Russian Revolution Lenin found himself in a position whereby he had to justify the application of Marxism to a backward country. To do this he had to alter Marxism, though scholars generally agree that Lenin neither intended to revise Marx nor did he ever realize the scope of his revision. After all, he was modifying Marx only for Russia and not in order to lay down new principles of revolution. But "lay down new principles" he surely did, and he has been used as an authority ever since, especially in other backward countries. Lenin has been particularly influential upon more recent revolutionists in several ways. For example, his emphasis on a tightly knit party which alone could provide insurgents with the necessary organization for survival, in both war and peace, has been adopted by many revolutionary socialists. According to Lenin the middle class in the 20th century is not progressive and capitalists are deadly parasites on society. Capitalism has extended itself via imperialism and, as such, will continue to expand and exploit. Capitalism can only be overthrown by violence; it cannot be reformed. The workers, not revolutionary enough themselves, need to be led by a party of professional revolutionists which would provide both leadership and ideology. Together they would prepare the world Marx had envisioned. Leninism helped to make Marxism meaningful in this century.

Both Marx and Lenin sought the destruction of capitalism. The differences that exist between them are significant, though they stem from Lenin's living and working in a setting different from Marx. For Marx revolution was an act of expropriation; it was an event which would be accomplished quickly and by which mankind would move into the realm of freedom. For Lenin revolution was a phenomenon of undertermined length. The destruction of capitalism would be a slow process of disintegration; the dictatorship of the proletariat would become a period of transformation and building during which socialism would be confined to one or more countries in an essentially imperialist world. In this sense, to the more vague image of the Marxian concept of revolution Lenin contributed a strategic and tactical realism.

World War I and the Russian Revolution itself further helped to point out the differences between Marx and Lenin. War, according to Lenin, played a major role in giving birth to revolution. Marx had questioned the value of war for revolution; but even where it played a role it was not as a spark but as a means—as in 1793 or 1871—to revolutionize the masses. Whereas for Marx industrial development was a more decisive factor, for Lenin it was war which would produce insoluble crises for capitalism and lead to revolution. As we have seen, Marx fully expected the proletarian revolution to begin in advanced capitalist countries. But for this Lenin substituted his important theory that power might be seized in a backward, unstable country; to adjust himself to Marx, Lenin said that after the revolution in such a country the new government would help the state to mature and become prepared for the new order. For Marx's notion that the proletariat would make its own revolution and rule itself, Lenin created the idea of an elite party, representing the workers and acting in their name; Lenin's party would be the only party of the proletariat while all others were merely bourgeoisie.

For Lenin winning the revolution in Russia was to become the first step in a world revolution. More wars and revolutions would then follow in which capitalism and imperialism would be overthrown and, after a while, socialism would be established everywhere. This was Lenin's vision for the future, though we might note that at the February, 1956 Soviet Communist Party Congress Chairman Nikita Khrushchev repudiated the dogma of "inevitable wars" between communism and capitalism, thus coming to terms, it seems, with the reality of the nuclear age.

II

Prior to 1917 the French Revolution of 1789 represented the prototype of a modern revolution; it was the first virtually total overthrow of a social and political order; it established liberty and equality as basic rights for the human race and as acceptable targets for political action. To be sure, this was more recently English (and especially Locke) in origin, but the French went beyond the English concept to an egalitarian ideology that was not forgotten. Moreover, the French Revolution had set its ideals in the future instead of the past.

If the French Revolution inaugurated the 19th century then the Russian Revolution may be said to have played a similar role for this century. Where the French Revolution established the idea of equality and brought to question the inherent naturalness of the social order, the 1917 Revolution was the first to establish social justice through economic direction, organized by political action. The Russian Revolution was a political revolution in an economically underdeveloped country. It was a revolution led by intellectuals who both learned from the past and planned for the future, who both prepared the conditions for the revolution and helped make it as well. In this sense, and in spite of its obvious spontaneous elements, the Russian Revolution was planned; this degree of self-consciousness has helped to give the Revolution its special place in history. Fundamental to the coming of revolution in Russia was the incompatibility of the tsarist state with the development of modern civilization; war was the accelerator which brought the crisis to a head.

In the years between the failure of the 1905 Revolution and the

outbreak of the 1917 Revolution there were three competing positions
among Russian Marxists as to the nature and prospects for the hoped
for revolution. There were the Mensheviks for whom revolution in
Russia would be bourgeois-democratic. The revolution would be led
by the middle class and would abolish the remnants of feudalism (i.e.,
Russian society was predominantly peasant), promote the full development of capitalism, and establish a bourgeois republic. Under such a
society socialists would assume power; they would propagate their
ideas and organize the working class for a second, socialist revolution.
But before the socialist revolution could begin the workers would have
to grow to become a majority. Until that time socialists should not join
the bourgeois government since this would involve their compromis-
ing their ideals and programs. Therefore, revolution for the Mensheviks meant eliminating the tsar, supporting the bourgeoise in its bid
for power, and exacting from the bourgeoisie the greatest amount of
freedom for the workers as part of a preparation for the second revolution. A second position was that advocated by Trotsky. For him revolution in Russia would take place too late in history to be solely
bourgeois; it would have to be both bourgeois and proletarian-socialist. Russia's weak bourgeoisie meant that the workers would have to
lead the first revolution, as well as their own, and the bourgeois revolution would develop into a proletarian revolution. Once in power the
proletariat would begin to socialize Russia. There would probably be
opposition at home and perhaps even foreign intervention. But
Trotsky expected the revolution to overflow Russia's boundaries to an
over-ripe West, which would keep it going both at home and abroad.
The third position was held by Lenin. Like the Mensheviks he believed
that Russia was economically ripe enough only for a bourgeois-democratic revolution, not a socialist one. Like Trotsky he believed that
Russia's bourgeoisie would be too weak to make its own revolution so
that the central role would have to be played by the workers. Lenin also
believed that socialists should enter any provisional government in an
effort to direct it.

   Lenin's ideas on organization and political strategy were different
from those of Marx and Engels. The latter thought in terms of a large
and relatively sophisticated proletariat which would seize power from
a comparatively small capitalist class. This was not a characteristic of
more backward Russia where the proletariat was comparatively small
and capitalism was just beginning to develop, not decline. Moreover,
Russia was predominantly a nation of peasants and they could not be

expected to produce that abundance of industrial products which, according to Marx, would be a precondition of socialism.

In realizing that Russia would need a bourgeois revolution before a proletarian one Lenin foresaw the workers as the prime movers. The proletariat, as the most revolutionary class, should work towards its goal (of proletarian revolution) and in the process it would carry through the bourgeois revolution. Lenin did not believe that the inevitability of revolution meant that encouragement or prodding were unnecessary or that the revolution would develop automatically while any interference would only destroy it. A perpetual wait-and-see policy would only lead to inaction. This is what Lenin's "theory of the spark" is about; the activity of the proletariat would set the bourgeoisie in motion and lead first to the latter's revolution and then to the former's.

In 1917 Lenin and Trotsky merged their ideas. Trotsky accepted Lenin's party machine to lead the revolution and represent the proletariat. Lenin accepted Trotsky's view that the conquest of power for a socialist revolution could be gained immediately. Lenin also accepted Trotsky's conception of a single-party dictatorship, which went perfectly with his idea of a minority dictatorship in the party. Both of these last ideas were based upon the assumption that the self-chosen elite, properly armed with Marxism, could run the state and avoid the pitfalls of totalitarianism.

III

The Russian Revolution began in February, 1917. It was a spontaneous uprising of the masses of Russians who were fed up with the burdens of war and the inequality that resulted from those burdens and from the tsarist regime. It was a popular revolution, supported alike by the masses and the middle and bureaucratic classes, all of whom had lost faith in the Romanov tsar and his autocratic, monarchical system of government. The revolution was not organized by any party or by any political leaders; in fact, most revolutionary leaders were abroad in exile or in Siberia. But although it was spontaneous the February Revolution was not an accident; years of propaganda, the bungling of the tsarist regime, intolerable conditions and a disastrous war effort brought Russia to her revolution.

The February Revolution was partly bourgeois and partly proletarian, but mostly it was neither. That is, the tsar and his government were brought down by a general strike and a mass insurrection of workers and soldiers. The initial Provisional Government was composed of middle class and aristocratic officials. None of the traditional Russian revolutionary parties played any significant role in the outbreak of the revolution; in fact, most, including Lenin who was in Switzerland, did not expect it. Even the establishment of the Petrograd Soviet of Workers was more or less a spontaneous creation and a non-party organization of a variety of groups which did not, at first, attempt to gain governmental power.

The Mensheviks were excited about the revolution; it had seemingly gone according to their expectations. The victory involved the masses with the industrial working class, rather than a narrow party of professional revolutionists playing a vanguard role. But the Mensheviks were soon to fail, not only because of the Bolshevik coup but because they persistenly refused to assume and exercise supreme power, and because they betrayed their own democratic program.

The October (Bolshevik) Revolution was a seizure of power by armed insurrection undertaken in the main centers, where power was concentrated. It occurred during a war which resulted in a national crisis when the government was weak and disorganized, conditions were confused, and the mass of people were ripe for change. The Bolsheviks seized power after successful preparations involving the encouragement of a revolutionary mood (e.g., their use of slogans, such as "land, peace, and bread," incited the population), the cultivation of widespread support, and the discrediting and isolation of their rivals, especially the Mensheviks. The actual Bolshevik coup was thus the climax of a process that involved mass agitation and propaganda, positioning for power within the soviets, and organized insurrection.

The February Revolution had failed to distribute land to the peasants and the Provisional Government proved unstable; the Bolsheviks provided an alternative. As far as peace was concerned only the Bolsheviks were prepared to make a decisive move; in pursuing peace they had to go against the grain of nationalist sentiment, although there was a patriotic element in the revolution in that it freed Russia from foreign domination and exploitation. (Interestingly, in the Chinese Revolution two decades later, as well as in other 20th century revolutions, the Communists led a nationalist struggle against foreign—Japanese—aggression.) And again, among Russian revolutionists only the Bolsheviks were willing and able to seize power.

The October Revolution, unlike the February Revolution, saw most people staying at home. The actual insurrection involved a comparatively small, but organized revolutionary force. The victory of so small a party may be explained by the events preceeding it: the spirit of revolution had had a chance to mature; the proletariat had grown increasingly discontented; and the bourgeoisie and other revolutionary forces proved too weak. By their perseverance the Bolsheviks earned the trust of the proletariat; in the process, they channeled the workers's revolutionary feelings and class consciouness to their advantage. In this sense, the October Revolution was a directed, not spontaneous revolution. Lenin defined the situation as a choice between a Bolshevik dictatorship (and with it an end to chaos, armistice and the redistribution of land) and counterrevolution; in fact, much of what the Bolsheviks were offering, especially peace and land redistribution, were little more than a recognition of reality.

Modifying Marx, Lenin regarded the peasant as a bourgeoisie whose grievances were sufficient enough to make him a revolutionist, if pushed far enough. A function, therefore of the proletariat in Russia would be to lead the peasant in the revolution. The revolutionary party, to secure the alliance of the peasants, would advocate the expropriation of the lands of the gentry and its redistribution among the peasants. The Bolsheviks made use of a peasant revolution alongside the proletarian revolution. They encouraged the peasants in their seizure of the landed estates and they helped in that success. Thus the peasants' insurrection was an important part of the October Revolution. But compared to the revolution in the major cities, such as Petrograd and Moscow, the peasants' insurrection was of secondary importance. However small in numbers the industrial workers were, along with the military, they constituted the most decisive element of Bolshevik support. In this way the October Revolution was proletarian, for without urban support it would not have occurred. But without the accompanying peasant support the Bolsheviks might not have survived in power.

As a result of the October Revolution much of the old order (e.g., tsarism, the old bureaucracy) was permanently destroyed, gentry land was redistributed to the peasants, church and state were separated, and the calendar was reformed. Shortly after 1917, of necessity, the Bolsheviks moved to the right and became less permissive. Their explanation for this (i.e., they were considered necessary setbacks, but they felt the road to socialism was still open) lies outside the purview of this book. Nevertheless, suffice it to say that the October Revolution achieved a revolutionary change in Russia.

IV

When the February Revolution erupted Lenin was in Switzerland. With the help of the German government he returned to Russia only to be forced into hiding after the Bolshevik-inspired disturbances in mid-1917. Lenin continued to write and guide his party until the Provisional Government was overthrown in October. The October Revolution eliminated Russia's budding parliamentarianism and prevented capitalism from developing within a bourgeois democracy. As the personification of the Revolution Lenin was refuting Marx's dictum that "no social order ever disappears before all the productive forces for which there is room in it have been developed, and new, higher relations of production never appear before all the natural conditions of their existence have matured in the womb of the old society."[2] Lenin's important role in the Revolution was due to the fact that he persuaded his party, upon returning to Russia, not to be satisfied with the establishment of bourgeois democracy and to oppose the Provisional Government. He also convinced the Bolsheviks, before October, that another revolution was possible and that they should be prepared for it; Lenin's program was based on the principle of overthrow by force when the situation is ripe. Whereas his ideas owe a great deal to Marx, Lenin's genius emerged in being able to determine the right moment to seize power.

In 1923, before his death, Lenin evaluated the October Revolution. It was not, he wrote, the triumphant entry into the promised land for which he had hoped. But it was the start of a long, difficult process of establishing the foundation on which socialism could be built. Lenin believed that he had been true to Marx's fundamental principles (i.e., the complete destruction of the existing social and economic order and the establishment of a proletarian dictatorship and a planned economy). Although this meant bypassing the bourgeois stage of the revolution Lenin argued that this was permissible since Marx's real objective had been to abolish capitalism and everything associated with it.

Earlier in his life Lenin developed the idea of a bourgeois-democratic revolution in Russia serving as the signal for a socialist revolution in Western Europe. A revolution in Russia would ignite a conflagration in Europe, whereupon the European workers, previously suppressed by bourgeois capitalist society, would rise up and show the Russians the way. Thus, the proletariat of the advanced capitalist countries would be in the vanguard once the Russians made a beginning. But by World War I Lenin no longer saw the bourgeois-democratic revolution in Russia as the first of a series of events which develops into a proletarian revolution in the West and then finally returns to Russia to initiate the socialist revolution there. The war revealed the possibility to Lenin that Russia might experience a socialist revolution simultaneously with the West. He also came to believe that the socialist revolution need not be victorious simultaneously all over Europe. Thus, Marx's model of revolution took on a new character.

With the failure of revolution to materialize in Western Europe after 1917, Lenin shifted his emphasis to the need to carry through the socialist revolution in Russia even if it did not coincide with one in the West. He justified the October Revolution on the grounds that the opportunity was at hand and not because it made sense in terms of long-range or world-wide developments. The relationship between the bourgeois-democratic and the socialist revolutions, said Lenin in 1921 on the fourth anniversary of the October Revolution, is that "the first grows into the second. The second, in passing, solves the problems of the first. The second consolidates the work of the first. Struggle, and struggle alone, decides how far the second will succeed in outgrowing the first." The October Revolution was the beginning of the world revolution, of a process that would conclude with the victory of socialism in all countries. The Russian Revolution, according to Lenin, was not merely a national revolution; it was a first, not a final victory. And the beginning of the world revolution meant that the revolutionary perspectives of all countries would have to be assessed on the basis of the fact that the world revolution had already begun.

Revolution for Lenin meant that the power of the state was to be used for the people, not against them. As he said in a later speech:

> Hitherto the whole creative genius of the human intellect has labored only to give the advantages of technique [i.e., technology] and civilization to the few, and to deprive the rest of the most elementary necessities— education and free development. But now all the marvels of technique, all the conquests of civilization, are the property of the whole people, and henceforth human intellect and genius will never be twisted into a means of oppression, a means of exploitation.[3]

But Lenin's Russia quickly evolved into a ruthless dictatorship. However, the very ruthlessness with which Lenin sought to secure his power is perhaps illustrative of his impatience at getting the problems of security out of the way and his eagerness to take on the job of establishing socialism.

V

The Russian Revolution was probably the first great revolution in history to be consciously planned and made, at least in some significant places. It was a revolution led by intellectual revolutionists, men who sought both to make the revolution and to analyze and prepare the conditions in which it could be made as well. It was a political revolution in an economically backward country. Russia possessed a small and mostly unorganized proletariat; in fact, the revolution did not progress very far at first because of the inadequacy of the proletariat. That is when the intellectual-led Bolshevik Party took over the revolution. Thus, the Russian Revolution was made by a party, not a class, although it was a party which claimed to be the representative and vanguard of the working class. In this sense, the Revolution was planned and was not, as Marx expected, the spontaneous action of a class. However much Lenin modified Marx, he was not in favor of a revolution by an elite alone. The party acted to lead and inspire the proletariat, to develop their latent class consciousness. Here lies the Bolshevik contribution to the concept of revolution. Revolution depends less on the means of production than on the role of a party. The Bolsheviks substituted the primacy of political action for the primacy of the forces of production. They merely camouflaged this change by retaining the vocabulary of the class struggle and by identifying the party with the class.

Since 1917 the Russians have considered the October Revolution as the beginning of a new era in history, the era of the downfall of capitalism and the establishment of communism. Subsequent 20th century communist revolutions have been seen by them as a continuation of the world revolutionary process initiated by the Russians; moreover, it is a process that will ultimately consume the whole world. Some scholars have argued that the Russian Revolution was merely a distinctive national event and not the beginning of an international trend. The truth of the matter, it seems, lies in the future.

NOTES

[1] Quoted in David Horowitz, *Empire and Revolution* (New York, 1969), p. 101.

[2] Marx, "A Contribution to the Critique of Political Economy" (1859), quoted in M. Drachkovitch (ed.), *Marxism in the Modern World* (Stanford, 1966), p. 8.
[3] Quoted in C. Hill, *Lenin and the Russian Revolution* (Middlesex, Eng., 1971), p. 157.

12

Non-Left Revolutions:
The Irish Revolution,
Gandhi's Revolution,
The Nazi Revolution

It is commonplace in the 20th century to identify revolutionary activity
with the ideologies of the Left. To be sure, the intellectual descendants
of Marx have, to say the least, generally included the possibility of
revolution as the means to a greater end, even though variations on
the Marxian theme have been and are numerous, similar to the sectarian variations which exist in Christianity. But there are other types of
revolutions and revolutionists. In this chapter we will deal with three
unusual types, "unusual" not only because they are frequently ignored
in socio-political studies of revolution but also because they are so very
different from what we have come to expect revolutions to be like. We
will look first at the Irish Revolution (1916–22) which, though it had
a socialist element, was a combined nationalist, anti-colonial and

minority revolution with little formal ideology. We will then treat the revolutionary philosophy of Mohandas Gandhi (1869–1948) which offered a startling alternative to revolution through violence. Finally, we will turn to the rightist revolution of Nazism, which may be of questionable character as a revolution but nonetheless is worthy of brief consideration.

I

After being dominated by the British for hundreds of years the Irish Free State became a reality in 1922. A look at the revolution that was precipitated by the Easter Rebellion of 1916 has a special bearing on the anti-colonial revolutions (or wars of liberation as they are also labeled) of this century. Many of the ingredients common to the troubles encountered by the West in the Third World were experienced first in Ireland: a conflict between an underdeveloped and a modern, affluent country; emerging nationalism and the problem of secession versus foreign rule; and declining and disappearing colonial empires (though, to be sure, the important racial element was missing). Thus, Ireland points the way to difficulties in Africa, Asia, Southeast Asia, the Middle East, and Latin America.

Protestant, industrial Britain was culturally distant from Catholic, agrarian Ireland. As such, Britain usually failed to react adequately to the needs of Ireland. Gathering momentum during the 19th century Irish nationalism developed as the rallying point for solutions to the nation's religious, social, economic and political problems. The British responded to Irish nationalism by generally doing what would mostly keep England undisturbed; British policy was at best politically expedient and unimaginative, and usually it was "too little, too late." By the turn of the century Irish nationalists were demanding a separate Irish Parliament. But as the British held fast Irish nationalism added to its demands, and home rule evolved into independence. The consequence was the violent Irish Revolution of 1916–22 and an independent, but not united Ireland.

In 1800 the Protestant minority which controlled Irish government agreed to accept union with Britain as a means to maintain its privileged, dominant position. The Catholic majority opposed this change which restricted it to second class citizenship. On the surface the conflict appears primarily religious, but religion only served to accent the division between the rulers and the masses. Generally speaking, the Protestants had the advantages of education, property, wealth and social and political dominance, whereas the position of the Catholics was the reverse. Religion was the emotional issue, but it was virtually inseparable from a minority's attempt, with foreign (British) aid, to maintain total ascendancy over a deprived majority. In the 19th century nationalism became the cause which promised self-respect and hope. In the 20th century nationalism became a revolutionary force.

After the start of World War I several, sometimes overlapping groups began to organize for a revolution against the British Government. Some hoped that a blood sacrifice for Irish independence would raise the level of nationalism among the people to a new, revolutionary height, spread throughout the country and eventually drive the British out and with them the humiliation of long foreign control. Others were less romantic and thought that a planned uprising would catch the British by surprise (while she was fighting on the Continent) and, with a rapid victory, rally the Irish masses behind the revolution and compel the British to leave.

The various revolutionary groups set Easter, 1916 as the time to start their revolution. Although racked by confused preparations and a divided leadership the revolution began as planned on Easter Monday in Dublin. The fighting was ferocious and the casualties heavy, but the Irish masses did not join in the fight; in fact, they even jeered the revolutionists after their defeat as they were marched off to jail. There followed then, massive, revengeful and terroristic reprisals which turned the "traitors" into martyrs and national heroes. The blood sacrifice had, indeed, worked. Irish nationalism intensified and constitutional methods to achieve Home Rule were replaced by revolutionary methods to win independence.

The British began to defend their interests by increasing the size of their forces in Ireland. The Irish, especially the Irish Republican Army (I.R.A.) utilized urban guerrilla tactics, striking at their oppressors and then disappearing into the civilian population. Such tactics, however unconventional, were the only practical way for a small nation with minimal resources to fight a war of liberation against a strong power. In this way, the Irish Revolution anticipated, among others, the Algerian Revolution almost a half century later.

In the end the Irish gained their independence, though without Ulster. The significance of the Revolution for later world events is beyond doubt. Ireland was the first country in the 20th century to liberate herself from foreign domination through her own efforts;

unintentionally, Ireland's fight for independence set a pattern for other revolutionary movements involving the underdeveloped areas of the world. However, there are some differences here, as there are in any historical analogy. Ireland is a white, European, Christian nation easily associated with the rest of the Western world. Ireland was a part of Britain, geographically very close, and not a colony in the usual sense of the word. Irish Protestants may have been a minority in Catholic Ireland, but Irish Catholics may be viewed as a minority in Protestant Britain. Thus, in addition to being nationalist and anti-colonial the Irish Revolution was the revolt of a minority and in this sense not totally unlike the position of blacks in the United States.

Still, the Irish Revolution was mostly a unique and native phenomenon. As fruitful as it may be to view it as a prototype of Third World revolutions or a minority problem, it should be viewed on its own terms as a nationalistic upheaval that was the culmination of centuries of abuse. It was a revolution influenced more by the course of history than by any specific revolutionary ideology. In this sense the Irish Revolution stands by itself, resisting typology.

II

In the 20th century the colonies held by Europe have sought their independence. An atmosphere of mistrust, hostility and hatred, clouded with envy and an uncertain future, blanketed the colonial world. Most colonial revolutionists resorted to violence in order to gain their national aims. As with Ireland, rebellion and guerrilla warfare were met with repression and tyranny. Passions became very intense.

The British controlled and dominated India from the middle of the 18th century. How India would free herself from the British yoke was unclear before the appearance of Mohandas K. (Mahatma) Gandhi. Gandhi initiated a revolution unique in the method it provided to achieve Indian independence. That method, known as *satyagraha*, literally meaning "truth force" or the force which is born of truth and love, employs mass civil disobedience and is based on the principle of converting the enemy through peace and love so that he would have to acknowledge your dignity and your rights. Gandhi made successful use of the concept of non-violence *(ahimsa)* and in the process led a revolution whereby India's masses, with humbleness and humility, freed themselves from British authority and oppression. Gandhi's significance lay in his attempt to release the power wrapped up in the suffering of the Indian people. One of the ways he did this was by identifying himself with the common Indian: by speaking the people's language, wearing similar clothes, eating the same kind of food. This was the secret of his hold over his people. Indians had drifted away from one another. Gandhi restored the contacts among the people and reestablished a unity among them. This was a monumental achievement which helped make his revolution possible.

Satyagraha is the way of life for those who hold steadfastly to God and dedicate their lives to Him; such people must resist evil in all forms. The weapon of *satyagraha* is non-violence. Gandhi derived his doctrine from many sources—including Jesus, Thoreau and Tolstoy—but the practical application of non-violence to broad social and political spheres involving masses of people (as opposed to individuals alone) was entirely his own. *Satyagraha* also involves appealing to the reason and conscience of one's opponent by inviting suffering on oneself. The aim is to make one's opponent a friend and it is based on the idea that this moral appeal will be more effective than the threat of force or violence. Gandhi believed that non-violence puts a permanent end to evil because it converts the evil doer, whereas violence to one's enemy merely suppresses evil for the time being only to have it emerge more dangerously later. In the political realm *satyagraha* means civil disobedience and mass resistance on a non-violent basis against a government after constitutional and traditionally democratic methods have failed. But *satyagraha* is not just for a passing moment; it is a way of life. It demands disciplined group action, a tremendous capacity for suffering without any thought of physical retaliation. And it involves obedience to leaders who have demonstrated "saintly" qualities and who must, in turn, be respected enough to be obeyed. *Satyagraha*, therefore, involves group cooperation of the highest degree; it means self-help and self-sacrifice.

With Gandhi *satyagraha* became a tool for social change which went beyond the limitations of mere civil disobedience. *Satyagraha* became more than a way of resisting a specific law; it became a technique of struggle for basic societal change. Added to non-violence and passive resistance, in Gandhi's hands *satyagraha* came to involve the objectives of independence and the ideal society which would follow.

Satyagraha follows three general stages for defeating (or winning over) an opponent. First, there is an attempt to persuade by reason. Failing this, persuasion is attempted through self-suffering; the people involved *(satyagrahi)* dramatize the issues and their goals by individual suffering. Finally, if these methods fail, the *satyagrahi* resort to non-violent coercion, such as non-cooperation and civil disobedience.

Satyagraha is characterized by adherence to a stated truth by means of behavior which is not violent, but which includes self-suffering. It attempts to effect social and political changes and it works in a conflict situation. It employs force, but it is not violent force. The notion of non-violent force is linked with the view of truth which uses as its measure the needs of man. In seeking and propagating truth the *satyagrahi* cannot possibly do harm to others since truth would otherwise lose its meaning. The *satyagrahi* must always be reexamining his own position for his opponent just may be closer to the truth. This brings to prominence the element of self-suffering which assures the sincerity of the *satyagrahi's* own views and restrains him from advocating uncertain truths. Therefore, the objectives of *satyagraha* are the discovery of truth and the victory over one's opponent by persuasion.

Why does *satyagraha* exclude the use of violence? Because, said Gandhi, "man is not capable of knowing the absolute truth and therefore not competent to punish."[1] Gandhi also said that "a non-violent revolution is not a program of 'seizure of power.' It is a program of transformation of relationships ending in a peaceful transfer of power."[2] Gandhi viewed revolution as the means to root out all that is inhuman and unworthy in man. As with socialists Gandhi sought political, economic and social equality for Indians. But where these are achieved by violence, Gandhi felt, they only bring the form and not the substance of freedom. He was aware that violent revolution often results in violent counterrevolution; consequently, if India could achieve freedom by persuasion she was less likely to lose it by force. He believed that the greater the violence the weaker the revolution. In violent revolution not all elements of society can take part, but in non-violent revolution there is room for contributions from all, even children, and in the process all will emerge stronger. Guerrilla tactics and conspiracy have no place in Gandhi's idea of revolution. Everything must be open because the *satyagrahi* wishes to win his enemy over to his side, not destroy him; *satyagraha* is essentially a defensive tactic to neutralize the actions of the oppressor. In this way the revolution becomes identified with all the people; it is especially for the oppressed who are subjected to unjustified restraints and are deprived of their birthright.

Violent revolutions can succeed only where the government is weak and disorganized. Non-violent revolution can win against even the strongest governments because *satyagraha* depends for its success not on the condition of the government but on the capacity of the participants to suffer in love and without ill will. "Ours," said Gandhi in 1920, "must be a progressively peaceful revolution such that the transference of power from a closed corporation to the people's representatives will be as natural as the dropping of a fully ripe fruit from a well-nurtured tree."

Part of the ideal of revolution for Gandhi was that each person should learn to be free, to rule over himself. When this happens you can convert your enemy after which there will be no need to expel him—he will just go—and thus there is no need for violence. For Gandhi, therefore, if India was to achieve independence only peaceful means could be used. He did not separate the means from the end; he insisted that the means be as pure as the end. Gandhi's efforts to give firm expression to this principle of the moral approximation of the end and means is an important contribution to the concept of revolution.

Gandhi's idea of revolution seems to have had its greatest appeal to subordinated groups which have sensed their powerlessness against a clearly identifiable oppressor. Gandhi himself has been lauded for his high moral character among revolutionists. Looked at in another way, Gandhi's advocacy of non-violent revolution was not only a question of morality but was, as well, the only realistic program he had available;[3] the morality was to a significant degree a rationale for a pragmatic program. Gandhi did not use guns because he had none, and had he had them he would not have had the people to use them; he found the Indian population generally submissive, bullied and crushed. He wrote in 1930: "Spiritually, compulsory disarmament has made us unmanly, and the presence of an alien army of occupation, employed with deadly effect to crush in us the spirit of resistance, has made us think we cannot look after ourselves or put up a defense against foreign aggression, or even defend our homes and our families."[4] Thus, if Gandhi had had guns and a people capable of using them he very well might have. Gandhi's successor Nehru later said that Gandhi never completely ruled out the use of violence and that he (Gandhi) was adaptable. (Nehru later used armed force against Pakistan over Kashmir in 1956 and eight months after independence the Indian National Congress outlawed passive resistance.) But, as it turned out, *satyagraha* was the wisest form of revolution the Indians could have utilized.

Gandhi converted a negative situation into a positive one as he organized his passive people and gave them a purpose with which they could cope. After all, the genius of any revolutionist lies in the ability to adjust ideology to circumstances. His greatness lay in his ability to transform India's weakness into a source of strength. Before Gandhi, Indians were collectively lethargic and apart from one another; an active, energetic revolution was not possible. Gandhi made use of this character of the Indian people. He accepted their fatalism and passivity and from it constructed a movement of non-cooperation in which passivity and endurance were turned into sources of energy and strength.

Satyagraha as a way of life pointed to a new method of revolution in which religion and politics were merged. Gandhi believed that society must be transformed and that the transformation could begin immediately. He believed that the political revolution was connected to social change and spiritual well-being, and these must all proceed together. Attaining political freedom, as with spiritual liberation, would only occur with self-purification. Thus revolution for Gandhi was total. Not only must the political order be transformed but so must each and every individual. Revolution is personal as well as societal. Gandhi did not know what the new society would be like, but the "new man" would develop both before and during the revolution, and not just be a product of the revolution.

Gandhi's view of revolution is a form of permanent revolution in that his philosophy of *satyagraha* is one of endless becoming and growing. Man and his society must always be improving because perfection is an attribute of God alone.

III

More than any other revolutionary movement Nazism appears out of place in this book. Not merely a movement from the right Nazism was a negative revolution. Technically it must be classified as a revolution since, with its coming, one form of government was replaced by another and significant changes in society were effected. It was a conservative revolution, begun legally (i.e., Hitler and his party were voted into office), to make the German world safe for small business, small farmers and those in small towns. It was conversely against big industry, big cities and big unions. Where the Nazis allied themselves with these "big" groups it was of necessity, not admiration. Oddly enough, however, for the time the Nazi Revolution was successful industry prospered and the age of the small businessman was postponed.

Before 1933–34 the Nazi Revolution went on from below. But by 1934 the victory of the Nazi Party was secure and the revolution continued from above. Its ideology was the doctrine of the superiority of the Aryan race. This doctrine was a basic theme in the Nazi protest against the current social disorder of post-war Germany. The very fact that social disorder could infect Germany was explained by declaring that Germany had failed to recognize the primary importance of the racial principle. The Nazis would correct this failure and make the racial principle the governing law of society. The Nazis sought the absurd aim of purifying the Aryan race. And, of course, Jews were the scapegoat on which the Nazi goal of establishing the dignity and beauty of a "higher" humanity would be built. Nazism sought to establish a new faith and a new way of life, but it became reactionary, regressive and racist.

NOTES

[1] Quoted in J. V. Bondurant, *Conquest of Violence* (Princeton, 1958), p. 16.

[2] Quoted in G. Dhawan, *The Political Philosophy of Mahatma Gandhi* (Ahmedabad, 1957), p. 233.

[3] See Saul Alinsky, *Rules For Radicals* (New York, 1957), pp. 37–42.

[4] Quoted in *Ibid.*

13

China in Revolution:
Sun Yat-sen, Mao Tse-tung
and the Cultural Revolution (I)

In the 20th century revolution came to play a crucial role in the history of China, and China came to influence revolutions elsewhere in the world. The giant of the East had been subject to major civil disturbances earlier (e.g., the Taiping Rebellion) and foreign forces had been penetrating China for some time. But, beginning in the early 1900's China took her first of several significant steps towards merging her history with Western influences through the vehicle of revolution. The effect of it all was to produce one of the world's most powerful and pivotal nations. In the process, the concept of revolution was expanded and made more meaningful to the modern world.

I

Ever since the 17th century when they came to power the Manchu rulers of China had been considered a foreign dynasty. Although the country had flourished under them and in more than 300 years they had become thoroughly Chinese, anti-Manchu sentiment remained an active ingredient of Chinese nationalism. It is perhaps for this reason that the Manchus presented themselves as guardians of orthodox Chinese traditions. All this coincided with the period at the end of the 19th and beginning of the 20th century when China was becoming more involved with the rest of the world and when the Manchus were decaying and outliving their heavenly mandate.

China was beginning to react to the challenges of the outside world. Structural and intellectual changes were taking place which resulted in greater political expression. The failure of the Manchus to protect the country against the intrusions of foreign powers was a sign of their inability to rule. The mandarins (i.e., public officials) were demoralized and many of the best scholars did not wish to serve the dynasty. A rebellion appeared imminent. But many Chinese, especially those influenced by both the West and Japan, believed that no traditional rebellion—which would only result in a new dynasty—would suffice. New dynasties had been founded before; this usually involved much fighting and disorder, and this time it could easily result in greater foreign intervention and perhaps partition. Chinese intellectuals were coming to believe that classical Chinese education was no longer serving the country adequately. They shared a deep dissatisfaction with the present, a sense that change was urgently needed, and an optimism about the future.

The ideas and programs of these intellectuals reached revolutionary proportions in the first decade of the 20th century. Although these new revolutionists differed among each other over details they shared a common spirit and vision. For example, they wanted some form of democracy; they wished to strengthen the foundations of the state by giving the masses a greater share of power and building up in them a greater sense of responsibility. Thus, it would be necessary not merely to change the personnel of the government but to regenerate the state itself by transforming the minds of the people. The masses would have to learn to regard affairs of state, not as the private business of the emperor and his officials, but as public business with which they should be concerned. The revolutionists propagated the idea that the government was not only failing to do all it could but also lacked the ability to satisfy deep grievances. Moreover, they argued, a new leadership, founded on different principles and institutions, was needed to do better. They predicted great improvements under a proposed Chinese republic. The goal of their revolution, therefore, would be a democratic republic administered by men who were familiar with Western learning. They articulated the desire of many for an improved life; and by expressing such possibilities they aroused new hopes and expectations.

In 1895, after a brief war, China was defeated by a smaller—and, to their way of thinking, inferior—but westernized Japan. The Chinese were shocked and the need for change and new ideas became more apparent. There were some efforts at reform and modernization afterwards but these failed to impress those in power or to create adequate popular pressure for change. A number of learned men emerged who preferred to advocate revolution instead of reform. Chief among these was Sun Yat-sen (1866–1925). A well traveled and educated man, Dr. Sun spent much of his time during these years in organizing for radical reform; a few years earlier, for example, he had established the Hsing-Chung-hui (Society to Revise China). His came to be a revolutionary republican program, and his followers were recruited largely from the middle classes. They worked from both within and without China developing a nationalist movement; nationalism provided revolutionary momentum for China and was characterized by a desire to change China's deteriorating civilization into a powerful, modern state. Political activity, such as boycotts and strikes, was used and although many failed, the movement gained a following. Sun came to favor revolution because he saw his people disunited, scattered and unable to resist the invasions of foreigners. Revolution would make it possible to restore China to a respectable place in the world.

In 1905 the T'ung-meng-hui was formed; it was a united, revolutionary alliance of many of the separate and smaller revolutionary groups. The T'ung-meng-hui later evolved into the Kuomintang or National Party; its first leader was Sun Yat-sen. The manifesto of the alliance provides a background for the Chinese Revolution of 1911. The revolution that was planned would be

> a continuation of heroic deeds bequeathed to us by our predecessors. .
> . . [But,] besides the driving out of the barbarian [Manchu] dynasty and
> the restoration of China, it is necessary also to change the national polity
> and the people's livelihood. And though there are a myriad ways and
> means to achieve this goal, the essential spirit that runs through them all
> is freedom, equality, and fraternity.[1]

It would be a national revolution of all the people, although a military government would be their agent. The manifesto outlined a four-point program: (1) drive out the Manchu; (2) restore China to the Chinese; (3) establish a republican government founded on equality with the president and parliament chosen by the people; and (4) improve economic and social organization so that in the state thus created all would be supported and satisfied. The manifesto also enumerated a three-stage plan for implementing the four points: a period of military government, followed by a period of a provisional constitution, and finally a formal constitution. Dr. Sun never explained how the constitution would be written or by whom, nor did he say how the transition from stage to stage would be achieved. But he did say that the aim of the revolution would be both to establish democracy and improve social conditions.

In any case, his ideas, as expressed in the manifesto, remained a part of his plans for China all his life and they were preserved by the Kuomintang (KMT, the governing party) in a modified form after Sun's death in 1925. They became known as the "Three Principles of the People": (1) Nationalism, which meant the elimination of foreign imperialism and domestic militarism from China and the formation of a united national state; (2) Democracy, which meant a form of government in which the people had the rights of election, recall, initiative and referendum, but in which only educated and qualified persons should be admitted to office; and (3) People's Livelihood, which meant the redistribution of land among the people who worked it, and state control of communications and industry for public benefit.

The revolution began in October, 1911 and spread quickly. In November a manifesto to the outside world was issued guaranteeing that international obligations would be safeguarded. The manifesto ended with the following plea for sympathy:

> We are fighting for what Britain fought in the days of old; we are fighting for what America fought. . . . We are fighting to be men in the world; we are fighting to cast off an oppressive, vicious, and tyrannous rule that has beggared and disgraced China, obstructed and defied the foreign nations, and set back the hands of the clock of the world. . . . We are trying to bring China into her own. . . . We have the right to win the laurels of freedom.[2]

In December a republic was declared and in the following February the Manchu dynasty formally abdicated. Imperial China was now history.

The goals of the 1911 Chinese Revolution may be summed up in the words "democracy" and "modernization." To this generation of Chinese "revolution" meant the overthrow of the alien Manchus and the establishment of a republic, with emphasis upon freedom, equality, self-determination, the need for popular participation in government, and respect for law. 1911 was a national revolution.

The Revolution of 1911 meant the final overthrow of a form of government and a system that had been weakened by Western interference from without and by discontent from within. The Revolution was not just a dynastic change (China had had many of these) but an attempt to terminate a 2000-year period of Confucianism (i.e., traditional China, the symbol of her culture and history) and the Confucian state. This part of the Revolution was necessarily destructive. The constructive part was to try to build a republic. The ideals of this republic were laid down by Sun Yat-sen in his Three Principles of the People, but they were theoretical and not at all practical to China's existing situation. Therefore, the success of the Revolution was followed by a period of internal conflict and disruption characterized more by attention to regional needs and the whims of the war lords (i.e., provincial despots) than to ideals. There were even a couple of attempts—in 1915 and 1917—to restore a monarchy but these failed; China was clearly not going to return to the old order.

The masses played only a passive role in the 1911 Revolution and the traditional social structure remained almost unaltered. But the new ideas slowly began to seep down among the people and the old order began to disintegrate. The Revolution, therefore, not only overthrew the monarchy but, more importantly, it inaugurated the process that eventually resulted in the destruction of the traditional order. The course of Chinese history could not stop in 1911; more changes would be necessary.

One of Sun Yat-sen's three principles had been "nationalism." As an admirer of the West his principle of nationalism was initially directed against the foreign rule of the Manchus, and not the imperialist powers of the West. Sun had expected, after 1911, that the West would give up its control in China so that the newly formed country could gain equality with the other states. Sun accepted the delay caused by World War I but after the Peace of Versailles (1919) and the Washington Conference (1921–22) it became clear that the Western powers had no intention of giving up their privileges in China. Sun's nationalism, therefore, then came to include the expulsion of the imperialist powers. (Sun's anti-imperialism was not Leninist in origin; imperialism he viewed as a tool of economic exploitation, not the final stage of capitalism.)

By the early 1920's, and until his death in 1925, Sun felt that one party, the KMT, should assume control, however dictatorial it might become, in order to create the right conditions for advancing his three principles, developing the Revolution and rebuilding the new state. But the KMT was not destined to be that party. Thus, in the final analysis, the Revolution of 1911 failed to achieve what the intellectuals had hoped. Many abandoned politics or cynically went along. But others decided to continue the Revolution and do more. The result, in brief, was that the revolutionary movement came to produce new revolutionary leaders in the period after World War I. The failure of these leaders, however, helps to explain the emergence of the Chinese Communists, who were themselves new revolutionists. In other words, each move towards modernization has had the way paved for it by a preceding one whose achievements were not significant enough to meet rising expectations and frustrations. This pattern would be followed again later in Chinese history.

II

The Chinese Revolution of 1927–49, led by Mao Tse-tung (1893–) and the Chinese Communist Party (CCP), was promoted not only by the ideology of Marxism-Leninism and nationalism, but by social, and especially rural problems and crises. These problems and crises were compounded by monarchical collapse, imperialist domination, war lord abuses, oppression by the landowning classes, and a sharp rise in population. Revolution, it seems, was the only way for China to resolve her problems. Given China's history in the 20th century revolution was a necessary fact of life in order to promote what many considered vital changes.

The success of the Russian Revolution in 1917, followed by Russia's renunciation of all her rights, privileges and commissions in China, helped give China's nationalism a new alternative. Theoretical Marxism had not been especially attractive in China until Lenin gave it a new shape in Russia. It came to be realized that in backward China, as in backward Russia, a numerically small proletariat, with proper organization and leadership, could depose a privileged ruling elite. As a result, China's nationalists soon became divided into protagonists of two rival ways of modernization and complete self-rule: capitalism and communism.

But before that division was formalized China witnessed another important episode known as the May Fourth (1919) Movement. It was a combined intellectual upheaval and nationalist movement in which socialist ideas played a subordinate role. Although the movement will not be a concern of this study, and it is doubtful that it was part of the world proletarian revolution of that time (as Mao stated), it should be pointed out that the May Fourth Movement, coming after the 1911 Revolution, further called into question the very basis of traditional Chinese society. The movement was a culmination of the influences of westernization and, while it further repudiated Confucianism, it provided the background for the social revolution of the CCP. The movement brought forth the ideals of progress, democracy, science and the potential of human reason; it was a virtual "Enlightenment" for 20th century China. In the process of opposing the old, Confucian culture the young, nationalist-minded Chinese were trying to save China, to give her strength to defend herself against exploitation and national disgrace. In short, it was a movement that combined pro-western culture and anti-western nationalism.

As alluded to above, many of China's intellectuals became advocates of Marxism-Leninism after 1917. In the summer of 1921 a small number of these intellectuals, including Mao Tse-tung, established the Chinese Communist Party. Their numbers grew rapidly (i.e., an estimated 60,000 in 1927) and they worked, of necessity, with the KMT for a while. The CCP, in the early 1920's, viewed the 1911 Revolution as a necessary prerequisite to their own forthcoming revolution; but the KMT, they said, was both militaristic and feudalistic, a block to further development, and must be eliminated. The CCP looked upon itself "as the vanguard of the proletariat," struggling "for working-class liberation and for the proletarian revolution. [But] until such time as the Chinese proletariat is able to seize power in its own hands, considering the present political and economic conditions of China's development . . . the proletariat's urgent task is to act jointly with the [KMT]."[3]

After the death of Sun Yat-sen in 1925 the new leader of the KMT was Chiang Kai-shek; he was conservative and less willing to work with the Communists. In 1927 Chiang turned on the Communists and the leaders of trade unions and workers' organizations arresting and executing thousands. The KMT and the CCP were now enemies in conflict. The latter was weak and beaten, and to many observers the Chinese Revolution was over.

Despite an initial advance towards improving the country the ad-

ministrative efficiency of the KMT proved little better than the old
Manchu variety. There was inflation and corruption, while the government was very authoritarian. Mostly though, the government failed to
do anything significant about China's main internal problem: the desperate poverty of the countryside. The landed interests blocked attempts at reform and the KMT became tied with the country's leading
capitalists (e.g., Chiang Kai-shek's two brothers-in-law were among the
wealthiest businessmen in China).

The CCP, under Russian direction, tried to form a proletarian base,
but failed consistently because of the lack of a cohesive urban elite.
Some Chinese Communists, however, began to organize the peasants
with the hope that they might provide the spark for the revolution that
would spread all over China and be guided by the proletariat in the
cities. One such organizer of the peasants was Mao Tse-tung, and such
organization was the key to the success of revolution in China, especially when contrasted with the Russian Revolution.

                                    III

By 1930 it became clear that the proletarian wing of the CCP was too
weak and lacked sufficient popular support to make any real progress.
In rural areas, however, the Party was acquiring territory and small
"red armies," using guerrilla tactics, were being successful. By 1931
Mao became the leader of Chinese Communism. The motivation for
his activity was based more upon observation than dogmatic assumptions.

Mao adapted Marxism-Leninism to the conditions of China as an
underdeveloped country which had experienced domination by the
West; and he remained emphatic in his awareness that Marxist doctrine would have to be adjusted to the reality of Chinese background
and experience. Here he was being consistent with Lenin's assertion
that Marxism be integrated with the actual circumstances in which it
exists. In 1938, in a report to the Sixth Plenum of the Sixth Central
Committee, Mao wrote that "we must not study the letter of Marxism
and Leninism, but the viewpoint and methodology of its creators, with
which they observed and solved problems." It was necessary to study
Marx and Lenin in order "to understand our historic inheritance and
to evaluate it critically by the use of the Marxist method [because] the
history of our great people over several millennia exhibits national
peculiarities and many precious qualities." To emphasize his point

Mao went on to say that *"there is no such thing as abstract Marxism, but only concrete Marxism,* [that is] *Marxism that has taken on a national form . . .* [and been] *applied to the concrete struggle in the concrete conditions prevailing in China."* In short, Marxism-Leninism must be Sinified to make certain "that in all of its manifestations it is imbued with Chinese peculiarities, using it according to the peculiarities."

More specifically, as his fellow countrymen have said, Mao changed Marxism from a European to an Asiatic form. This has not been to deny the basic truths of Marxism, but it has been to assert that China's problems need specific attention. Thus, according to Chinese Maoists, Mao used Marxist-Leninist principles to explain Chinese history and problems, which may be applicable to other Asian peoples with similar conditions and problems.

There has been considerable dispute among scholars over the question of Mao's originality. Although he was not a theorist like Marx, Mao's fundamental contribution to the revolutionary thought of Marx and Lenin lies in his application of that thought to actual Chinese conditions. For the moment, suffice it to say that Mao (1) shifted the focus of revolution from urban centers to rural areas, (2) developed a communist party based on the peasantry, not the proletariat, (3) emphasized class alliances and "united front" tactics, and (4) concentrated on a prolonged military conflict based on rural guerrilla warfare. In these ways—which will be elaborated upon in the next chapter—Mao's Revolution differed from the Russian Revolution and gave added dimension to the Marxian concept of revolution.

Before proceeding with the details of Mao's views on revolution there are a couple of other points we wish to mention. For Mao, as for Lenin, revolution would have to be stimulated and encouraged rather than simply awaited. For Marxists like Mao and Lenin, just as for Calvinists, the order and fate of the world may be inevitable (or predestined) but it is not the job of believers to be mere fatalists. However optimistic they may be it is the task of the faithful to struggle to achieve the desired ends. This was a most meaningful creed to Lenin as it has been to Mao.

Finally, it can be noted that there are two separate but related strands that run through Mao's thought. First, he has pursued radical social change. Second, he has been intent on restoring Chinese national independence and dignity after the humiliation of Western domination. Thus, he has been both a revolutionist and a nationalist (and anti-imperialist); these are related since justification for revolution has been found in the belief that the nation can only be restored by a change in the political and social system. This has made Mao more radical than other revolutionary nationalists—such as Nasser, Nkrumah and Sukarno—who did not subscribe to Marxism-Leninism and who regarded revolution only as a means of strengthening their nations and not as an end itself.

NOTES

[1] "The Manifesto of the T'ung-meng-hui" (1905) in Ssu-yü Teng and John K. Fairbank (eds.), *China's Response To The West; A Documentary Survey, 1839–1923* (Cambridge, Mass., 1961), p. 227.

[2] "The Revolutionists' Manifesto to the Foreign World on the Aims of the Revolution and the Provisional Government" (November 17, 1911) in Vera Simone (ed.), *China in Revolution; History, Documents, and Analysis* (Greenwich, Conn., 1968), pp. 111–14.

[3] "First Manifesto of the CCP on the Current Situation" (June 10, 1922) in *ibid.,* pp. 157-61.

[4] Mao Tse-tung, "On the New Stage" (October 1938) in Stuart R. Schram (ed.), *The Political Thought of Mao Tse-tung* (New York, 1969), revised and enlarged edition, pp. 171f.

14

China in Revolution:
Sun Yat-sen, Mao Tse-tung
and the Cultural Revolution (II)

.

As a Marxist, Mao has said that all modern revolutions are proletarian, of which there are two types: (1) there are those occurring in advanced industrial societies with a strong proletariat, and (2) there are those in colonial, semi-colonial (i.e., nominally independent but still under foreign influence) and semi-feudal (i.e., part feudal, part capitalist) countries in which the majority of people are peasants. In the former type the workers, by whatever means available, initiate a revolution and overthrow the bourgeoisie. Peaceful revolution is essentially impossible since the ruling classes virtually never relinquish power voluntarily. In the latter type, the type with which Mao was both concerned and involved, the revolution develops in two stages: the first bourgeois-democratic and the second proletarian-socialist. The bourgeois-democratic stage of the revolution is led by the proletariat and relies on a "united front" of all "progressive" forces (e.g., peasants, workers, intellectuals) in the country; this stage seeks to overthrow imperialism and feudalism, achieve political independence, and nationalize the main sources of public wealth. But, while it "overthrows the rule of the imperialist, traitors, and reactionaries . . . [it] does not destroy any section of capitalism which is capable of contributing to the anti-imperialist, anti-feudal struggle.[1] When all this is achieved the second stage can be initiated. In this, the proletarian-socialist stage of the revolution, capitalism is overthrown and socialism is introduced. The aim of the first stage is to transform a colonial country into a strong, independent one; the aim of the second state is to eliminate domestic reaction and advance the country along socialist lines. Although the two stages are distinct they are part of a single process, with the first providing the conditions for the second.

For ages, wrote Mao in his 1940 work describing the "new democracy" of the first stage, Chinese society, politics, economics and culture were feudal. With the invasion of foreign capitalism the country changed into a colonial, semi-colonial and semi-feudal society. It was against this system that the Chinese Communist Revolution was being directed. China, he said, must first become an independent, democratic society before the Revolution could be carried forward to build a socialist society. "The state system, a joint dictatorship of all the revolutionary [and anti-imperialist] classes and the system of government, democratic centralism—these constitute the politics of New Democracy."[2] This "new democracy" will own the big banks and big industrial and commercial enterprises. Also, the land of the landlords will be confiscated and distributed to the peasants having little or no land.

The bourgeois-democratic revolution is to be distinguished from the "old" democratic revolutions, such as the French Revolution of 1789. The old, according to Mao, sought to establish a capitalist bourgeois state under bourgeois leadership and direction.

> China's economy must develop along the path of the 'regulation of capital' and the 'equalization of land ownership,' and must never be 'privately owned by the few'; we must never permit the few capitalists and landlords to 'dominate the livelihood of the people'; we must never establish a capitalist society of the European-American type or allow the semi-feudal society to survive.[3]

The "new democracy" is led by the proletariat and seeks to establish a transitional state under the dictatorship of a united front of several revolutionary classes (i.e., proletariat, peasants, petty bourgeoisie and soldiers).

It should be pointed out that Lenin had stated that revolution in a pre-capitalist country would have two stages, a bourgeois-democratic one and a socialist one. But Mao built on this by declaring that in China the first stage would be his "new democracy" and this was different from Lenin's first stage by the fact that it would not be led only by the bourgeoisie, but by the "joint revolutionary-democratic dictatorship of several revolutionary classes." Here is an example of Mao adjusting orthodox Marxism-Leninism to fit China's specific needs. To be sure, Lenin had written of a "revolutionary dictatorship of the proletariat and peasantry" and, if necessary, of even including the bourgeois nationalists. But Mao, by including the bourgeoisie from the start, was invariably moving towards the "people's dictatorship" proclaimed in 1949. Mao transformed industry and commerce into mixed public-private industry and commerce; he transformed capitalists into share-holders and he transferred the administration of private enterprises into party and government hands. This, moreover, helps to explain the post-1949 mixture in China of capitalist and socialist elements, a mixture that contained in it the seeds for the conflict that resulted eventually in the Cultural Revolution in 1966.

Thus, Mao's "new democracy" was a four-class alliance. Original or not, this four-class concept questioned the Leninist insistence upon the dominance of the proletariat, although Mao was careful to keep his position somewhat vague by mentioning, every so often, that "without the workers the Chinese revolution will not be able to succeed, for it is they who are the most revolutionary." It should be added that the four-class alliance was also based on national feelings, which were magnified from 1937 with Japan's invasion of China.

The Chinese Revolution, said Mao, is a national revolution. This too put him at odds with traditional Marxism. But, as Mao has repeated many times, "the universal truth of Marxism must be combined with specific national characteristics and acquire a definite national form if it is to be useful, and in no circumstances can it be applied subjectively as a mere formula."[4] According to Mao in 1940 the Chinese Revolution was only in its bourgeois-democratic stage. At a later date the socialist stage would arrive and China would enter an era of true happiness. But socialism would be out of the question until imperialism and feudalism were completely eliminated from China. The two stages were to be part of the same ideology, except that one was for the present (i.e., Chinese Revolution, 1927-49), the other the future. The entire process would be one of uninterrupted revolution, unfolding continuously from beginning to end. Although there are two stages to the revolution they form a single process, the aim of which "is to bring about a socialist and communist society."

Mao's theory of "uninterruped revolution" differs from Trotsky's theory of "permanent revolution" in several significant ways: (1) Trotsky distrusted the peasantry whereas Mao, as we shall see, did not; (2) Trotsky questioned the feasibility of a working alliance with the bourgeoisie whereas Mao, as we have seen, did not; (3) Trotsky thought it possible to by pass the bourgeois-democratic revolution whereas Mao did not since that was the stage in which the Chinese Revolution was engaged in the 1930's and 40's; (4) Trotsky questioned the possibility of a joint revolutionary dictatorship whereas, as we have seen, this is what Mao was planning after victory; and (5) Trotsky rejected the possibility of building socialism in one country in favor of a "permanent revolution" that would seek to establish socialism on an international level whereas Mao saw the necessity of binding Marxism to suit national needs.

II

Marx wrote that the legitimacy of the "Dictatorship of the Proletariat" rested on the belief that the dehumanization of the proletariat makes the working class most conscious of its mission of historical redemption. Lenin did not trust the workers to act in their own best interests without the leadership of a small, elitist, disciplined party. Mao's position was that the party's claim to legitimacy was based on its aid to the proletariat and its commitment to the liberation of the workers. This echoed Lenin's idea, to be sure, but Mao went further and said that the party must not only lead and arouse the consciousness of the masses, but also learn from them and join with the masses in achieving the revolution. Although by themselves the masses lack political consciousness, claimed Mao, without mass support the party cannot lead the revolution to victory. The party must convey its policy into the action of the masses and create the belief among the masses that the party line is really a reflection of their own views. Therefore, Mao persistently identified the party with the masses. The attainment of socialism was not to be a class or party interest alone, but a national (collective) interest.

Mao came to believe that the central task of revolution was to seize power by armed force; this, he said, was a universal principal of Marxism-Leninism. But the Revolution in China was different from the one, say, in Russia because China was neither independent nor democratic, had no parliament to make use of and no legal right to organize the workers to strike. Thus, "the task of the Communist Party here [in China] is not to go through a long period of legal struggle before launching insurrection and war, and not to seize the big cities first and occupy the countryside [afterwards], but the reverse."[5] In short, the task of the party would be to unite with all elements in the country to defeat the nation's enemies both within and without.

III

"The broad peasant masses have risen to fulfill their historical mission. . . . The democratic forces in the rural areas have risen to overthrow the rural feudal power. The overthrow of this feudal power is the real objective of the national revolution."[6] So wrote Mao in his important 1927 report on the peasants in Hunan province. From that time on revolution in China came to mean "peasant revolution"; the force behind the Revolution was not to be the workers in the cities but the poor, rural peasantry.

Marx had little more than contempt for the peasantry because they were far from the major centers of political and economic power and therefore essentially incapable of concerted action. Other Marxists, including Lenin and Stalin, considered the peasantry an important revolutionary force, but none recognized the peasantry as capable of action independent of the proletariat or the revolutionary bourgeoisie. Stalin had spoken of revolution *for* the peasants, and the Russians before 1927 had advised the CCP not to overlook the peasants. But official Communist policy regarding the role of the peasants remained on the books only, while the central focus of activities was on the urban proletariat. Still, China in the 1920's had hardly any industrial workers so that when Mao turned his attention to the peasantry as the major revolutionary force—revolution *by* the peasants—he was not exactly discovering an unknown factor. Nevertheless, where only lip service had been paid to revolutionary activities in rural areas—they were only isolated events to Lenin and Stalin—Mao took it to heart and attributed an initiative role to the peasants. This much was new and different with Mao; it was still Marxism-Leninism but with adjustments necessary to suit the Chinese situation. This adjustment helped Mao to become the leader of the Chinese Revolution.

With the destruction of the CCP's urban base in 1927 Mao really had little choice but to utilize the peasants. He set himself the task of creating an organization almost totally peasant in origin, even though it called itself the party of the proletariat and Mao continued to talk about "proletariat leadership" being "the key to the victory of the revolution." For Mao not only were the peasants more revolutionary and effective, but they needed to be recognized as such by those Chinese intellectuals who styled themselves as leaders of the Revolution. The peasants were, by themsleves, advancing in a revolutionary direction and the choice of the intellectuals was whether they would acknowledge this and lead the peasants or not acknowledge it and end up out of the picture. Although Mao never said it outright, the peasantry became, for all intents and purposes, the new "revolutionary vanguard." Mao further emphasized the role of the poor peasants. Without them "it would never have been possible to bring about the present state of the revolution in the country-side. . . . Without the poor peasants there can be no revolution."[7]

Mao's ideas on revolution here can be viewed as an extension of the Leninist theory of the weakest link. He relied on the peasants because it was among them that government control was weakest. Along with his followers he came to believe that only a mass-based and popular revolutionary movement would have a favorable chance to defeat a local army or forstall or defeat foreign intervention. A politically conscious mass support was a vital prerequisite for successful revolution. For Mao revolution meant a protracted struggle involving rural revolutionary bases; it was peasant guerrilla warfare led by the CCP. The idea of rural base areas was a contribution of Mao to the Marxist-Leninist strategy of revolution. In order to survive, wrote Mao, a rural base requires "(1) a sound mass basis, (2) a first-rate party organization, (3) a Red Army of adequate strength, (4) a terrain favorable to military operations, and (5) economic strength sufficient for self-support."[8] In this way Mao formulated, and later carried out, the prototype of rural revolution.

Mao's technique was to start the revolution in the countryside with an armed struggle, then establish rural bases and increase the size of his forces, and then encircle and finally seize the cities. Guerrilla warfare is less a military techinque—though, to be sure, it involves a favorable geography, mobility, etc.—than it is a political condition; it is also civilian warfare. The guerrilla faced with a professional army needs the active support of the people. Mass backing allows him mobility and his ability to fight where and when he wants. An overtly neutral

but covertly involved population is vital. The population aids the guerrillas by freeing them from logistic anchors, providing them with intel-
ligence, and hiding fugitives. As Mao stated: "Because guerrilla warfare basically derives from the masses and is supported by them, it can
neither exist nor flourish if it separates itself from their sympathies and
cooperation."[9] Mao's guerrilla's were instructed to abstain from steal-
ing food and from molesting women; they were not to be bandits but
representatives of a new order. The guerrilla's strength depended on
his ability to operate behind the enemy's rear as well as his front line.
This is possible only if guerrillas are able to move among the population, said Mao, like fish in the water.

IV

By the late 1920's and early 1930's Mao and his followers had formed
local soviets which fought against the existing order, especially in
central and southern China. In the process they developed a strong
Communist power base with a well organized army. Mao's leadership
came as a result of his political and military successes; for lack of an
alternative Russia raised no objection. The KMT, in the meantime,
sought to eliminate the CCP. In 1934 the success of the government
compelled Mao and the "Red Army" to escape in what has become
known as the "Long March" through a number of Chinese provinces.
Only after a great effort and heavy losses did the Red Army succeed
in avoiding destruction by government troops. The "Long March" was
a major military achievement; it acquired martyrs and a myth of its
own, and it brought the survivors closely together. During the "Long
March" the Red Army used every opportunity to publicize its revolution; it treated the masses well and gained considerable sympathy. In
time it was able to develop a new power base in the north which came
to be the starting point for the eventual conquest of China and the
success, in 1949, of the Chinese Revolution.

During the 1930's the KMT appeased the aggressive Japanese in
order to buy time to fight the Communists. But appeasement failed
and the KMT had to join with the CCP to fight Japan. The CCP
successfully placed itself at the front of the peasantry and later became
the political beneficiary of peasant mobilization. By 1937, mobilized by
the military challenge from Japan and lacking the traditional centers
of authority, the peasantry was ready to resist the foreigners; leadership was provided by the CCP which was militarily competent and
committed to war as the vehicle for social change. The pre-war CCP

program (e.g., alteration of the system of land tenure) was superceded by an ideology of patriotism, national liberation and self-sacrifice.

During World War II the conflict between the CCP and KMT was transformed into a contest for national leadership. The KMT grew corrupt and inept, and their fighting capability was inefficient. The CCP strengthened its forces and gained supporters. It worked behind Japanese lines within China spreading its gospel and setting an example of devotion and self-sacrifice. It moved carefully to offer advantages to the majority, yet mildly enough to avoid threatening the wealthier classes. It avoided appearing as an organization of extreme radicals, and moderation became the keynote; this, coupled with the idea of a national fight against the Japanese, helped the CCP gain considerable support. What also helped was that the Communists redistributed expropriated land among the landless, organized rural cooperatives, offered educational opportunities, and gave a large share in public life to women. Liberation meant not only China's independence, but also freeing the masses from the oppression of landlords, the bureaucracy and capitalists.

Mao called for a coalition of classes from which the landlords, bureaucrats and collaborators with Japan would be excluded. Small landowners and national capitalists were to be admitted in a broad national front. By the end of the war the Communists were the strongest force in China.

The KMT emerged from the war with the allies (i.e., the United States, Great Britain, and the Soviet Union) all recognizing its rule as the legitimate Chinese government. But it was still weak, corrupt and inefficient, and the masses were impatient. The Communists pressed for control. A civil war erupted that finally, in 1949, resulted in the CCP succeeding in gaining power.

                                    V

Revolution, Chinese Communist-style, succeeded, in part, because it prescribed solutions for China's internal needs. It also—simultaneously—seemed to prescribe solutions for China's external problems by criticizing the imperialist West, fighting relentlessly against imperialist Japan, and promising that socialism would enable China to catch up with and eventually surpass the capitalist countries. Because China was semi-colonial and semi-feudal, before she could achieve social revolution, she needed a national, anti-imperialist revolution. This is what Mao and the CCP provided between 1927 and 1949.

From the time of the Russian Revolution of 1917 such revolutionary struggles had been conceived in relation to the organization of an urban mass insurrection. But the Chinese came to rely on the capacity of a people's army, led by the Communist Party, to liberate the countryside, after which would come the liberation of the cities. The specific Chinese contribution was to make the military struggle inseparable from the political, to shift the focus of political and military organization from the urban to the rural areas, and to rely on a protracted armed struggle rather than a decisive sudden confrontation.

If we could put Mao's concept of revolution into one sentence it would be the following: a peasant army, led by an elite Communist Party, operating from the countryside, struggles to achieve political power. There may be little that is original in Mao's thought, but this by no means implies that there was nothing original in his *application* of Marxism-Leninism. Mao's contribution lies less in his writings than in his deeds. The greatest value of his thought is derived from its practical base; it is a reflection and extension of Mao's and China's revolutionary problems.

Mao's strategy was based on common sense and the reality of China itself. He had to reverse the roles of the proletariat and the peasantry; otherwise; adhering to orthodox Marxism on this matter would have resulted in failure. This may have been foreseen by Lenin, but Mao put it to practice. Mao has been a revolutionary nationalist; that is, he has been politically anti-Western and he has possessed the will to work for the transformation of society. Unlike the anti-nationalist Lenin, Mao saw real positive value in nationalism.

The old Chinese Confucian society, in which the key word was "harmony," had dissolved in the 20th century into a society, especially by the late 1940's, in which the key word was "struggle." The Chinese Revolution was, indeed, a struggle. But it was a struggle, according to Mao, with a special significance. Not only has he viewed it as a continuation of the Russian Revolution but he has also stressed its unique appeal to colonial and semi-colonial countries; it is a model to be followed by other backward countries. As Mao said in 1951:

> Just as the Chinese people have done . . . the colonial peoples of the East can hold big or small base areas and maintain revolutionary regimes for an extended period, carry on protracted revolutionary war to encircle the cities from the countryside, and proceed gradually to take over the cities and win nationwide victory.[10]

The CCP has envisioned itself as a national revolutionary instrument to industrialize and modernize China and transform its peasantry into a proletariat (which will ultimately destroy capitalism), and as an international revolutionary instrument to assist similar proceedings elsewhere in the world. Only when imperialism is defeated and the whole capitalist system is overthrown can lasting peace be achieved. Mao's writings on revolution have revealed a commitment to and confidence in the power of the masses. Being armed with the thought of Mao has meant for the Chinese a conviction of future victory, a strategic formula that envisions the revolutionists as eventually more powerful than their opponents, and the confidence to struggle for victory.

To Chinese Communists revolution has been a long, continuous process in the creation of a new man. They foresee the radical transformation of a whole people from old ways to new possibilities. Industrialization, education and revolution will produce a socialist society and lead to the perfection of man.

VI

The victory in 1949 was not the victory of a socialist revolution. It was, instead, a triumph over a feudal past and the evils of imperialism and foreign intervention. It was not aimed against capitalism and private enterprise; in fact, after 1949 considerable ordinary capitalist development took place. Then, during the 1950's private property was eliminated and the economy began to be socialized. But differences developed among China's leaders as to the best strategy and emphasis' that should be placed on ideological discipline. These differences became acute, as did the need to consolidate China's socialist economic base. By the mid-1960's Mao became somewhat disillusioned with the activities and direction of the CCP and the way in which it was leading China. He felt that the Party had become more concerned with its own self-preservation and prestige than with carrying forth the Revolution; it had, in other words, become institutionalized. The Party had become excessively bureaucratic and lost contact with the masses. Moveover, Mao feared that the Party's recruitment policies, which favored skills over ideological qualifications, would result in further bureaucratization and, perhaps, revisionism. Even the Communist Youth League (YCL), a creation and extension of the Party, appeared entrenched and conservative. The results was the Great Proletarian Cultural Revolution (1966-69).

The Cultural Revolution was not just a power struggle but a struggle over how best to translate the commonly agreed upon ideals of Communism into reality. It began as a cultural purge of writers, teachers and artists, then spread upwards to include Party leaders and downwards to involve the masses; it was a revolution in that many principles by which the CCP had been ruling China were either turned around or adjusted. Whether or not the magnitude of the Revolution was justified by Mao's charge that revisionism had penetrated all of China is unknown. But it does show the importance Mao attached to the cultural and ideological development of the people's minds. In this respect, the Cultural Revolution was a conflict between Maoist and anti-Maoist approaches to socialism. The Cultural Revolution did not come about as a result of social, political or economic crises, at least not in the usual way as with other revolutions. Economically China was doing quite well in 1966, but this was partly where the problem lay. China was on the verge of expansion and inside China a conflict arose over the direction that expansion should take. Other differences arose (e.g., over defense and foreign policy) and they all came to a head in 1966.

The Cultural Revolution should be viewed within the general context of revolution in China in this century. As such it was an extension of the other revolutions, or a revolution within an on-going revolution, with Mao trying to preserve the revolutionary character of China, to prevent the goals of the long-range Chinese Revolution from being abbreviated. The motivation, from the perspective of Marxist-Leninist theory, was that class struggle must continue even after a communist party was in power and even after it had collectivized the means of production and reorganized the labor force. It was feared that bourgeois, counterrevolutionary efforts would be attempted to return the country to capitalism—as had occurred, Maoists argued, in Soviet Russia—unless the bourgeoise were totally defeated.

Although Mao's role in the Cultural Revolution is not entirely clear, suffice to say that he provoked the struggle to seek both primary and secondary goals. Of a secondary nature was his wish to purge certain people and shake up the bureaucracy and the CCP. His primary goals were the training of a successor generation in revolution by allowing and encouraging young people to wage "revolution from below," the creation of a new morality and superstructure in China (i.e., the reinstating in practice of the revolutionary ideals of equality and mass participation) and the transformation of the nature of the CCP. The Red Guards, composed of many younger and lower-class students, was created to attack the corrupt institutions and symbols of society (e.g., the educational system which had restricted them and the upper classes and officials who looked down on them) in such a way that the contradictions within Chinese society would be turned against one another in a crusade for a new order. As such, the Cultural Revolution was not a comprehensive socio-political revolution in the sense of the earlier Chinese Revolution (1927-49). Rather than attempt to repeat the earlier revolution the Cultural Revolution sought to revitalize it. For example, the attempt was not made to eliminate the ruling class, but to prevent it from becoming fixed and entrenched, and the attempt was not made to change the economic structure but to deemphasize the individual's pursuit of material gain. Thus, in this regard, the Revolution was something new in practice. It was a revolution against history, against the usual course of successful revolutions in that it was an attempt to perpetuate the ideals of the earlier movement rather than lose sight of them. Mao's idea of uninterrupted revolution meant the continued stress upon egalitarian and mass participation after the main revolution succeeded. The challenge of creating participatory institutions to deal with contemporary problems was at the core of the Cultural Revolution.

The Revolution was also a spiritual movement to mold China in Mao's image of total struggle, a perpetual "Long March" of romantic, fighting communism. About half of China's population had been born since the success of 1949. If young Chinese nursed on the bottle of bureaucracy failed to experience the equivalent of the Long March and the struggle against the KMT, China's future leaders would be revolutionary in name only. Propaganda alone would not revolutionize the younger generation. As a breaststroke champion once said: "We learn to swim while swimming." The status quo within the CCP and the YCL threatened to destroy Mao's vision for the future. Without genuine revolutionists to be potential successors the past would have been an exercise in futility. With this in mind, it has been suggested that Mao saw that his revolutionary romanticism might die and with it would come his own extinction. As such, Mao needed to regain control over the fate of China to insure the continuation of his ideals after his death. Therefore, another aim of the Cultural Revolution was purification, a purging of those reactionaries within the CCP. It was Mao's grand design to save China from the dangers of revisionism with a wave of terror and turmoil. Actually, the Cultural Revolution may have only been first of other cultural revolutions all of which, theoretically at least, will be attacks on regimes that have lost their revolutionary fervor.

In sum, it seems that the Cultural Revolution was not so much a struggle for power as a struggle for policy and direction. It was Mao's attempt to preserve the principles of egalitarian socialism in the face of "creeping" capitalism. And it was an attempt to change the minds of the Chinese people to accept revolution if any government betrays the ideals of the "new man" in China.

NOTES

[1] Mao Tse-tung, "The Chinese Revolution and the Chinese Communist Party" (December 1939) in M. Rejai (ed.), *Mao Tse-tung on Revolution and War* (Garden City, 1969), p. 92.

[2] Mao Tse-tung, "On New Democracy" (January 1940) in V. Simone (ed.), *China in Revolution* (Greenwich, Conn., 1968), p. 243. Democratic centralism is a political form that combines a democratic process in selecting government personnel with an obedience of the people and lower levels of authority to higher levels.

[3] *Ibid.,* p. 244.

[4] *Ibid.,* p. 249.

[5] Mao Tse-tung, "Problems of War and Strategy" (November 1938) in Rejai, *Mao Tse-tung,* p. 62.

[6] Mao Tse-tung, "Report of an Investigation into the Peasant Movement in Hunan" (February 1927) in S. R. Schram (ed.), *The Political Thought of Mao Tse-tung* (New York, 1969), p. 252.

[7] *Ibid.,* p. 255.

[8] Mao Tse-tung, "The Struggle in Chengkang Mountains" (November 1928) quoted in A. A. Cohen, *The Communism of Mao Tse-tung* (Chicago, 1964), p. 53.

[9] Quoted in Chalmers A. Johnson, *Peasant Nationalism and Communist Power* (Stanford, 1962), p. 186.

[10] Quoted in Cohen, *The Communism of Mao Tse-tung,* p. 72.

15

Latin American
Revolutions and Revolutionists:
Mexico

I

A study of Latin American history reveals that revolution has been a major vehicle for bringing about changes in the control and exercise of power. Generally, revolution, almost invariably accompanied by violence, has been of three varieties in Latin America: (1) the revolutionary wars for independence during the first several decades of the 19th century; (2) the struggles for political power (usually coups d'etat) which have characterized most of the so-called "revolutions" during the 19th and 20th centuries; and (3) the more monumental social revolutions involving basic changes in the political structure accompanied by significant changes in the social, economic and cultural spheres.

Those early 19th century revolutions sought freedom and independence from the European countries; they were largely white settlers' revolts. They were revolutions like the American Revolution in that they were wars of independence; but they were little more, although they did mouth the grand phrases about liberty and equality borrowed from the United States and France. Very little was done to alter the political and social structures of the new nations. The struggles were led mostly by conservative forces concerned with maintaining their own interests in the new nations, and not in upsetting the existing order by establishing a democratic republic. Thus, the masses, who contributed greatly to these national struggles, received few benefits and were treated poorly. Essentially what happened was that a "native" elite replaced a "European" elite. For this reason, among others, successive revolutions became virtually inevitable.

One Latin American revolt of this period, though, was significantly different from the rest. In 1794 the black slaves of Haiti, despite illiteracy and persecution, rose in revolt under the leadership of Toussaint l'Ouverture. Although inspired by the ideals of the French Revolution the Haitians were put down by the French. But then in 1804 these descendants of the freed slaves joined with the others and expelled the whites. Although we will not deal any further with this uprising, suffice it to say that Haiti became the first independent black nation in modern history.

The second kind of Latin American revolution, the revolutionary coup d'etat, has been the most common. Although they have been political in nature they have not been mass movements. The main combatants have been rival military and/or political leaders and their close followers. Usually, some members of the landed oligarchy and leaders of the Church might participate, but most of the population has been unaffected. Only a change in the top layers of government has been involved; for the masses all that has occurred has been a change in masters. Often the country finds out about the coup after it is announced as an accomplished fact. These revolutions have been little more than palace revolts—a kind of in-fighting among the members of the ruling classes. Since the interests of those in power, both before and after successful coups, has been usually the same, not very much could be expected by way of major changes in society. For these reasons most of Latin America's revolutions have achieved very little for most Latin Americans. But their frequency has provided an alternative to governmental longevity, an outlet for dissent and protest, and a cathartic experience to release pent-up hostilities and aggression.

These challenges to power, even those which failed, often have resulted in at least some concessions to the opposition, especially in this
century as the middle classes have become involved.

In spite of the success of the early 19th century revolutionary wars
of independence and the many revolutionary coups of the 19th and
20th centuries, Latin American countries continued, in many respects,
to be colonial; political colonialism may have disappeared, but the
economic, social, cultural and even psychological variety remained.
Thus, the third type of Latin American revolution, broadly speaking,
the social revolution, has become a phenomenon—rare, but not unexpected—in this century. These revolutions have been consequences of
growing national feeling. They have sought not only to gain control of
their governments but to reorganize society as well. Only Mexico,
Bolivia and Cuba have had this type of revolution in Latin America,
and although their degree of success may be questionable, especially in
Mexico and Bolivia, they have achieved some impressive results.

II

Before treating these social revolutions and the ideas of some of their
leading revolutionary theorists it might be instructive, by way of introduction, to discuss those characteristics they have had in common.
Dealing with some uniformities in a summary fashion should help
eliminate unnecessary repetition and provide an overview at the same
time. Although part of what follows pertains to the unsuccessful social
revolution in Chile (1970-73), it will be discussed separately because
it was a different kind of social revolution (i.e., an attempt at legal
revolution). The Bolivian Revolution (1952) will be included in this
section but, for reasons of space, will not, as with the Mexican Revolution (1910) and the Cuban Revolution (1959), be analyzed any further
except insofar as Che Guevara's unsuccessful attempt at revolution in
Bolivia (1967) is concerned.

Social revolution per se has occurred only in Mexico, Bolivia and
Cuba among Latin American nations. In each of these countries the
revolutions resulted in fundamental changes in property relationships,
the distribution of national income, the methods of exercising political
power, and in social structure, policies and values.

In all three countries, before the revolution, agriculture was suffering from an intensive exploitation, inefficiency, and the usual social ills
related to underdevelopment. Agricultural conditions alone did not

cause the revolutions in these countries since such conditions existed elsewhere as well. But the demand for land and the need for agrarian reform played major roles. The following comment on the Bolivian Revolution could easily apply to the other two, if not all of Latin America:

> Agrarian reform is the cornerstone of the National Revolution. Social justice demanded it. Economic development was impossible without it. Advance toward a democratic society was inconceivable until it had been accomplished. Bolivia would not truly be a modern nation until agrarian reform had been achieved.[1]

As alluded to above, nationalist and anti-imperialist forces played a role, but one that is difficult to measure. To be sure, subordination to foreign domination was one of many reasons behind the demands for change, and there was popular criticism of economic dependence on foreign nations and the priviliged position of foreigners, but the "anti-imperialist" elements in the revolutionary programs of the nations concerned were more evident after the seizure of the government than before. Moreover, the leadership of all three of these revolutions lacked a carefully articulated doctrine or ideology, especially when compared with the Russian and Chinese Revolutions; their conflicts were more moral than ideological. None of the leaders owed allegiance to any foreign government or imported ideology—although in Cuba one was employed and modified afterwards.

In all three countries the governments in power, before the revolution, denied the electorate the chance to select its own leadership. For example, presidential candidate Francisco Madero was arrested on the eve of the 1910 election in Mexico; Bolivia's military refused Congress the permission to carry out the electoral mandate of 1951; Batista usurped power on the eve of the 1952 Cuban election. Such defiance was not only a breach of the legal constitution but also revealed a contempt for the people by those in power. These rulers discredited themselves by relying on force and, as such, provided moral and political justification for revolution. Thus, a fundamental cause of all three revolutions was the growing distance between the majority and the ruling elite.

In these revolutions the middle classes dominated, but other classes participated as well. For example, in Cuba the peasants played an important, but not decisive role while in Bolivia miners and urban laborers participated actively. But in each revolution it was the middle class which provided the core of the leadership. Moreover, the revolutionists won more because of the weaknesses and vices of the old elites than their own strengths and virtues. They triumphed because they were able to attract or neutralize the mass of the°population. And each revolutionary group succeeded in defeating or outmaneuvering the regular army on at least one occassion after which they were able to capitalize on their victory.

Given the similarity of conditions in many Latin American countries it seems that there were successful revolutions in Mexico, Bolivia and Cuba only because they were founded on broad social, moral and ethical principles which reached the souls of the people as well as their stomachs. In each case the government that was overturned rested more on corruption and injustice than legitimacy. As such, force, and not popular approval, was their basis. The more they tightened the screws of their positions the more pressure was exerted on the threads of popular reaction until the whole thing burst in revolution. The leadership in these revolutions popularized simple programs to gain many followers and alienate as few as possible. For example, Madero and his supporters spoke of "no re-election" and "effective suffrage"; Bolivia's revolutionists attacked the government and made promises to most segments of society; Castro and his followers actively sought the support of all sectors of Cuban society. And all the revolutionary groups claimed to be the legitimate heirs of a heritage which had been betrayed; in the process they gained the support, active and passive, of most of the nation.

III

The Mexican Revolution was the first and, until the time of Castro and Cuba, the most famous of the Latin American revolutions in this century. It was a nationalist revolution aimed at identifying the people of Mexico with their nation and its history and culture. It aimed at giving unity to a people who had always been divided by race, class, language and culture; it tried to blend disparate elements into a cohesive unit and form a true, unified Mexican nation. From the time of her independence in the 19th century until the thirty-five-year presidency of Porfirio Diaz, Mexico was riddled with perpetual turmoil and frequent government changes. Although Diaz provided some stability he did so at the expense of liberty and he employed any means necessary to get himself elected repeatedly. Such was the situation in 1910.

The Revolution began as a political upheaval aimed at eliminating

Diaz's dictatorial regime and establishing a more democratic system. But it developed over the following decade into a social and economic revolution which sought to alter radically the roles played by the military establishment, the Catholic Church and foreign capitalists. More importantly, the Revolution attempted to make great changes in the social class structure, to abolish the system of large estates (i.e., the haciendas), to initiate agrarian reform, and to stress the value of education. The Revolution aimed at taking a politically independent nation which would be controlled by Mexicans for the benefit of all the people.

Mexico in 1910 was a society out of tune with itself. Revolution was about to become accepted as a necessary vehicle to achieve peace and natural stability. As one contemporary observer said: "We must consider the revolution as a natural event, entirely natural; we must march with it and not against it. To place obstacles in its course is like attempting to quiet the sea or blot out the light of day."[2] Mexicans were attempting to terminate their subservience to and imitation of foreign ways; they were also fighting for pride. They knew what they needed to abolish but were often uncertain and confused about the society they wished to create.

The Mexican Revolution did not have a monolithic character; it was really many different revolutions. It neither burst forth as a cohesive movement nor did it evolve in one direction only; in fact, it was local and regional before becoming national. Much that transpired throughout the Revolution was experimental and pragmatic, though this was primarily because it was not accompanied by any substantial ideology. It was a political upheaval against dictatorship, an economic revolt against the land-holding structure, a national reaction against foreign influence, a religious revolution against a conservative Church, and finally, a social struggle against the propertied classes. At first the revolutionists fought the Diaz government. Then, with victory, they fought among themselves to try and lead the Revolution.

Three common pre-conditions of revolution were absent from Mexico in 1910: (1) the ruling class believed it could maintain itself; (2) the masses were only barely, if at all, thinking in terms of revolutionary change; and (3) there was no revolutionary party or organization to act as a stimulant. Yet, in November, 1910 revolution came to Mexico. It was led, nominally at least, by Francisco Madero (1873-1913), a large land owner.

The previous month (October 5) Madero had issued his "Plan of San

Luis Potosí," the theme of which was that in order to establish "liberty and justice" it would be necessary to throw off the oppressive "tyranny" of the Diaz regime. "Throw the usurpers from power, recover your rights as free men and remember that our ancestors left us a heritage of glory which we are not able to stain. Be as they were: invincible in war, magnanimous in victory."[3] This was the Plan with which Madero summoned Mexico to revolution. It was not an imposing political document, nor was it intended to be. It was concerned primarily with administrative positions, not political philosophy or socio-economic doctrine. The Plan, in fact, was not a program for reform but a guide, a means by which the government could be changed; Madero believed that with the establishment of political democracy Mexico would have the machinery to treat all her other problems.

Although all the revolutionists participated for any number of personal reasons, some merely for private gain, others to effect fundamental changes in society, the Revolution at the outset had no central, clearly defined idea except the overthrow of Diaz. There was actually little basis on which to build a new government. But this was Madero's task. He did not "make" the Mexican Revolution, although he did help prepare public opinion and popular support for it. He came to epitomize the need for change in all areas.

The Madero phase of the Revolution aimed first to defeat Diaz and then place younger men in office. That it was fundamentally political can be seen in its slogan, "Effective suffrage, no re-election." Much of the activity in this early period was spontaneous and uncoordinated. Madero merely symbolized the upheaval of local groups each led by their own leaders. But the urge for a more complete revolution evolved as the people of Mexico began to break down their laws, habit of obedience and traditions. It became a mass uprising that both directly and indirectly repudiated the basis upon which the old order rested. The people came to believe that they were now the government and that they had been denied such status under the previous regime. Mexicans began to turn from the educated, well-born and rich to find solutions to their problems as offered by men who came from among themselves. It was men of peasant origin, men such as Emiliano Zapata, Pancho Villa, Alvaro Obregón and Lázaro Cárdenas, who exerted their personalities and programs upon Mexico.

From the time of Madero's success until 1917 Mexico suffered through a troubled, violent period. But the great social and economic ideals of the Revolution sprang from this period and reached a climax with the formulation of the Constitution of 1917. That Constitution, which was proclaimed on February 5, 1917, embodied the goals and purposes of the Revolution. It established a norm or guideline for Mexico, and the Revolution from that point on has been the gradual implementation of its directives. The Constitution sought to ensure that government would carry through social and economic programs, the absence of which had been a cause of the Revolution. It put the hopes and aspirations for which the Revolution had been fought into the law for all Mexico. But the 1917 Constitution was also a reaction to the excesses of laissez-faire capitalism in that it strengthened the active role of the state, especially in social and economic areas.

Of particular importance for understanding what the Revolution meant for Mexicans are three of the provisions of the Constitution. Article 3 provided for free, compulsory primary education not based on any religious doctrine. Article 27 set forth agrarian reforms and asserted that the nation is the primary owner of all the land and its riches; individual ownership of land was not destroyed but it was now to be subjected to the public good. Article 123 gave a special place and constitutional guarantees to labor; as with property, the strength of the state was enhanced by giving it power to control the activities of labor and industry so as to make the state virtually a part of all contracts, disputes and regulations.

Clearly, the Constitution had contradictions in it. While preserving federalism it enlarged the power of the central government. While preserving the division of powers it gave greater prerogatives to the executive. While defending personal liberties it was society oriented. And while maintaining private property it stressed the principle of the equitable distribution of wealth and national ownership. These contradictions explain, perhaps, why different Mexican governments have often pursued contradictory policies.

After the Constitution of 1917 revolution passed into evolution. The lack of a predetermined ideology, plus alternatives, compromises and contradictions in the original revolutionary period, 1910-17, allowed for the flexibility and continuity of the Mexican Revolution. The doctrines of the Revolution changed periodically so that overall it was eclectic and pragmatic. Like English Common Law the developing ideology of the Revolution has been a combination of history, precedent and time. Beginning as a political protest it ended—if it has ever ended—by working out a new social system. It provided the Mexican people with a set of somewhat utopian goals toward which they could keep moving, and it absorbed old aspirations with new ones as it mingled ancient elements with modern ones.

But for all the good it achieved it should not be overlooked that the Revolution, all ten to twenty years of it (i.e., the imprecision here is because there is no uniformly accepted terminal date), was characterized by chaos and disorder. For most of the time the country was either torn by physical conflict or was in some state of preparation for its continuance. Local *caudillo's* (i.e., leaders) appeared whom the government often failed to challenge for fear that they and their followers might be stronger than the government itself. When some semblance of stability was achieved it came as a result of the restless determination of a few presidents. The Revolution also wrecked the economy of Mexico, cost close to two million lives, destroyed most domestic communication, and added a tremendous debt to the people. At the same time, however, the Revolution produced a new Mexico now able to pursue reasonable social and economic change free from the bondage of the past. Although by the mid 1920's the nation was as poor as it was before 1910, almost as uneducated and with not many more political rights, the Revolution laid an institutional, intellectual and psychological base for modern times. It created conditions under which it would be possible to propose solutions to the basic problems facing the country.

In sum, therefore, the Mexican Revolution was a nationalist revolution that sought to guarantee both domestic and international independence. It was an agrarian revolution that sought to destroy the landholding oligarchy and to distribute land among the people. And it was a bourgeois revolution that attempted to establish a democratic regime and a more equitable capitalist system that would both recognize workers' rights and the advantages of state intervention.

According to Mexicans their Revolution was a complexity of events.

> [It was] a complex phenomenon, not a little mysterious, and above all, home grown. . . . Complex—because its roots reach into every field of sociology. Mysterious—because it constitutes a vital impulse toward the *future* which surges up spontaneously and almost intuitively despite the perils which have beset it, and it continues. Home grown—because it came about without foreign influence of any kind, the result of the people's hunger—. . . hunger for justice, hunger for bread, hunger for land, and hunger for liberty.[4] By 'revolution' we mean not only the social reforms that necessarily had to undergo an initially destructive stage, such as the agrarian reform, but we also consider as revolutionary all those actions that aim to provide the nation with an infrastructure. . . which will allow industrial, agricultural and cattle-raising development. The word

'Revolution' in Mexico (and we capitalize it to make the point). . . means
that the ideals of the Revolution of 1910 are still the same today, that is,
that the ideals say: 'the land belongs to the man who toils on it, the worker
has the right to strike, the subsoil wealth belongs to the nation, [and]
public services should be nationalized.'[5]

The general characteristics of the Mexican Revolution were to en-
trust to the State—in contrast to the individual or private enterprise—
the promotion of the general welfare of the country, to make the
general welfare the main goal of the State. Whereas effective democracy has increased in Mexico since the Revolution so has the legal and
economic dependence of the people upon the State. But for the Mexican people, perhaps the heart of their Revolution was the notion that
the individual could and should improve his lot.

[In the years of the Revolution] large numbers everywhere felt that
exalted sensation of man turned into a god, of man with creative genius
and will, with the faith that from his hands may come a new, great,
brilliant, harmonious and kind world; faith, also, that nothing is
impossible and that anything may be achieved by simply willing it.[6]

This was the Mexican Revolution.

NOTES

[1] Robert J. Alexander, *The Bolivian National Revolution* (New Brunswick,
1958), p. 57.

[2] Manuel Gamio quoted in Frank Tannenbaum, *Peace By Revolution: Mexico
After 1910* (New York, 1966), p. 112.

[3] Quoted in Stanley R. Ross, *Francisco I. Madero; Apostle of Mexican Democracy* (New York, 1955), p. 116.

[4] Jesus Silva Herzog quoted in Howard F. Cline, *The United States and Mexico*
(Cambridge, Mass., 1961), p. 58.

[5] Ramon Beteta quoted in James W. Wilkie and Albert L. Michaels (eds.),
Revolution in Mexico: Years of Upheaval, 1910–1940 (New York, 1969), pp.
13f.

[6] Daniel Cosío Villegas, *Change in Latin America: The Mexican and Cuban
Revolutions* (Lincoln, Neb., 1961), p. 29.

16

Latin American
Revolutions and Revolutionists:
Cuba, Castro, Che

I

The Cuban Revolution (1953–59) was different from most previous
Latin American revolutions. Not only was it a political revolution, as
the others were, but it was social as well. Most earlier Latin American
revolutions were in countries where a military or civilian strongman
ruled and remained in office by a variety of means. Force was all any
opposition could resort to in order to overthrow the government. The
army became involved and was usually a decisive factor. Success of the
revolution usually meant another strongman and the process would
begin again. Latin American revolutions were generally like this because politics was dominated primarily by the military and a small
upper class. Thus, revolutions were primarily political, involving a
change of personnel, but barely affecting the mass of people. The

Mexican Revolution, as we have seen, was different, but it was a special case without immediate consequences elsewhere. Juan Peron's seizure of power in 1945 in Argentina was a forecast of things to come in that large numbers of people assisted Peron in obtaining power. The Bolivian Revolution of 1952 was also an event influenced by the actions of the common people. But the Cuban Revolution was the first full social revolution in Latin America since 1910 and its influence elsewhere is unquestionable.

Cuba in the first half of the 20th century had suffered from chronic political instability and economic exploitation; she also had a tradition of political violence. Irresponsible leadership had done little to improve the credibility of the existing institutions and American interference was always in evidence. Economically, Cuba was not especially backwards—in fact, she had one of the highest standards of living in Latin America—but her economy was unstable, fluctuating with the tourist season and the international sugar market; moreover, the government did little to stimulate the economy. The Cuban masses had seen enough of the society around them to know that their poverty was neither inevitable nor necessarily perpetual (i.e., they had experienced a significant degree of relative deprivation). They thought in terms of progress and a better life if only certain structural changes could be introduced and new leadership provided. The middle class saw the future of the economy under the existing government of Fulgencio Batista as being bleak.

Cuban society on the eve of the Revolution was splintered. At the top there was a wealthy, affluent sector, which identified with American capital, while at the bottom there was a large working population, better off than elsewhere in Latin America but still exploited. Below the affluent sector were middle groups, also dependent upon American capital and working to become more wealthy. The Catholic Church and the military were loosely tied to the status quo, but they were not as important as in the rest of Latin America. The dictatorship of Batista ran the country in the 1950's while the only opposition group of any strength was the Popular Socialist Party (PSP, the Communist Party).

The roots of Cuban nationalism extended back into the 19th century and the island's struggle for independence, achieved—on paper—in 1898. But American intervention in Cuba during the Spanish-American War in 1898 and the establishment of an official U.S. protectorate until 1902 frustrated Cuban nationalism. Furthermore, the U.S. insisted that the Platt Amendment, an imperialist-motivated measure passed by Congress making Cuba an unofficial American protectorate, be incorporated into the Cuban Constitution, which was promulgated in 1901. This was viewed with considerable resentment because it came on the heels of the 1898 Teller Amendment by which the United States Congress promised "to leave the government and control of the Island to its people." The Platt Amendment, which lasted until 1934, gave America control over Cuban foreign affairs and Cuban coaling and naval stations; it was humiliating to Cuban nationalists and in-stilled in Cubans an imposed inferiority complex which was not forgot-ten in the 1950's. Perhaps more than anything else the Platt Amendment—and what was done in its name—was responsible for the rise of Cuban nationalism and its specific anti-American tone.

Thus, the Cuban Revolution was not a sharp break with the past but the climax of a long historical struggle. That struggle, especially in the three decades prior to 1953, involved the Cuban workers and the PSP. It is perhaps because of the activity of the Cuban Communists that circumstances had evolved by the 1950's to such an extent that it was possible for the actions of the revolutionists, though the Communists could not have been among them (because of the pressures of the Cold War), to receive an increasingly favorable response from the people. The propaganda and the political work of Cuban Communists over the years helped to make the political takeover of the cities—especially Havana, which was seized peacefully—possible, as it no doubt did the transition to socialism which began in 1960. But the Revolution was successful not simply because class consciousness led to revolutionary unrest. The corruption which characterized Batista's regime and the methods of terror and torture he used to hold power led to increasing revulsion among the population. This, more than anything else, paved the way for the triumph of the Cuban Revolution.

II

On July 26, 1953 a disenchanted young Cuban lawyer named Fidel Castro (1927–) and a band of followers made an unsuccessful attack on Fort Moncada. This event marked the beginning of the Cuban Revolution. Castro was captured and put on trial. In an explanation of his actions, Castro sounded like a middle class reformer. He spoke of social justice and he emphasized those goals that would appeal to the urban bourgeoisie: economic progress, law and order, and national pride. Cuba, he said, "should be the bulwark of liberty and not a shameful link in the chain of despotism."[1] He spoke of full employment and a decent livelihood for all. Public liberty and democracy would be immediately restored and the problems of land, industrialization, housing, education and health would be met.

Practically from its inception the nature of the Cuban Revolution has been a cause for dispute among observers. Was it a peasant revolution, or a workers revolution, or a middle class revolution? If it was not any one of these in particular, than what role did each of these classes play? Castro and some of his followers were bourgeois, whereas others were workers; yet, their use of guerrilla warfare brought them into contact with the peasants. Arriving at an accurate description is important not just for an understanding of the Cuban Revolution itself but for coming to grips with the course of revolution in all of Latin America since the Cuban experience has been so influential.

Even though Cuba turned communist in 1960, the Cuban Revolution was not a revolution of either the Russian or Chinese variety. It was not an outright peasant-based revolution in which a small guerrilla force came from the mountains to liberate the cities. Although the peasants were involved, much of that involvement was unintentional or forced. The guerrillas resembled the peasants among whom they moved and therefore the latter were involved automatically, while the guerrillas themselves worked on aggravating the peasant's relations with the government. Therefore, Castro may have had peasant support, but the nature and extent of that support is not clear enough to say simply that the Cuban upheaval was a peasant revolution. There is hardly any question about the Revolution not being a proletarian, urban conflict. But, as alluded to above, the years of activity by the Cuban Communist Party and the urban workers contributed to the overall success of Castro and his followers. Their role was not, as many have charged, simply passive or even anti-revolutionary.

By the same token, to say that the Revolution was essentially a self conscious middle class movement with clear middle class objectives is also misleading. Rather, the Revolution had urban middle class support and even leadership, but this sector had no common program. Ultimately, Castro and his followers imposed their program—which only developed during the course of the Revolution—on the others. The guerrillas were supported by the middle class because the latter had come to despise Batista. It was the government's weakness, plus discontent in the army, which were the decisive forces along with middle class resentment.

In sum, the Cuban Revolution was the work of a small minority, supported by the sympathies of a growing majority. It had no particular class overtones—especially in a traditionally Marxist sense—and the revolutionists were not of any one class or consciousness. They were the unemployed and discontented of the cities and the countryside; they were students, professionals, workers and peasants. They were bound by nationalism which enabled them to oust the old order, with its close ties to foreign capital, and to summon national pride and ambition. As it unfolded, the Revolution became a movement for all classes involved, though to be sure, after its success, the middle classes lost most of their privileges, wealth and property.

By 1958 the successes of Castro and his guerrillas caused Batista, in a desperate move to destroy the Revolution, to react with counter-terrorist tactics. Interestingly, the Cuban Revolution had not begun with any thought to guerrilla warfare; Castro himself did not believe it would be a key to victory (and it only became a theory for revolution in Latin America after 1959). But Castro ended up resorting to guerrilla tactics—following Cuba's own 19th century revolutionary tradition —such as bombings, sabotage and hit-and-run raids. Unfortunately for Batista, his terror was indiscriminate and greatly frightened the middle class. Resentment of the government became massive and, in the process, the army disintegrated. Guerrilla warfare, therefore, served the end of encouraging Batista to react to terror so violently that life for average citizens became intolerable.

Because of its post-victory conversion to communism the Cuban Revolution can be classified too easily as a communist revolution. But to do so outright is to misread historical and sociological evidence. Castro and his followers embarked upon a revolutionary course with no clear program or ideology. By taking up the national cry of anti-imperialism and joining it with the cries of democracy and economic and social change, Castro was able to place himself within Cuba's national tradition; he was merely following earlier Cuban nationalists such as Antoneo Maceo and José Martí. In this way he was able to appeal to the overwhelming majority of the Cuban people.

As Castro became a revolutionist his concept of revolution stood for ridding Cuba of Batista (who had repeatedly violated the Cuban Constitution), establishing honest government and economic reform, and making Cuba truly sovereign. The revolution he was making, he said in 1953, was to be an independent one, free from foreign control. He dedicated himself to the sacred will of the people in conquering the future that they deserve. The revolution is the decisive struggle of the people against those who have betrayed them . . . [It will assure all the people] the introduction of a complete and definitive social justice based on economic and industrial advancement.[2]

Even prior to victory Castro's program was vague; but this was all to his advantage since it gave the Revolution greater magnitude. By being imprecise about its goals the Cuban Revolution gained a mass following and did not arouse the hostility of Cuba's neighbors, especially the United States.

Even when he successfully entered Havana in 1959 Castro apparently only had a general idea of the direction the Revolution was going to take. "We ourselves [the revolutionists] knew little about the real possibilities of our country and we lacked a strong political organization."[3] But that general idea had come to include making radical changes in the social, economic and political spheres. Since Castro and Cuba did become communist it appears, therefore, that circumstances and not ideology propelled the Revolution to the left.

Why, then, did Castro turn communist? Before answering this question it should be noted that communist activity had played a definite role in Cuban life and history throughout the 20th century. Marxists had organized Cuban labor in the 1920's and were active in the literary and artistic life of the country long before the 1950's. Communism, therefore, was a native phenomenon before the Revolution. Moreover, some Cubans looked to the Mexican Revolution and argued that it had failed because it had stayed within the framework of capitalism, thus making Mexico subject to American imperialism. If the Cuban Revolution was to succeed, the argument continued, it would have to avoid these circumstances and break any kind of neo-colonial relationship with the United States. Thus, Castro became a communist for three fundamental reasons: (1) he feared U.S. foreign policy which, he believed, opposed his goal of a genuine social revolution; (2) he needed popular support from organized labor; and (3) he came to believe that communism would best provide the answers to Cuba's social and economic problems. In addition, Russian support would make nationalization of the sugar estates possible, especially since Russia would be a market, and Russian oil would make possible the expropriation of American owned refineries that had kept Cuba supplied with fuel. And the Communist Party in Cuba presented Castro with both an ideology and the political machinery to commit the population to the revolution.

III

Fidel Castro, like Lenin, Mao and Ho Chi Minh, has been one of those rare figures in the history of revolutions who has successfully survived and thrived during the several stages through which his revolution has progressed. He has been, for example, (1) an agitator who has aroused his followers and directed their attention to specific goals, (2) a prophet who, with distinct authority, has revealed to his people a new message, a new philosophy of life and a social myth, (3) a statesman who has formulated policies and suggested ways to carry them out, and (4) an administrator-executive who actually has administered the state. To be sure, Cuba's political and economic conditions were largely responsible for Castro's success, but without doubt the Cuban Revolution would have been different without his leadership and charisma. He was able to rise above class differences and establish a relationship with the Cuban people based more upon his personal charisma than his ideas. This served him well, especially after 1959, since he could change his ideas without altering his relationship with the people. As a talented politician who claimed to be following in the footsteps of Cuba's earlier national heroes Castro captured the loyalty of large numbers of people.

From Lenin's writings and actions have emerged Leninism and from Mao's Maoism has emerged. Castroism, however, has been different. Where Castro viewed the Cuban Revolution as "humanistic," providing for the masses both bread and freedom, Castroism has only been a theory of revolution in retrospect. As we have seen, Castro's ideas were vague and general until after 1959. Only when he took power did Castro and his followers (whose ideas collectively comprise Castroism), especially Che Guevara, begin to ask themselves what they had done and how they had done it. We shall elaborate upon this in the final section of this chapter in discussing Che Guevara, but a few words are in order now.

As a revolutionist Castro mixed idealism and pragmatism. Revolution for him "is not made for the sake of revolution itself; it is made in order to create the best conditions for the development of the material and spiritual activities of the human being."[4] At the same time, he recognized that revolution is work only for men who have faith in man. On an abstract level, Castroism has stood for stimulating the consciences of a people and satisfying their material needs. Revolution has become the sole origin of justice and law. For Latin America, Castroism has given the word "revolution" new meaning; it has come to stand for more than a return to the status quo ante (i.e., the establishment of a new dictator), but a new beginning and a new hope for the mass of people. However, to make the revolution requires leadership because the masses have to be "launched into battle." Thus, Castroism holds that the objective conditions for revolution exist in most Latin American countries and only the subjective conditions— the handful of guerrillas willing to launch the struggle—are lacking.

IV

The Cuban Revolution saw a small group of revolutionists, helped by the increasing anxiety and disenchantment of the people, overthrow the Batista dictatorship. It was a revolution unaided by any internal coup, external assistance, serious economic crisis, defeat in war, or active mass movement. Cubans from a variety of backgrounds, collectively calling for national and economic independence, social justice and rapid modernization, led the revolution as it blended democratic and socialist elements. As the Revolution moved more towards socialism after Castro's victory it did so without a civil war or a change in leadership. Because of immediate humanist attempts to provide benefits for the mass of poor people—often at the expense of future development—the Revolution remained popular and was able to proceed without terror. To be sure, the Revolution brought suffering and losses to some, but to the revolutionists this was just about the only way to bring an end to tyranny, corruption and injustice.

Unlike traditional Marxist-Leninist revolutions the Cuban Revolution was neither initiated nor led by a communist party but by a charismatic leader. It passed through a humanist phase in which benefits were bestowed quickly upon the masses and it moved from its democratic to its socialist phase peacefully and without a change of leadership. Because Cuban politics and politicians were bankrupt and essentially dependent upon foreign support, the structure of society crumbled quickly. It is probably that without a weak government and a shaky social structure Castro would not have succeeded so easily.

After a visit to Cuba, Jean-Paul Sartre said: "The originality of this Revolution consists precisely in doing what needs to be done without attempting to define it by means of a previous ideology."[5] In this sense it was the first Marxist-Leninist revolution (i.e., we call it that in retrospect only) led by independent radicals throughout its most decisive phases. Even after they identified themselves with the international communist movement and fused with Cuba's old communists, they still retained the initiative and gained for Cuba a unique place among communist states.

The Cuban Revolution was fortunate in that it did not have to face the forces of counterrevolution in any major degree. Unlike Mexico, Cuba's ruling class had no significant social base to mobilize as allies to defend its own interests. Batista had little or no accepted legitimacy and the influence of the landed upper class had been mostly expropriated by the development of capitalism; Cuban capitalism was absentee owned and foreign controlled. Because Cuban capitalists were dependent on American support they too lacked legitimacy. In addition, there was among the working class a socialist political culture which had existed for many years. The outlook of many workers was impregnated by socialist ideas so that a vision of the future without capitalism was not foreign. All these factors helped Castro.

Finally, to the rest of Latin America the Cuban Revolution has had hemispheric importance. As Chile's then Senator Allende, a socialist, wrote in 1960, perhaps echoing the sentiments of many other Latin Americans:

> Cuba's fate resembles that of all Latin American countries. They are all underdeveloped—producers of raw materials and importers of industrial products. In all these countries imperialism has deformed the economy, made big profits and established its political influence. The Cuban revolution is a national revolution, but is also a revolution of the whole of Latin America. It has shown the way for the liberation of all peoples.[6]

However, since that was written the governments of the United States and many Latin American countries have learned the "lessons of Cuba" to such an extent that it is highly possible that a Cuban-style revolution will never be repeated, precisely because of its success. That is, Latin America's middle classes will be cautious about believing the moderate aims of revolutionists, as will the United States. Moreover, with the aid of American training, Latin American governments are more prepared to handle guerilla movements—all of which leads us to Che Guevara.

V

Ernesto "Che" Guevara (1928–67) was, in many respects, the perfect revolutionist. He had an unbending belief in the righteousness of his cause—the cause of revolution and the betterment of mankind—and he never compromised his ideals. He was a charismatic leader who set an example of self-sacrifice and who usually showed the way to his followers by pushing himself to, and even beyond, his limit. Che was also a perpetual revolutionist. Throughout most of his adult life he was involved in the making of or preparation for revolution. Civilian jobs were not satisfying. Had he not been killed in Bolivia, where he was attempting another revolution, it is highly probable that Che would have continued to immerse himself in revolution.

In 1955 Che met Fidel Castro and the other Cuban exiles in Mexico. Castro was planning a new start to his revolution after his release from prison following the unsuccessful attack on Fort Moncada. Che, an Argentinian, was a part of the Castro group when it reentered Cuba in November, 1956 to launch the ultimately triumphant phase of the Cuban Revolution. It was during this time that Che probably became a communist. His conversion, however, was not simply the result of ideological conviction; instead, he shared with the Communists an opposition to conditions in Latin America. Actually, Che considered himself a "pragmatic" revolutionist since he did not bind himself to the strict ideological interpretation the Communists held regarding Latin American society. His ideas on revolution were formed as much —if not more—on the basis of his experiences during the Cuban Revolution as on the works of Marx, Lenin and Mao. Moreover, he came to believe that the Cuban Revolution demonstrated that a socialist revolution in the underdeveloped areas of the world would be initiated without the direction of the official Communist Party or without the revolutionists being fully versed in Marxist-Leninist theory.

Lenin wrote that "without a revolutionary theory there is no revolutionary movement." That this was not the case with the Cuban Revolution, said Che, made it unique. Although Cuba's revolutionists had no coherent theoretical criteria they had a "profound knowledge of reality, a close relationship with the people, the firmness of the liberator's objective, and . . . experience [which] gave to those leaders the chance to form a more complex theoretical concept."[7] Che went on to say that the Cuban experience simply took up Marx

> where he himself left science to shoulder his revolutionary rifle. . . . We are simply adjusting ourselves to the predictions of the scientific Marx as we travel this road of rebellion. . . . We, practical revolutionaries, initiating our own struggle, simply fulfill laws foreseen by Marx. . . . [which are present in the Cuban Revolution] independently of what its leaders profess or fully know of those laws.[8]

In 1960 Che had published his book *Guerrilla Warfare*. In it, and in several other pieces he wrote, he put forth his key ideas on revolution and guerrilla warfare. There were, he wrote, three ways that the Cuban Revolution contributed to revolutionary theory in Latin America:

> (1) Popular forces can win a war against the [professional] army. (2) It is not necessary to wait until all conditions for making revolution exist; the insurrection [by a guerrilla force] can create them. (3) In underdeveloped [Latin] America the countryside [as opposed to the city] is the basic area for armed fighting.[9]

In this and other ways Che's ideas were in sharp contrast to the teachings of Marx and Lenin.

For Che, revolution and guerrilla warfare were virtually synonymous; revolution without the guerrilla was inconceivable. Other factors are important, to be sure; for example, the peasant, not the proletariat, would seize power from the bourgeiosie and build socialism. But the guerrillas were the prime movers of the revolution; the guerrillas were the real vanguard, the self-chosen elite who would perform the duties of the party and the military command. Thus, Che implicitly rejected Lenin's thesis of the need for a highly trained, organized and disciplined political party based upon and leading the proletariat in the revolution. This also subordinated political considerations to military ones, again contrary to Lenin's teachings.

Che believed that a nucleus of some thirty to fifty devoted revolutionists could establish a revolutionary guerrilla *foco* (i.e., the focal point or center of guerrilla activity) anywhere in Latin America as long as they had the cooperation of the people and a precise knowledge of the terrain (neither of which Che had in Bolivia in 1967). Moreover, the people must be of the conviction that peaceful means are fruitless or else they would not support the guerrillas (which they did not in Bolivia).

Che did not believe that the masses in the cities had to be mobilized as a prerequisite for revolution. Revolution in the cities would be difficult because it was there that the might of the established regime could be concentrated and utilized most effectively. In rural areas, however, the professional army would be more at the mercy of a mobile guerrilla band supported by the peasantry. Without the support of the rural masses, asserted Che, the revolution would surely fail. Therefore, the revolution is not merely the guerrillas gaining power for themselves but the guerrillas acting as catalysts to propel the population to fight the government. This view reflected Che's almost naive faith in the magic of guerrilla warfare. He believed that a guerrilla force, no matter how small or weak at first, could eventually generate the means to its own success just as Castro's forces had during the Cuban Revolution. But, at the very least, this view neglects the fact that in Cuba the guerrilla activity was a part of the general popular feeling against Batista and worked in accordance with that feeling.

The guerrillas, Che went on, will be able to gain the support of the rural population by representing their grievances and standing for the correction of social, economic and political injustices. They must become the conscience of the people, and as such their moral behavior must be perfect. Ideally, Che believed, the guerrillas should be native to the areas in which they are fighting (but this was not the case in Bolivia). In this way they will be familiar with the terrain and be known to the population to whom they could turn for help.

The goal of guerrilla warfare is the defeat of the army and the seizure of political power by the guerrillas on behalf of the people. But guerrilla warfare is only the first step in the revolution. In order to defeat the enemy completely guerrilla warfare must evolve into conventional warfare. When this happens the guerrillas merge with the rural masses to become a people's army. Together they move towards the cities, and when the urban masses join them success is at hand. After seizing power the building of the new order can begin, but not under a dictatorship of the proletariat or the peasantry, or even both together. What results is a dictatorship of the classless guerrillas.

In a 1965 letter to a Uruguayan journalist Che elaborated on the need of the revolutionized society to create a new man with a new kind of social consciousness before a true cooperative society would be possible. During the period of the construction of socialism the new man would be born. The process proceeds parallel to the development of the new economic forms as "men acquire more awareness every day of the need to incorporate themselves into society and . . . of their [own] importance as motors of that society."[10] The masses follow the lead of the vanguard of advanced men, many of them former guerrillas.

> The vanguard has their sight on the future and its rewards, but these are not envisioned as something individual; the reward is the new society where men will have different characteristics — the society of communists man.[11]

The task of the vanguard would be to keep the first revolutionary generation, which is maladjusted by its conflict and background, from becoming perverted and perverting the new generations. The best workers would make up the party, and the party would be the vanguard that helps to elevate the masses to its own level. As the party is the vanguard for the masses, Che said, Cuba is the vanguard of all Latin America on the road to full freedom.

This last sentence was not idle rhetoric for Che. Of all the leaders of the Cuban Revolution Che was the most prolific writer and his influence spread throughout Latin America and the world. His aim, like Lenin's and Mao's, was not to be a new theorist of revolution but to adapt established Marxist theory to Latin America. He did this by explaining the Marxist-Leninist-Maoist nature of the Cuban Revolution and by providing guidelines for revolution elsewhere. Revolution was a global phenomenon—not unlike Trotsky's concept of permanent revolution—for Che viewed the Cuban Revolution as part of a larger revolutionary struggle that would soon involve all of Latin America. Unlike Mao, Che was sometimes more romantic than realistic, and he lacked the roots in the peasantry that Mao had and which were necessary for victory with the support of the countryside. The dreamer in Che expected successful revolutions in all Latin America in the 1960's or shortly thereafter; he could literally taste the future.

There was no nationalism in Che's concept of revolution. In contrast with Mao, Castro, Ho Chi Minh and many other revolutionists, Che thought nothing of making revolution in a country not his homeland. Throughout his adult life Che was a foreigner trying to make a revolution in someone else's country. However much he regarded all of Latin America as his homeland the absence of a national base undoubtedly hindered Che. Although it had not mattered much in Cuba where he was only one foreigner among many Cubans, it did matter in Bolivia.

NOTES

[1] Fidel Castro, "History Will Absolve Me" (1953) in Bruce Mazlish, et al (eds.), *Revolutions: A Reader* (New York, 1971), p. 382.

[2] Castro, "Manifesto of the Revolutionaries of Moncada to the Nation" (1953) quoted in Herbert L. Matthews, *Fidel Castro* (New York, 1969), p. 65.

[3] Quoted in K. S. Karol, *Guerrillas in Power* (New York, 1970), p. 478.

[4] Quoted in Lee Lockwood, *Castro's Cuba, Cuba's Fidel* (New York, 1967), p. 180.

[5] Quoted in Leo Huberman and Paul M. Sweezy, *Cuba: Anatomy of a Revolution.* Second edition (New York, 1968), p. 145.

[6] Quoted in Boris Goldenberg, *The Cuban Revolution and Latin America* (New York, 1965), p. 311.

[7] Ernesto "Che" Guevara, "Notes for the Study of the Ideology of the Cuban Revolution" (October 8, 1960) in Mazlish, *Revolutions,* p. 400.

[8] *Ibid.,* p. 401.

[9] Guevara, *Guerrilla Warfare* (New York, 1969), p. 1.

[10] Guevara, "Socialism and Man in Cuba" (1965) in Mazlish, *Revolutions,* p. 412.

[11] *Ibid.,* pp. 412f.

17

Latin American
Revolutions and Revolutionists:
Che in Bolivia,
Debray, Chile

I

In 1966 and 1967 Che Guevara attempted a revolution in Bolivia based upon the theories he formulated during and after the Cuban Revolution. Our purpose here is not to trace the course of that futile effort but to examine it insofar as it has influenced the concept of revolution. It will also have a bearing on our discussion of the theories of Régis Debray which we will treat in the next section.

Bolivia has been a country rich in natural resources but underdeveloped and poverty ridden. In 1952 she experienced a genuine social revolution that began a radical transformation of the traditional social order. The *Movimiento Nacionalista Revolucionario* (MNR or National Revolutionary Movement), with the support of many workers, defeated the professional army and began to transform the country so that the masses were given a real stake in society. The Revolution of 1952 was based on a widespread sense of nationalism. The major foreign-owned mining companies were nationalized, universal suffrage was introduced, and a national land reform program was initiated. Although the success of these programs was limited, especially in terms of their economic impact upon the masses, they did succeed in convincing most Bolivians that their Revolution was a special event worthy of their support and defense. Just nationalizing the mines was enough to justify the new government's claim that the national wealth was no longer in the hands of foreigners but in the Bolivian people themselves. Universal suffrage gave the masses a voice in government they never had before and a real feeling of citizenship. And the land reform, carried out by the peasants themselves, not only gave them small amounts of land but considerable self-esteem. All this was of major importance for an understanding of Bolivian politics. The Bolivia in which Che sought to make a revolution was populated by a people, especially in the countryside, who had a strong sense of national consciousness.

In 1964 there was a successful coup in Bolivia. Although it sought to depoliticize the country the new government was able to establish a base for its power among the organizations of peasants. The new regime, though hardly democratic, was at least not counterrevolutionary since it still acknowledged moving towards the goals of the 1952 Revolution. It was generally moderate in its political outlook (i.e., political opposition was permitted, including communist groups) and it gained in strength and status. Bolivia was clearly not the country in which to attempt another revolution, but that is precisely what Che did.

Che's revolution was launched in 1966, though fighting did not begin until March, 1967. The number of guerrillas never totaled more than forty-four; although half were Bolivians most of the remainder were Cubans who occupied the leadership positions. By October Che was captured and killed; his revolution and his life were over, but his ideas and his influence have survived.

Che was well aware that it is vital for the success of any guerrilla force to have the support of the local population. This Che lacked in Bolivia and is a fundamental reason for his failure. Active popular support counts for more than tactics in a struggle where guerrillas hope to defeat a larger, superior professional army. Che mistakenly believed that the Bolivian masses would provide a popular base for his forces. But even the army was generally accepted by the people since they had been participating in economic development projects from 1952 and had thus earned great respect. Che overlooked the strong national sentiment among the peasants and their dislike of foreigners. The Bolivian peasants looked upon the guerrillas as foreigners. Simultaneously the government appealed to patriotic sentiments to defeat them. Che tried to offer the peasants land but they already controlled the countryside. Although their economic situation was still poor, the peasants recognized that they were nevertheless better off than before. Che also failed to recognize that the Bolivian government was not typical of Latin American regimes; it was not hated because it offered the population hope for further improvement. Che's belief that military elements are more important than political elements led him to forfeit the support of leftist Bolivian groups which, if nothing else, would have been useful for propaganda purposes and would have served to offset the charges of foreign (especially Cuban) intervention.

Thus, by a combination of failing to understand the realities of the Bolivian situation and of approaching Bolivia with preconceived ideas, it was impossible for Che to succeed. Isolated guerrilla *focos* without a mass base of support, regardless of the skill of the guerrillas, cannot defeat professional armies. Without political support in the cities *and* a broad base of support in the countryside a guerrilla force will probably fail.

It appears therefore that Che did not pay sufficient attention even to his own writings on revolution. He had written that a guerrilla force cannot succeed in a country where the regime had been established popularly, seemed to be legal and gave the population the impression of working for their best interests. Thus, in many respects, Che defeated himself. He also brought into question the validity of his views on revolution as well as those of Régis Debray.

II

Debray (1941-) is a French philosopher-journalist of upper-class origins. A student of Marxist thought he visited Cuba in 1961 (and again in 1965-66) and then travelled throughout Latin America. After writing a series of essays on Latin American revolutionary movements in the mid-1960's and publishing (in Havana in January, 1967) his book *Revolution in the Revolution?* he went to Bolivia in April, 1967 to assist Che Guevara. The actual role played by Debray, and his conduct both before and immediately after his capture, are suspect; there seems to be a question of his bravery and fortitude that cannot be resolved since Che is dead and Debray is not likely to defame himself. In any case, he was arrested after leaving the guerrillas on charges of aiding their revolution; he was not released from prison until late 1970.

Most of Debray's ideas, clothed in Marxist terminology, have as their foundation the experiences of the Cuban Revolution. During his visits to Cuba he spoke with many of those who participated in that revolution, including Fidel Castro; he also had access to numerous unpublished documents. Debray wrote with the following maxim in mind: the duty of a revolutionist is to make revolution. Using the Cuban experience, his Marxist training and his own observations Debray formulated what he thought would be correct revolutionary practice for most of Latin America. He came to believe that revolutions in that part of the world could not follow either the Russian or Chinese examples, but that there needed to be a third way, modeled after Cuba. The lesson of the Cuban Revolution, to which Debray has subscribed, is that

> revolution is an indefinite process, without 'separable phases', which if it cannot start from socialist demands, inevitably leads to them. . . . But the Cuban experience also suggests that *the nub of the problem lies not in the initial programme of the revolution but in its ability to resolve in practice the problems of state power before the bourgeois-democratic stage, and not after.*[1]

In summary fashion Debray's ideas on revolution may be listed as follows: (1) The peasantry, although passive at first, have the potential to be the main force in Latin American revolutions. (2) The national bourgeoisie do not play an important role in the making of a revolution. (3) The working class also plays little or no role since it has been corrupted by life in the city; because "cities are graveyards for revolutionary individuals" the revolution must be waged in the countryside. (4) Students and intellectuals have the potential to play dominant roles. (5) A small group of dedicated guerrillas alone can have the power to arouse the masses against the government; the "small motor" sets the "big motor" into motion. (6) In this process the regular communist parties of Latin America are of little value; both political and military leadership must rest with the guerrilla leaders during the revolution, not with a Leninist urban party. (7) The *foco,* the isolated guerrilla group, is the only form of armed struggle likely to succeed in Latin America; by striking from mobile, flexible, remote *focos* guerrillas can gain mass support and destroy capitalist regimes. (8) It is the activities of the guerrillas which create the revolutionary vanguard, and not the reverse—this is the revolution in the revolution. (9) Subjective conditions (e.g., the role of key individuals) must be added to previously present objective conditions (e.g., imperialism, poverty, oppression) to spark the revolution.

Debray broke with the Marxist tradition. He said it is not possible or desirable to engage in revolutionary activity without being assured of large-scale disaffection and, at least, some desire for fundamental change among oppressed classes. In *Revolution in the Revolution?* Debray argued that neither the working class nor the peasantry alone, neither professional political revolutionists nor city poor, but armed guerrillas made up of students and revolutionary intellectuals will "initiate the highest form of class struggle." Debray apparently rejected the Marxian concept that without a revolutionary theory there can be no revolutionary movement. Instead, he adhered to the value of spontaneity, the notion that revolutionists are made on the scene as a result of participation in military conflict. This idea, together with his playing down the role of political and ideological leadership and his theory of the *foco,* are the result of his belief that the mass of people are passive and will only join a revolution when an elite few show the way by their heroic military actions.

"Revolutionary guerrilla warfare aims at total war by combining under its hegemony all forms of struggle at all points within the territory."[2] For Debray, as with Che, the fight is everything. "The socialist revolution is the result of an armed struggle against the armed power of the bourgeois state."[3] Such an armed struggle is the only way forward for Latin America. Thus violence plays a necessary part in the establishment of a new social order. Violence is to be expected not only because the established government will not give up real power without a struggle, but also because any revolution which fails to challenge the ruling elite's monopoly of violence will be incapable of social energy that is necessary to establish a new order of society. For Debray, therefore, "political struggle and armed struggle go hand in hand; where one is weak, so is the other."[4] (Although Debray asserted that the guerrilla force is the political vanguard and from its development a real political party will emerge—and not the reverse—this is not what happened in Cuba. Castro's group was highly motivated politically and it was sustained by the people in the countryside and the towns. Moreover, the present Cuban Communist Party is a result of the merger between the old PSP and Castro's forces.)

But Debray was hostile towards the Communist parties of Latin

America for their lack of militancy and their inability to seize power; he differed from Marxists, therefore, regarding the role of the revolutionary party. Traditionally, for Marxists, the party has been vital because it embodied the theoretical and ideological thrust of the whole movement. For Debray, however, the party has counted for little; an ideology and a party will come from the guerrilla force itself.

> The political and military are not separate, but form one organic whole, consisting of the people's army, whose nucleus is the guerrilla army. The vanguard party can exist in the form of the guerrilla *foco* itself. The guerrilla force is the party in embryo.[5]

To support his view he quoted Castro as saying that the people and the guerrilla revolutionists will make the revolution in Latin America, with or without a party.

> Fidel Castro says simply that there is no revolution without a vanguard; that this vanguard is not necessarily the Marxist-Leninist party; and that those who want to make the revolution have the right and the duty to constitute themselves a vanguard, independently of these parties.[6]

This idea of the military force giving rise to the political, along with the *foco* theory, is fundamental to Debray's concept of revolution.

The guerrilla force must be organizationally separate from the civilian population; it does not blend in "like fish in water." It must live like a nomad band moving from camp to camp. Because of Latin American conditions the guerrillas must cut themselves loose from all sectors of the population until they win over the masses. Eventually they must gain mass support or they will be defeated, but, "before enlisting them directly, [they] must convince them that there are valid reasons for [their] existence so that the 'rebellion' will truly be. . . a 'war of the people'."[7] The revolutionary goals and programs of the guerrillas must be constantly explained to the people until their support is gained, and only then can the guerrillas "pass over to direct action against the enemy."

The *foco* theory, said Debray, is the form and the force of revolution for Latin America. (He saw a somewhat similar social structure in all of Latin America, stemming from a common history of oppression; thus, the *foco* theory could be applied anywhere.) He believed with Che that "it is not always necessary to wait until all conditions for making revolution exist; the insurrection [or *foco*] can create them." To wait for ripe conditions does not necessarily work. Revolution is a project and as such is protracted in nature. Since all necessary preconditions never exist revolution becomes a "long march." Debray has stated that a dedicated group of guerrillas can, by themselves, produce revolutionary situations in Latin America. The guerrillas need only to create a *foco* which spreads like "an oil patch. . . through the peasant masses, to the smaller towns, and finally to the capital."[8]

The guerrilla *foco* offered the masses an alternative to the status quo. In a given area the *foco* breaks the power of the establishment, liberates and stabilizes it, and then follows with a program of reform. The *foco* would be one of many *focos* comprising an overall strategy for national liberation.

> In order for the small motor [of the *foco*] really to set the big motor of the masses into motion, without which its activity will remain limited, it must first be recognized by the masses as their only interpreter and guide, under penalty of dividing and weakening the people's strength. In order to bring about this recognition, the guerrillas must assume all functions of political and military authority."[9]

But none of this is to presume that the *foco* seizes power on its own, by one audacious stroke; it does not. Nor does the *foco* aim simply to conquer power militarily by itself. Rather, the *foco* "only aspires to enable the masses themselves to overthrow the established power. It is a minority. . . [which] aims to win over the masses before and not after the seizure of power, and which makes this the essential condition of the final conquest of power."[10]

This, then, has been Debray's contribution to the concept of revolution. But Debray is still a young man and his experiences in prison and afterwards, especially his subsequent visit to Chile, have caused him, it seems, to modify some of his earlier views. For example, he said in a 1969 interview that "each people must seek out and take the road [to socialism] which suits it, without however forgetting the experiences of other people which previously took this road."[11] He is quoted in another interview, though he later denied it, as declaring his book, *Revolution in the Revolution?*, to be "so fragile, so debatable, so limited to a particular situation and a particular moment of Latin American history."[12] Was Debray questioning his previous insistence on armed struggle and the *foco* as the only means for revolution in Latin America? Was he suggesting that his book is more a description of the Cuban Revolution than a blueprint for other revolutions? It is too early to be certain. Only the future actions and writings of Debray will give us insight into his position.

III

The attempted "revolution by the ballot" in Chile is over, defeated by a military coup in September, 1973. Although it is usually the victors who dominate history, we have here such a fascinating and unique example of a peaceful effort to socialize a country that it warrants our attention. Even in defeat Chile's example is bound to have a profound influence on the concept and course of revolution. Our observations, here more than elsewhere, are based on recent events. Our conclusions are necessarily tentative and subject to serious modification depending on tomorrow's headlines.

Following the election of the Marxist government of Salvador Allende Gossens (1908-73) in September, 1970 one story in an American newspaper began with the following lead: "Chile Has Elected A Revolution." Many will question the validity of a "legal" or "electoral" revolution but, as Debray has written: "A complex gestation has begun [in Chile] which no one can be certain at this stage will not end by giving birth to a really new society freed from exploitation and foreign domination."[13] The Revolution may have failed but the possibility for its sucess did exist.

When Allende, the leader of the Socialist Party and a candidate of the Popular Unity coalition, became president Chile did not instantly become a socialist country; that would have taken more than the six years of Allende's legal term in office. Moreover, the bourgoisie did not simply hand over power to its "class enemy," the proletariat. After the election segments of Chile's Right sought to create an atmosphere of chaos. The commander-in-chief of the army was assassinated and there was economic sabotage and considerable anti-regime terrorism. Subsequently, but prior to September, 1973, there were strikes in the private sector, public distress, resignations of key officials, two attempts on Allende's life and even two aborted coup d'etat. In addition, Allende's government was only a minority regime and the masses never wrested full power from the privileged classes. Nevertheless, in its beginnings the Chilean Revolution was otherwise non-violent—especially when compared to the "usual" violence of revolutionary periods—and Allende and his supporters gained the reins of government legally, without firing a shot or threatening the use of force.

This phenomenon can best be explained by an understanding of Chile's history. Although economically underdeveloped, as with most other Latin American countries, Chile had been politically sophisticated. Chileans prided themselves on their constitutional form of government and they regarded their constitution as sacred. The army had remained non-political, supporting any government so long as it guaranteed the constitution. Political parties had traditionally operated within the legal framework with communists and socialists participating in governments since the end of World War II. Leftist parties attempted to take over only from within the government, though they would instigate strikes to pressure the various regimes to move more towards socialism. Allende and his party were almost elected in 1958 but were narrowly defeated by a coalition between the Center and the Right. Allende barely missed victory again in 1964 while losing to Eduardo Frei. But the Frei Adminstration created an expectation of dramatic change which was not fulfilled, thus probably contributing to Allende's victory in 1970. Allende had campaigned on a program of Marxism with liberty; this meant more nationalization of industry (which had been going on since the late 1930's) and more state control with the aim of redistributing Chile's wealth and giving much of it to the poor.

As a Marxist, Allende did not forget the principle of the class struggle. His government aimed to change the system "to form a government in order to obtain the power to carry out the revolutionary transformation which Chile needs. . . . As for the bourgeois State at the present moment, we are seeking to overcome it. To overthrow it!"[14] Revolution for Allende was not a question of violence but of "the transfer of power from a minority class to a majority class,"[15] and this meant changing the constitution legally. Allende saw his government as one of reform, but reform which would open the road to a revolution that would create a democratic, national and popular government and eventually lead to socialism. He believed that socialism could not merely be imposed by decree.

Allende did not try for political control as it is exercised in other Latin American countries; Chile was not a police state. It was the opportunity of free political choice that gave the Chilean Revolution its significance. For the first time in the more than a century since Marx warned the world of the spectre of communism a somewhat advanced and politically mature country attempted to experience a socialist revolution in terms of democratic consent.

Allende saw a chance for Chile to play a significant role in history by initiating the *via Chilena,* a second way to socialism without the waste of revolutionary violence. But all this came to a violent end on September 11, 1973 in a military coup. Allende allegedly took his own life as his government was ousted, climaxing months of unrest and conflict. The coup was exceptionally violent, even by Latin American standards; several thousand were killed or injured. A conservative military junta, swearing allegiance to itself and not the constitution, took office. It was the first time in forty-six years that the traditionally nonpartisan Chilean military had overturned a freely elected civilian government.

Allende had been elected in 1970 with only 36.3% of the votes. In a congressional election two and one-half years later his supporters received some 44%, a significant increase and a blow to his opponents. But instead of improving, conditions deteriorated. Allende may have been idolized by the masses of peasants and workers, but Chile's middle and upper classes despised him, especially because his socialist fiscal policies were hurting rather than helping the country's economy. For example, imports rose because his land reform programs reduced production, inflation squeezed the country and foreign business turned away. Moreover, Russian assistance was minimal, and the decline in world copper prices, with a cruel touch of irony due to an end of the war in Viet Nam, hurt the economy. The Chilean military, egged on by hostile middle and upper classes seeing their living standards and hopes crumble, felt it had no choice but to act. Even though socialism in Chile may not have been succeeding and Allende was only a minority president with no clear mandate, the counterrevolutionary coup has overshadowed the gains and losses of the regime.

John F. Kennedy once said: "Those who make peaceful revolution impossible will make violent revolution inevitable." As Lenin suggested, peaceful revolution is still a contradiction in terms. With its coup the Chilean military has unwittingly presented further justification for violent revolution rather than legal, peaceful progress towards socialism. Where the masses of Latin Americans—if not the world—become discontented with their exploitation and choose to do something about it they will no longer have the Chilean alternative as a precedent. Revolution by the ballot appears to be an anachronism. Revolution by the bullet may be the only way.

Where the death of Che Guevara signaled the end of one kind of revolutionary struggle in Latin America—guerrilla warfare in the countryside—Allende's demise possibly signals the end of another revolution—within a constitutional system. If so, the future of revolution in Latin America lies elsewhere.

IV

Latin American revolutions in the 20th century have followed several
major paths. There are today, no doubt, those who would favor that
kind of revolution that would simply destroy those obstacles that have
impeded progress toward a way of life similar to that in the United
States. Such revolutions, like the Mexican Revolution, would establish
a regime that is politically democratic, economically mixed (i.e., with
private and public investment, and state planning), and socially capable of merging the population into a reasonably contented national
unit. The Chilean example stands out as a unique experiment in radical, but legal societal transformation. However, with its defeat it is
unlikely that any effort will be made in the near future to repeat it
elsewhere.

The Cuban-style revolution, involving guerrilla activity in rural
areas, has not been succeeding. The emphasis of Castro, Che and
Debray upon the countryside rather than upon the cities as the base
for revolutionary movements appears to be faulty and has not worked
well since the Cuban Revolution. Peasants tend to be apolitical, hostile
and suspicious towards outsiders, and they resist change for fear of
losing all. Guerrillas have not received a positive reception from peasants who more often are willing to help the existing government. In
addition, properly trained Latin American armies have shown themselves adept at defeating guerrillas in rural areas.

The failure of Che in Bolivia has resulted in the Latin American
Left's grounding its strategy and tactics in local reality. That reality
seems to exclude the Che-Debray model of the guerrilla *foco.*Even the
extreme Uruguayan group, the Tupamaros, has through their violence, been trying to build a mass political consciousness and to politi-
cize and radicalize the people. Equally important is the fact that it
appears that the cities are the best breeding grounds for revolution.
Disgruntled peasants have moved to the cities where unemployment
and poverty have led to greater frustration and discontent.

It seems, therefore, that the future of revolution in Latin America,
especially with the failure of Chile's "electoral revolution," lies fundamentally in the urban areas where a popular based, many-sided revolutionary force will be necessary for successful armed insurrection. In
other words, a new form of revolution—and with it a new theory of
revolution—can be expected to blend the ideas and spirit of Che and
Debray with more traditional Marxism (i.e., urban revolution utilizing
the proletariat) and local realities. With such developments the concept of revolution will be modified once again.

NOTES

1 Régis Debray, "Castroism: The Long March in Latin America" (1965) in Debray, *Strategy For Revolution; Essays on Latin America* (New York, 1970), pp. 71f.

2 Debray, *Revolution in the Revolution?* (New York, 1967), p. 30.

3 *Ibid.*, p. 19.

4 *Ibid.*, p. 50.

5 *Ibid.*, p. 106.

6 *Ibid.*, p. 98.

7 *Ibid.*, See also "Castroism: The Long March in Latin America" in *Strategy for Revolution*, p. 40.

8 "Castroism: The Long March in Latin America" in *Strategy For Revolution*, p. 39.

9 *Revolution in the Revolution?*, p. 109.

10 "Castroism: The Long March in Latin America" in *Strategy For Revolution*, p. 39.

11 Quoted in Jack Woddis, *New Theories of Revolution* (New York, 1972), p. 275.

12 Debray to Oriana Fallaci (1970) in *Evergreen Review* (April 1971).

13 Debray, *The Chilean Revolution; Conversation with Allende* (New York, 1971), p. 15.

14 *Ibid.*, pp. 81f.

15 *Ibid.*, p. 116.

18

African Revolutions
and Revolutionists:
Guinea-Bissau and Cabral

Most attempts to examine the revolutions and revolutionists of an entire continent will invariably exclude many. In this particular instance the process of selection is not without design. We will first engage in a discussion of the nature and variety of anti-colonial revolutions. This will apply to most of Africa and obviously to much of the underdeveloped world as well. In addition, it will serve to focus some attention on African countries and their leaders not otherwise examined here. Then we will deal specifically with two revolutions and two revolutionists. One of the former, the Revolution in Guinea-Bissau (which was also known as Portuguese Guinea or Guiné), is now completed; independence was proclaimed in September, 1973, with the revolutionists in control of more than two-thirds of their West African country—Portugal yielded more than a year later. The

Revolution is occurring in a sub-Saharan nation whose indigenous population is black. The other, the Algerian Revolution, has been politically over (i.e., independence was achieved) for more than a decade; it occurred in a North African nation composed mostly of Moslem or Arab inhabitants. Of the two revolutionists whose ideas will be analyzed one, Amilcar Cabral, the organizer and leader of the Revolution in Guinea-Bissau until his assassination in January, 1973, has been a lesser known figure but one whose value to all of Africa, through his example and his writings, has been underrated. The other, Frantz Fanon, participated in the Algerian Revolution and has become, especially since his death in 1961, a revolutionary theorist of world renown and monumental importance.

I

Anti-colonial revolutions, or wars of national liberation as they are also called, have as their purpose the termination of oppression and exploitation, the achievement of self-determination and the fulfillment or completion of an existing society, not its destruction as in more completely internal revolutions—although certainly the destruction of the rule of the imperialist or foreign power is sought. These revolutions have been both nationalist and social in that they have aimed to convert each colonized nation into an independent, modern and progressive welfare state. As a representative of the Revolution in Guinea-Bissau expressed it:

> National liberation requires that there be a profound change in the process of the development of the productive forces, that is to say, it necessarily corresponds to a revolution. . . . [It] takes place when all the productive forces have been freed from every kind of foreign domination. The liberation of productive forces implies that there is a free choice of the mode of production, according to the evolution and concrete situation of the liberated people. Each people's right to self-determination is the basis of national liberation.[1]

The anti-colonial revolutions of the Third World (i.e., the underdeveloped areas, also the non-white people of the world) have been more than attempts to assert political autonomy and to end European domination. They have also been social and economic revolutions, often brought about by a Western-educated elite who have attempted to make their countries more modern, with industrialized economies. For this reason they have sometimes been labeled "revolutions of modernization." The countries of Latin America, for example, which have been nominally independent for a century and a half, have fought against economic domination and for social change on a level similar to the newer nations in other parts of the world.

Third World revolutions depend a great deal on ideology (i.e., a set of ideas about man's nature, society and history which is capable of eliciting the support of large numbers of people to the cause of political and social change). These revolutions, in order to achieve the goal of bringing their people into the modern world, often must create a nation. They must instill a sense of nationality that is often in conflict with more traditional loyalty to a tribe or local community, and they must do this quickly. Compared to nationalism in Europe, time has been a factor working against them, especially in Africa. The leaders of these revolutions, usually intellectuals who became politicized from education and training abroad, have had to infuse a hope and a faith that great things can be done by their new nation. This is the indispensable role of ideology.

As much as the revolutionary goal of independence requires ideology, so does the longer run aim of economic and social development. Third World countries usually have either a small or no native middle class to work on economic development and they usually have little usable capital. The goal of amassing capital and mobilizing society for long-term development is another crucial role of ideology.

Anti-colonial revolutions do not necessarily involve the simple conflict between "communism" and "capitalism." Instead, they involve the conflict between rich and poor, the economically developed and the underdeveloped, the technologically and industrially competent and the "backward" areas. Economic development is an important factor in understanding the revolutionary ideal in the Third World. That is, through modernization and industrialization social equality, educational opportunity and adequate styles of living can be achieved. To be sure, this does not mean that the developing nations do not care whether they modernize via capitalism or communism. Most revolutionary leaders in Africa, as well as in Asia and Latin America, would agree that capitalism as it developed in the West is unsuited to conditions in their area, but that socialist means are probably best to achieve economic growth. For moral as well as economic reasons capitalism is rejected and socialism accepted; capitalist ethics, for example, are viewed as unnatural by Africans. It is generally believed that a revolution along socialist lines would best establish a society based on justice, planning and comprehensive national growth. Socialism is not merely an imported theory.

This is not to imply that the socialist-oriented anti-colonial revolutions will result in offsetting the world balance of power in favor of the East. These revolutions are also, and perhaps more importantly, nationalist revolutions. In terms of the world political picture this means that resulting new nations are interested in establishing their own identity and, for reasons of security, in not becoming entangled in a cold war between the East and West. The socialism of these emerging nations is neither all communistic nor all anti-capitalistic. The Third World finds Marx's analysis of the dehumanization of man by capitalism to be attractive, as they do the Marxian notion that man can remake himself and eliminate alienation by revolutionary action. But they generally reject the concept of the class struggle as the locomotive for revolution in the Third World. They also reject Marx's theory of the state as an instrument of class domination. They are not interested in the theories regarding the dictatorship of the proletariat or the withering away of the state. Many see their countries as almost classless (or at least the differences among classes as not being especially great) and their new states as speaking for all the people. Having no industrial proletariat to speak of—and not anticipating one either—Third World ideologies probably will never be simply Marxist-Leninist. But, especially in Africa, they are anti-capitalist since they have rejected the capitalist mother countries which subjugated them.

Calling their systems by different names (e.g., "communocracy" by Sékou Touré of Guinea—not to be confused with neighboring Guinea-Bissau—or "democratic, socialist, cooperative democracy" by Gamal Abdul Nasser of Egypt) Africa's nationalist leaders have hoped to combine planning and central control with some degree of private enterprise. They want somewhat less competition as well as collectivism. Kwame Nkrumah of Ghana called his system "consciencism":

> The philosophy that must stand behind this social revolution is philosophical consciencism; . . . [it is] the disposition of forces which will enable African society to digest Western and Islamic and the Euro-Christian elements in Africa, and develop them in such a way that they fit into the African personality. . . . [It is] that philosophical standpoint which, taking its start from the present content of the African conscience, indicates the way in which progress is forged out of the conflict in that conscience. . . . The restitution of African humanist and egalitarian principles of society requires socialism.[2]

Thus, African leaders have generally agreed upon the need for some kind of humanist socialism adapted to African realities, though they differ in their interpretation of socialism itself.

For Touré individualism and liberalism have no place in African revolutions. Instead of individualism, the African must focus on the sovereignty and solidarity of the people. Collective values are above individual needs and individualism is equated with selfishness. By emphasizing the participation of all people in politics Touré arrived at a theory of "popular dictatorship" in which formal rulers do not constitute the source of authority and in which politicians must obey the popular interest. The party which heads the dictatorship must be in the vanguard of the masses as well as in their midst. In contrast to communist parties the African party is supposed to be a mass, not an elite organization.

Revolution, for Africa's leaders, has not meant political independence alone, but the means to more meaningful goals, such as self-respect, spiritual and economic development and cultural emancipation (i.e., identity). Self-government is the first step on the road to full independence, which will be attained when African economies are freed from excessive dependence on the developed countries and when African societies have regained their spiritual and cultural values.

African revolutionists (and consequently the revolutions they espouse) can be divided into several overlapping categories: (1) "Revolutionary nationalists" seek to effect basic changes within their own country and to initiate a foreign policy based upon their own country's particular needs; not only do they seek the elimination of foreign rule but they have ideological commitments to seek major societal changes as well. The two revolutions we will be discussing below, in Guinea-Bissau and Algeria, were led by revolutionary nationalists. (2) "Regional revolutionary nationalists" belong to ethnic or regional groups in revolt against established national political systems which allegedly dominate and refuse autonomy to them; they are basically separatists and their movements often have religious overtones. For example, Biafra's attempt to break away from Nigeria was a movement of this type, clouded by a contrast between Biafra's Christian affiliations and Nigeria's Islamic faith. (3) "Revolutionary pan-nationalists" believe in the priority of a revolutionary movement that encompasses a larger geographic area than just one country. Nkrumah and Fanon were Pan-Africanists. Nasser was a Pan-Arabist. (4) "Marxist-Leninist revolutionists" aim to create communist states; they reject nationalist and even pan-nationalist aspirations, and they oppose political neutrality in favor of one of the communist camps. But there are also "national communists" (as in Egypt and Algeria) who hope to establish single-party systems of government in their countries. (5) "Islamic revolutionists" view themselves primarily as Moslems and they oppose other kinds of revolutionists. As one of them said: Islamic socialism is "not a step toward communism, nor is it an evolution from capitalism. ... It aims at social justice and is based on Islam, a great religion which has its own principles for the organization of society as well as of individual lives."[3] (6) "National liberation revolutionists" aim to free the African majority from white minority rule in their country. They refuse negotiation and, of necessity, are committed to violent conflict. Many are also "revolutionary nationalists" and their groups are really united-front organizations. Such revolutionists exist in South Africa, Rhodesia, Angola, Mozambique and Guinea-Bissau.

II

Independence has been achieved by most African nations during the past two decades. But few of Africa's revolutionary movements have realized additional success primarily because they have been unable to merge their efforts for national liberation with the task of a social revolution. Often the post-decolonization governments have been more loyal to the former mother country than to their own people. Coups d'etat have occurred substituting military for civilian regimes, but little else has changed. In most cases, African governments have lacked a firm social base and their connections with the imperialist powers have prevented them from strengthening their national independence to any significant degree, especially by means of establishing a foundation for social and economic development. But this has not prevented them from trying and some success has been achieved in Mali, Tanzania, the Congo and Ghana.

The struggles of Guinea-Bissau, Angola and Mozambique were anti-colonial revolutions. Under the subjugation of Portugal these nations were classified as mere provinces or extensions of the European country and the natives were treated as a labor force with few rights. Portugal had been continuously losing control of Guinea-Bissau and, were it not for the impact on morale in her other colonies and in Portugal itself, the mother country might have given up the colony long ago since it was costing more than it was yielding. To lose Guinea-Bissau might have meant losing Angola (from which Portugal got oil, coffee and diamonds) and Mozambique (from which she got sugar and cotton). To give up her colonies would have forced Portugal to recognize herself as a small, backward state; and this she did not do willingly. Portugal, supported by NATO, had been fighting three wars at once, but victory now lies with the Africans.

In the 1950's the road to reform was being blocked by the Portuguese in Guinea-Bissau. Natives had the choice of quiescence or revolt. In 1956 the African Party for the Independence of Guinea and Cape Verde (PAIGC; the Cape Verde Islands are some 600 miles offshore and considered part of Guinea-Bissau) was formed clandestinely by a handful of men led by Amilcar Cabral (1925-73), a Lisbon trained agronomist. Cabral was one of only fourteen Guineans who had attended Portuguese universities before 1960 and one of only three-tenths of one percent of the entire native population which was literate after more than 400 years of the Portuguese "civilizing mission."

The PAIGC built up a party organization carefully and secretly. Cabral had used his position as an agronomist during 1952–54 to travel about his country and acquire an intimate knowledge of the life of his people. Thus, in a new way he was laying the groundwork for a later time when he would combine the theory and practice of revolution. The movement spread, and slowly but surely the idea of independence and of a struggle became popularized among the urban masses. At first, peaceful means to gain independence were tried, but these got nowhere. Then, in 1959, the forceful crushing of a dock workers' strike signaled that other methods would have to be employed.

> In the beginning, we thought it would be possible to fight in the towns, using the experiences of other countries, but that was a mistake. We tried strikes and demonstration, but . . . realized this would not work. The Portuguese hold us by force of arms. There is no choice; we must do the same.[4]

Cabral then began to create a guerrilla organization that would concentrate on both armed struggle and political organization; he did not separate the two. Part of Cabral's genius was in transforming a small group of anti-Portuguese dissidents into an effective political and military force.

By 1960 PAIGC members were out in the countryside explaining their aims and mobilizing the people; Cabral believed that their struggle would need massive rural support before the revolution began.

This experience of the PAIGC seems to contradict the *foco* theory of Che Guevara and Régis Debray (i.e., a guerrilla force, by itself, can initiate the armed struggle and gain support from the countryside as it develops.) It also demonstrates that armed struggle probably could not have been initiated if a lengthy period (two years, in this instance) had not been devoted previously to preparatory political work. In fact, because Guinea-Bissau had no large working class and no large peasant population deprived of land (i.e., exploitation came through price mechanisms, not land ownership) the revolution could not be based upon other revolutions. By carefully building an ever widening base of political education, by creating and fostering a national consciousness among the masses, and by insisting that the revolution not begin until the educational campaign was successful, Cabral has made an important contribution to the development of revolutionary theory.

The Revolution in Guinea-Bissau began in 1963; it continued and succeeded because of the organization and leadership provided by the PAIGC, which saw the struggle as an anti-colonial, socialist revolution.

> To be masters of our destiny, that's not simply a question of having African ministers. What we need is that our work, our riches, should belong to all of us, to the people who labour to create this wealth. . . . If we make this war only to chase out the Portuguese, then it's not worth the trouble. Yes, we make it to chase out the Portuguese, but also so that nobody shall exploit us, neither white men nor black men.[5]

According to Cabral his people have been fighting to win material benefits, to live better and to see their lives go forward. Revolution for him and his people was a process of structural change which would overcome both direct colonial subjugation and indirect or neo-colonial subjugation. The struggle was violent because that is the nature of imperialism. Revolution does not involve merely raising a flag or singing an anthem or elevating an African elite. It is an indigenous development to be conducted by and for the people to regain their history and "to change radically the economical, social and cultural situation of our African people."[6]

By the time Cabral was assassinated in January, 1973 the PAIGC was in control of about two-thirds of the country (this was verified by a United Nations observer team). A 120-member National Assembly had been created, some 200 schools had been established to serve 20,000 students, and four hospitals and 200 clinics had been built. A declaration of independence was imminent and, of equal importance, a new nation was emerging from the revolution. As one member of the PAIGC summed it up:

[We] are living in freedom and dignity regained in strife. Thanks to the struggle the situation in our country has changed to the benefit of the popular masses. . . . We have consolidated our moral and political unity aimed at establishing a new life and raising our civil and political consciousness at the same time we are fighting. . . . A new consciousness and a new man are being created in the struggle: people also are aware of their rights and their duties, of being human and African.[7]

III

Although not widely known outside Africa and limited intellectual circles, Amilcar Cabral stands out as one of History's few great revolutionists and revolutionary theorists, even though an assassin terminated his life before his work was done. Cabral's thought blends a combination of reflective theoretical analysis with a careful application of theory to the real problems of winning a revolution and building a new order. His writing is not bloated with rhetoric and is based upon experience and thought which give it tremendous value. His greatness lies in his insistence on the need for careful study and analysis of the particular historical situation of each struggling nation. "We . . . know that on the political level our own reality—however fine and attractive the reality of others may be—can only be transformed by detailed knowledge of it, by our own efforts, by our own sacrifices."[8]

The first task of every African revolution, said Cabral, is independence and the elimination of foreign economic domination. But revolutionists should look beyond the liberation struggle to the future economic, social and cultural evolution of the people and, above all, neocolonialism (i.e., a native ruling class acting as a front for foreign domination) must be avoided. National liberation is the inalienable right of every people to have its own history, and the objective of national struggle is to regain this right previously usurped by imperialism. National liberation must aspire to do more than replace a foreign ruling class with a native one doing their work. It must become a revolution and regain its own history. In other words, the struggle for national liberation involves not only political independence but also the fight against neocolonialism.

Therefore, according to Cabral's analysis, revolutions can occur in two situations in Africa: the colonial and neocolonial. In the former, the nation as a class fights the forces of the colonizing country and fights for a national solution, which is independence and the economic structure which suits it best. In the latter situation the African working classes and their allies struggle against foreign businessmen and the native ruling elite who serve them. Since independence has previously been achieved a national solution is not sought; instead, the capitalist structure is to be destroyed since it was implanted by imperialism and a socialist solution is begun.

Cabral's analysis of the role of social classes is of great importance for Africa and the concept of revolution . Because of its political development and moral awareness the petty bourgeoisie, or at least the revolutionary minded among them (as opposed to those committed to or compromised with colonialism), are the only group, according to Cabral, capable of leading the revolution (colonial or neocolonial). It is nationalist minded and was the source of the idea for the national liberation struggle (Cabral among them). It is the group which most rapidly becomes aware of the need to free itself from foreign exploitation because, among other factors, it has more frequent contact with colonialists and thus more chance for being humiliated. In order not to betray the revolution the petty bourgeoisie must strengthen its revolutionary consciousness, reject the temptation of becoming more bourgeois, and identify itself with the working classes.

> This means that in order to fulfill the role in the national liberation struggle, the revolutionary petty bourgeoisie must be capable of committing suicide as a class in order to be reborn as revolutionary workers, completely identified with the deepest aspirations of the people to which they belong.[9]

Cabral states that this is the dilemma of the petty bourgeoisie in the struggle. It is also, it seems, the dilemma of the revolution itself and can mean its success as a socialist revolution or its failure, in which case it would become a neocolonial society ripe, sooner or later, for another revolution.

After analyzing the social structure of his country Cabral and his supporters agreed that for their national liberation struggle to be successful they would have to unite all the people of Guinea-Bissau. This is why they created the PAIGC. One of the primary functions of this party was to minimize the conflicts and contradictions among the various groups and classes making up the struggle. Although the Revolution has been based on the peasantry Cabral did not recognize them as a revolutionary force per se. The peasantry comprises the vast majority of the population. It is a large physical force which controls most of the nation's wealth, but it is not eager to fight. Unlike the peasantry in China the peasantry in Guinea-Bissau had no tradition of revolt and the revolutionists did not find the same kind of welcome among them as did the Chinese revolutionists among theirs. The *dé-classés* (or lumpenproletariat who were, according to Fanon, a radical revolutionary force) were not to be trusted because of the assistance they usually give to the Portuguese. Yet, many of the young, former peasants among them, astute enough to compare their standard of living with the colonialists, have the potential for revolutionary consciousness. In addition, the African workers in the towns (though they are hardly a traditional proletariat) have been more inclined toward the revolutionists because they can see more clearly their own exploitation (e.g., they earn less money for the same work performed by Europeans) even though they are exploited comparatively less than the peasants. Thus together the young, former rural dwellers among the *déclassés,* the "little proletariat," as Cabral calls the workers, and the petty bourgeoisie make up the backbone of the revolution.

Cabral did not consider himself a Marxist. "We agree that history . . . is the result of class struggle, but we have our own class struggles in our own country; the moment imperialism arrived and colonialism arrived, it made us leave our history and enter another history."[10] Thus, the class struggle has continued but in a different way. Africa's struggle is against the ruling class of the imperialist countries, and this has given the class struggle a different connotation and it has meant a different evolution for the African people. What class or classes, then, will be the agent in the African Revolution? All will, since the unity of all classes is a prerequisite for success. No one class can succeed on its own. Therefore, the class struggle, in a traditionally Marxist sense, is out of place in colonial countries.

The problem for revolutionists is to see who is capable of taking control of the state when the colonial power is destroyed. The peasantry is a non-revolutionary class, the proletariat is an embryo, and there is no economically viable bourgeoisie. All that is left is the African petty bourgeoisie who have been in the service of imperialism and have learned to manipulate the apparatus of the state. "So we come to the conclusion that in colonial conditions it is the petty bourgeoisie which is the inheritor of state power. . . . The moment national liberation comes and the petty bourgeoisie take power we enter, or rather return to history."[11] But, as Cabral was well aware, this presents a potential problem. The petty bourgeoisie has the option of allying itself with either the forces of imperialism (in which case we have neocolonialism) or the workers and peasants. This is a crucial choice, the pivot upon which the success of the revolution turns. In allying itself with the peasants and workers the petty bourgeoisie may, as stated above, be committing suicide, "but it will not lose; by sacrificing itself it can reincarnate itself, but in the condition of workers or peasants."[12] Cabral had faith that the petty bourgeoisie would more easily identify itself with the peasants and workers than with the imperialists.

As for the question of the respective roles of political and military leadership Cabral wrote that in Guinea-Bissau (as in Angola and Mozambique) the political party built the armed forces, and not the reverse (as it was for Che and Debray). "The political and military leadership of the struggle is one: the political leadership. . . . We are political people, and our Party, a political organization, leads the struggle in the civilian, political, administrative, technical, and therefore also military spheres."[13]

Finally, for Cabral the armed struggle was important, but it was not everything. Until the end, it seems, he always looked ahead to the future, after the revolution.

> [It is most important] to have an understanding of the conditions of our people. Our people support armed struggle. We must give them the certainty that those who have arms in their hands are the sons of the people and that arms have no superiority over working tools. If one carries a rifle and the other a tool, the most important of the two is he who carries a tool. For one takes up arms to defeat the Portuguese, but if we want to chase out the Portuguese, it is to defend those who use tools.[14]

Amilcar Cabral was a practical, sensible and farsighted revolutionist. His ideas on revolution just may, in the long run, be wiser and more valuable than his more famous contemporary Frantz Fanon, with whom we will deal in the next chapter.

NOTES

[1] Cruz Pinto, "Guinea-Bissau's Liberation Struggle Against Portuguese Colonialism," *Freedomways,* 3 (1972), p. 189.

[2] Kwame Nkrumah, *Consciencism; Philosophy and Ideology for De-Colonization,* revised edition (New York, 1970), pp. 79, 77.

[3] Libyan Premier Qadaffy in an interview with the (London) *Observer* (January 1972) quoted in Colin Legum, "Africa's Contending Revolutionaries," *Problems of Communism,* XXI, 2 (March-April 1972), p. 9.

[4] Quoted in David A. Andelman, "Profile: Amilcar Cabral," *African Report* (May 1970), p. 19.

[5] PAIGC statement, quoted in Basil Davidson, *The Liberation of Guiné* (Baltimore, 1969), p. 29.

[6] Amilcar Cabral (October 1972) quoted in *The New York Times* (January 28, 1973).

[7] Pinto, "Guinea-Bissau's Liberation Struggle," p. 192.

[8] Cabral, Address to the first Tricontinental Conference of the peoples of Asia, Africa and Latin America (January 1966) in Cabral, *Revolution in Guinea* (New York, 1969), p. 92.

[9] *Ibid.,* p. 110.

[10] Cabral, Text of a seminar held in the Frantz Fanon Center, Milan (May 1964) in *Revolution in Guinea,* p. 68.

[11] *Ibid.,* p. 69.

[12] *Ibid.,* p. 72.

[13] Cabral, Interview in *Tricontinental* magazine (September 1968) in *Revolution in Guinea,* p. 146.

[14] Quoted in Jack Woddis, *New Theories of Revolution* (New York, 1972), p. 29.

19

African Revolutions
and Revolutionists:
Algeria and Fanon

I

The Algerian Revolution (1954-62) was both an anti-colonial (i.e., anti-French) revolution and an attempted socialist revolution; it was successful as the former, but has failed as the latter. Actually, the Revolution was socialist only insofar as the revolutionists voiced some socialist phrases and as the burden of the conflict fell mostly upon the peasants, who were being guided by bourgeois intellectuals. The peasants themselves, however, fought as much to gain posession of their own land as they did against imperialist forces.

Prior to the Revolution there was a lack of unity among Algerians. There was little substantial nationality or national feeling and it took the fight for independence to begin to weld the people together. But this lack of unity, especially among military and political groups, was evident throughout Algerian history. It was probably a cause for the failure of the Revolution (after driving out the French) to achieve additional goals.

Where the English in their dealings with their colonies were primarily interested in trade and were more or less willing to grant independence when it was insisted upon so long as the trade would continue, the French were different. French colonial policy emphasized the country's "civilizing mission." France in the 19th and 20th centuries sought not only foreign territory and trade, but also to spread French civilization, which in turn would help make France great. Algeria, however, was a special colony. French occupation of this land across the Mediterranean Sea from her began in 1830. Algeria became a legal extension of the French mainland so that holding this particular colony was viewed as exceptionally important for French national pride and the position of France in the world. Losing a colony is somewhat comparable to a parent losing a child to maturity and adulthood; it might be difficult to adjust to but that strange feeling of loneliness usually disappears. But losing Algeria was to the French like losing a limb; the pain might eventually subside but the resulting disfigurement would forever be a source of weakness and embarrassment for the world to see. The French position in Algeria was further complicated by the fact that the Algerian Moslems, a majority with only minority rights, were rendered subservient to a substantial local French population.

The French settlers in Algeria, the *colons,* dominated the country in the first half of the 20th century. During this time there emerged a Moslem awakening, coming indirectly as a result of the little French education available and directly due to the political renaissance of the whole Arab world. Arab nationalism was fed by the racism of the *colons* and the failure of various French governments to override the *colons* and impose meaningful reforms. France's defeat at the hands of the Germans in 1940 helped the Algerians to lose their awe and fear of the French, whereas the latter, to salvage her wounded pride, held on tenaciously to her colonies, especially Algeria. At the same time, continued French indignities only resulted in increased hatred. Also prompting the outbreak of revolution were the successful struggles for independence of neighboring Tunisia and Morocco.

After World War II the Algerians found themselves between two conflicting worlds: that of the modern West and that of their Moslem, Arab past. Feeling somewhat alienated from each the Algerians began revolution that was an attempt to gain the best of both; that is, the

Algerian Revolution was an effort by Algerians to enter the modern
world and blend it with Islamic values. Simultaneously, the Revolution
was a rejection of France and much of Algeria's own recent corrupted
history. This Janus-faced picture, which generally characterizes anti-
colonial revolutions, was particularly stark because of several factors:
the length of French domination, the especially strong influence of
French culture on the Algerian elite, the proximity of Algeria to
France, and the degree of *colon* economic and social life in the country. Algeria was separated from her past because of the significant
degree of her westernization. Yet, the masses were poor and illiterate
and had an enormous distance to travel to bring their past closer to
the present. Finally, because of the long and involved French occupation of Algeria, it was almost inevitable that the conflict would be
intense, prolonged and brutal.

The colonial structure in Algeria was such that no native political
group was able to achieve its aims legally and, thus, peacefully. Attempts by moderate reformers for greater equality were rejected by the
colons. Attempts by nationalists to organize a mass-based political
party were undermined and doomed to failure. Even the extremists'
initial use of violence almost failed, while in the end it took a regroup-
ing of all these forces to gain independence. Most of the leaders of the
Revolution were a French-educated native elite; they were followed by
the Algerian masses who were mostly ignorant of French and Western
civilization, but who were the recipients of its evils. The Algerian
Revolution was also a part of the cultural and political rise of Islam
which was fostering national consciousness as it attempted to merge
with some facets of socialism.

The Algerian Revolution began in November, 1954. The previous
month the National Liberation Front (FLN) had come into being as the
successor to another secret, revolutionary organization that had existed from 1947. Since the French had continuously refused to give up
their hold in Algeria and since legal and extra-legal means had failed,
the small number of patriots who made up the FLN decided on a war
of liberation. Judging from the activity of the previous half century it
was clearly a gamble. At first, the FLN was a body with no mass
following, few and even primitive weapons, and a program calling only
for independence and collective leadership. At no time was the organization a tightly knit party and, interestingly, it did not survive the
transition to independence. No foreign aid reached the revolutionists
until 1956. Many of the leaders realized that military victory was at first

impossible, but they were hoping instead for a psychological shock that would change the mood of the masses from apathy and disillusionment to hope and action. They believed that French colonialism could only be destroyed by a violent and concerted effort, and this helped keep them together.

By 1956 the FLN and its military branch, the Army of National Liberation (ALN) had increased its mass support, established a complex organization and, more importantly, had succeeded in uniting other revolutionary groups. The Algerian masses became more radicalized as they became aware that the entire colonial society is what needed to be overthrown. This was vital since mass support remained one of the most crucial tasks of the revolutionists. Popular support is based upon the moral alienation of the masses from the existing governmental system and the aim of revolutionists is to activate and perpetuate it until it is complete and irreversible.

The French government toyed with the idea of reforms, but to the threatened *colon* population in Algeria any reform, even token reform, was looked upon as a sell-out. What the *colons* really wanted was simple: the elimination of the FLN. Between 1956 and 1958 the FLN became more entrenched all over the country. In the city of Algiers direct urban guerrilla warfare was practiced. From December, 1956 until the Fall, 1957 the struggle in the capital came to be known as "the battle of Algiers." The terrorism of the French became an excuse for the same kind of tactics by the FLN. The escalation of brutality was frightening.

Meanwhile, in 1956 the FLN issued its declaration of the Soummam Congress.

> The Algerian Revolution wishes to conquer national independence in order to establish a democratic and social republic guaranteeing true equality to all citizens of the same country without discrimination. . . . [The Revolution] is a national struggle to destroy the anarchic regime of colonization and it is not a religious war. It is a march forward in the historic sense of humanity and not a return towards feudalism. It is, finally, the struggle for the rebirth of an Algerian state in the form of a democratic and social Republic and not the restoration of an obsolete monarchy or theocracy.[1]

Between 1960 and 1962 tension grew worse. On December 11, 1961 the FLN successfully staged mass demonstrations in Algiers, thus showing the French the degree of support they had. This date was perhaps a turning point since it provided a tremendous psychological boost to the Algerians and a scare to the French. Far outnumbering the Europeans the Algerians showed that they had the potential to overwhelm the *colons* and the French forces. Then, on March 19, 1962 an issue of *el Moudjahid,* the official newspaper of the FLN, ended with the following: "The cease-fire conference is being held at Evian from the 7th to the 18th of March; on the basis of political agreements reached. . . the Algerian Revolution attains the first part of its objectives and decides to stop the armed struggle."[2] Independence came on July 5, 1962. The Revolution was over.

During the Revolution there had been no attempt made to establish a program for the future, and both personal and ideological differences had been minimized. However, after independence these differences reemerged more violently as the various groups which had come together to drive out the French demanded a share in the power. In the process, the Revolution consumed many of its own, which has had consequences that have seriously impeded efforts at reconstruction. Interestingly, Fanon has claimed that the violence of revolution binds a colonized people together. But this did not happen in Algeria, or at least it did not last beyond independence as Fanon anticipated. Ideologically, Algeria moved towards Marxism after the Revolution as she tried to make it compatible with Islam. As former President Ben Bella said, the Revolution would go as far as possible toward scientific socialism, provided Allah remains.

Algeria was not the first African country to demand or achieve its independence. But it was the first to begin a total revolutionary war of national liberation and to make an international issue out of what France would have preferred to limit as an internal problem. As such, the Revolution was an event of crucial significance for the Third World. Revolution came to be viewed as the tool that a colonized people could use to decide their fate. Algeria became the standard bearer for revolution in Africa. She was simultaneously converted into a training center for African revolutionists and she became a haven for political exiles from other parts of the world (e.g., Eldridge Cleaver and Timothy Leary).

The success of the Algerian Revolution cannot be explained by rising nationalism alone. Foreign rule was resented and acute grievances existed which, it seems, could not be satisfied except through violence. But discontent alone is not sufficient for a revolutionary situation to emerge. What existed in Algeria (and in Viet Nam as well, as we will see in the next chapter) was a sense of desperation and a fierce determination to end injustice and humiliation. Patience, pro-

longed suffering, mass militancy and a conspiracy of silence were all
necessary for victory. Although the French won most of the battles, the
Algerians won the revolution because they became determined to win
or die.

II

Frantz Fanon (1925-61), a black man born on the Caribbean island of
Martinique, studied medicine in France and became a psychiatrist.
During the Algerian Revolution Fanon worked in an Algerian hospital
where he soon found himself supporting the cause of the revolutionists. From his experiences there and his subsequent travels throughout
much of the rest of the continent he came to consider himself an
African. His ideas on revolution are contained in his writings, the most
important of which is *The Wretched of the Earth* which he wrote just
before he died from cancer.

   Much of Fanon's thoughts on revolution and liberation were formed
by the Algerian Revolution and his experiences there. Revolution to
him meant more than a struggle for political independence. It was part
of the process of the regeneration of man and society, of self-liberation
and rebirth. Through revolution a suppressed people could undo the
negative effects of colonization. In Algeria Fanon had been an editor
and contributor to *el Moudjahid.* A theme that runs consistently
through most of his articles is that an anti-colonial revolution is the
beginning of a larger movement for a democratic and social revolution. But in pursuing this movement, Fanon warned, none of the
nations of the Third World could afford to imitate Western and capitalistic ways of life; in fact, none should *dare* imitate the West because
it would only lead to a similar moral and spiritual debasement. He tried
to minimize the differences between Arab Africa and Black Africa.
Their boundaries were the artificial creation of 19th century European
competition. Moreover, the entire subdivision of Africa, which in no
way reflected tribal differences, geographic realities, or economic and
social factors, was a legacy of imperialism. Destructive national rival-
ries were the gift of Europe to Africa, as well as to all the Third World.
To be sure, Fanon was aware of the differences and problems between
Arab and Black Africa. Nonetheless, he believed, with a greater optimism than history apparently warrants that their common interests
(e.g., preservation of independence from Europe) dictated a negation
of such conflicts. In his last years Fanon struggled to emphasize the
common goals of all Africa.

The relatively peaceful, cooperative practices of decolonization employed by Britain and even France, Fanon distrusted as a sophisticated brand of neocolonialism. He was leery of cooperation with former imperialist powers because the only purpose of such a policy for the West, he contended, was to strengthen its own interests. In like fashion, Fanon had no faith in those Third World leaders who opposed revolutionary change. The goals of liberation were not limited to national independence. Revolution for Fanon—the complete process—would achieve the liberation of colonial men, restoring their integrity and pride, as well as their past and future.

Fanon wrote about revolutions more to encourage their occurrence in Africa that to analyze them. His works, especially *The Wretched of the Earth,* appeal to the passions, not the intellect. This helps to explain some of the contradictions in his writing, the generalizations and the lack of precision and much supportive evidence. Unlike the tomes of Marx, the more limited fruits of Fanon's labor were not intended to be detailed analyses of economic conditions and change. They were meant instead to be a part of the larger war against colonialism and imperialism; they were a means by which the once degraded natives could reconquer themselves. Analysis for the sake of analysis is for intellectuals; Fanon wrote to arouse, to anger and to warn against the dangers of exploitation. As a propagandist for revolution he was highly effective. Where Lenin had examined the relationship between imperialism and revolution from the point of view of their impact upon the imperialist powers, Fanon looked at the other side, at their impact upon the colonized people. In fact, it might not be too unfair to say that an effective study could only have been written from the inside looking out.

Fanon contended that true anti-colonial revolutions must proceed along two stages. First, there is a period of guerrilla warfare during which a national program has to emerge to act as a unifying element in order to achieve independence. Second, after independence the energies of the revolution must be directed into building a socialist state. Fanon did not encourage a chauvinistic type of nationalism. As a Pan-Africanist he recognized that it was necessary to hold a people together. But he did favor a nationalism based upon the genuineness and individuality of the indigenous culture which would, in turn, unite with other anti-colonial and socialist movements.

Fanon's affinity for socialsim was, like Cabral's, primarily the result of circumstance; he was not doctrinaire about it nor did he feel that traditional Marxism-Leninism was completely suitable to Africa. Specifically, neither Marx nor Lenin dealt with the question of race, probably because it never occurred to them. Fanon took aspects of Marxism-Leninism and injected the notion of racism: "you are rich because you are white, you are white because you are rich."[3] Although he did not consider himself a Marxist he was sympathetic with the Marxist approach to revolution, to which he added his own training as a psychiatrist. But Fanon differed from Marx in that, among other ways, he emphasized "underdeveloped countries" as the agency for change, not "social class." Moreover, not only did Fanon wish to be free from capitalism but also from any institutionalized form of communism as well. In point of fact, he looked to the Third World to create a humanistic society, apart from and independent of capitalism and communism. As such, Fanon has been an inspiration to colonized people and to much of the New Left, especially among those American blacks who have called for counter-violence, reparations and cultural identity.

One of the themes that runs through Fanon's works is that freedom is not something that the colonial power gives; freedom is seized, it is fought for, it emerges only in the struggle and birth of the new nation. In this process violence is necessary because the very structure of colonialism is essentially violent.

> Decolonization, which sets out to change the order of the world, is obviously, a program of complete disorder. ... [This is because colonialism] is violence in its natural state, and it will only yield when confronted with greater violence.[4]

In the process, asserts Fanon, the natives must "vomit up" foreign values, the effect of which upon them is positive in a moral, ideological, psychological and organizational sense.

> Decolonization is the veritable creation of new men. ... Violence alone, violence committed by the people, violence organized and educated by its leaders, makes it possible for the masses to understand social truths and gives the key to them. Without that struggle ... there's nothing but. ... [the masses], still living in the middle ages, endlessly marking time.[5]

Thus, struggle and violence are not only rewards in themselves, but means to a greater end as well.

Through violence Africans come to realize that the settlers are no different from themselves, that their lives and their skins are the same. This discovery, according to Fanon, "shakes the world in a very necessary manner. All the new, revolutionary assurance of the natives stems from it."[6] Of course, as much as the settlers have been saying that all the native understands is force—and thus the necessity of "legitimate" colonial force—so "by an ironic turning of the tables it is the native who now affirms that the colonist understands nothing but force."[7] Like Mao Tse-tung and Che Guevara, Fanon was less interested in the process of violence than where it led. Since colonialism was built upon a foundation of coercion Fanon's view revolved around the cleansing effect of violence. Decolonization could only be effective where the native not only seized his freedom in the course of revolution, but also participated in physical violence to purge himself of the negative effects (e.g., inferiority, submission) of colonization.

Thus, his advocacy of violence was no mere rhetorical device for Fanon; he was not trying to justify violence for the sake of violence. He wrote only of a reactive violence that was an integral part of justice and non-compromise; it was a testimony to the havoc the white man rained upon Africa.

It is in his analyses of the roles of social classes in the anti-colonial revolution that Fanon differs mostly from Marx and Lenin, as well as Cabral. Most of recorded history, as well as traditional Marxism, has indicated that the peasantry make the poorest revolutionists. However, in this century, especially in China and Viet Nam, the peasantry have become revolutionary when provided with an appropriate ideology, capable leadership and efficient organization. Unlike Cabral, for Fanon "it is clear that in the colonial countries the peasants alone are revolutionary, for they have nothing to lose and everything to gain."[8] Peasants are outside the class system and are first among the exploited to discover that only violence pays. All other groups in society have to be evaluated and utilized in terms of the peasantry whose thinking is pure and unhampered by the inconsistency and compromise of the city people. Where Mao also assigned a key role to the peasantry Fanon went further and was eager to give them the central role in the post-revolutionary period as well; the new society should revolve around them. The masses must be educated so they can form the politically decisive arm of the revolution. When this is achieved the nation will become a living reality to all its citizens.

Although the peasants in the countryside are ripe and ready for action they are without adequate intellectual leadership. This will come from the revolutionary elite in the cities who otherwise would have no base for action. What Fanon finds wrong with most political parties in colonial countries is that they are reformist and are alienated from the peasant masses; instead, such parties restrict their activity to the urban proletariat (i.e., skilled workers and civil servants) who are only a small portion of the population. Here, for Fanon, Marxism does not work. The proletariat in colonial countries is not the same as the suppressed industrial workers in European countries. Instead, the colonial proletariat, in whom Cabral saw potential, Fanon found to be the "most pampered," much like the bourgeosie in industrial countries and, being small in number, "is in a comparatively privileged position. . . . In the colonial countries the working class has everything to lose."[9] To rely on the urban proletariat is to try to transpose European conditions on Africa.

For the revolutionary elite who would identify with the masses, Fanon developed the idea of radical or illegal party. These two groups, with the party acting as the ideological vanguard and the masses as their numerical base, provide a real political force. The illegal party is composed of deviant nationalists who react against the enclosed character and limited nature of the traditional national party. They are pushed out of the city to the countryside where they discover that the peasants, unlike the urban proletariat, are not indifferent. They discover that the peasants accept the view that national liberation must be violent. In this way the role of the peasants is crucial. Like Che and Debray, Fanon had little use for traditional parties. However, for Che and Debray the guerrillas who form the nucleus of the revolutionary party come from the cities and transform the countryside. For Fanon the revolutionary party is a product of a fusion of the peasants with the revolutionary elite; the peasants play an integral, not a subordinate role in revolutionary activity.

To the combined revolutionary force of the peasants and the elite Fanon added a politicized lumpenproletariat (i.e., the term he used for the mass of former peasants settled in the poorer urban areas). Having been galvanized, the lumpenproletariat, the group Marx thought incapable of any constructive political action, would play a major role in the revolutionary activity of the cities: "that horde of starving men, uprooted from their tribe and from their class, constitutes one of the most spontaneous and the most radically revolutionary forces of a colonized people."[10] Fanon was distrustful of the traditional proletariat, whom he considered to be the rearguard of the establishment, but also of the international Left and world worker solidarity. During the course of the Algerian Revolution he had seen the lumpenproletariat transformed from a lost mass into a reservoir for revolution.

The bourgeoisie, or at least the revolutionary minded among them in whom Cabral placed much faith, were a useless, parasitical class to Fanon. In fact, it is not a true bourgeoisie but a "greedy caste, avid and voracious. . . . It remembers what it has read in European textbooks and imperceptibly it becomes not even the replica of Europe, but its caricature."[11] And unlike in European countries, the bourgeoisie phase in the history of underdeveloped countries is a useless one, not even promoting an economy to make a socialist revolution possible. Because the bourgeoisie, or "national bourgeoisie" as he called them,

> is strung up to defend its immediate interests, . . . sees no further than the end of its nose, [and] reveals itself incapable of simply bringing national unity into being, or of building up the nation on a stable and productive basis. . . .[it] should not be allowed to find the conditions necessary for its existence and its growth.[12]

The bourgeoisie only try to replace the colonial class that had been removed by revolution, whereas for Fanon the aim of revolution is to re-distribute the productive energies of the nation, not substitute black bourgeoisie for white. Where the bourgeoisie acts selfishly it must be removed since in exploiting the country it is endangering the future.

Fanon resented the various national bourgeoisie for another reason. As a Pan-Africanist his view of nationalism was one of ambivalence; nationalism was a means of liberation and no more. He wanted revolution to overflow national boundaries to create a new humanism in all of Africa. National bourgeoisie, he said, put obstacles in the path of this "Utopia," of this attempt at unity of all Africans "to triumph over stupidity, hunger and inhumanity. . . . This is why we must understand that African unity can only be achieved through the upward thrust of the people, and under the leadership of the people, that is to say, in defiance of the interests of the bourgeoisie."[13]

Fanon had tremendous faith in the revolutionary movements of all of Africa, and even most of the Third World. But he has been criticized for emphasizing the revolutionary role of the peasants and denigrating the working class. Such criticism has been leveled by Third World leaders as well as European Marxists, many of whom believe that even though the peasants may compose the majority of the revolutionary force, the urban proletariat is still best placed to direct the revolution. Nevertheless, Fanon's influence has grown because his writings reach down and touch sensitive emotions and long frustrated hostilities. Moreover, it seems that urban revolutionists the world over have assumed that Fanon was addressing them as well as the peasants.

As with most revolutionary theorists Fanon was more concerned with making the revolution than with predicting the future in much detail, but he thought he knew the direction in which revolution would propel African society. Although he was an advocate of the value of violence he was not simply a nihilist. His goal was to build and reconstruct. Decolonization—and the necessary violence that went with it—would not only end the colonial system but also make possible a reconstruction of human relations, the production of a new society and, eventually, a new man. "Humanity is waiting for something from us other than an imitation [of Europe]. . . . For Europe, for ourselves, and for humanity, comrades, we must turn over a new leaf, we must work out new concepts, and try to set afoot a new man."[14]Fanon was simultaneously a prophet of violence and hope.

NOTES

[1] Quoted in Irene L. Gendzier, *Frantz Fanon; A Critical Study* (New York, 1973), p. 176.

[2] *Ibid.,* p. 138.

[3] Frantz Fanon, *The Wretched of the Earth* (New York, 1968), p. 40.

[4] *Ibid.,* pp. 36, 61.

[5] *Ibid.,* pp. 36, 147.

[6] *Ibid.,* p. 45.

[7] *Ibid.,* p. 84.

[8] *Ibid.,* p. 61.

[9] *Ibid.* pp. 108f.

[10] *Ibid.* p. 129.

[11] *Ibid.* p. 175.

[12] *Ibid.* pp. 159. 174f.

[13] *Ibid.* pp. 164.

[14] *Ibid.* pp. 315f.

20

The Vietnamese Revolution

In the 1960's and early 1970's the United States found the small Southeast Asian country of Viet Nam to be a quagmire. The name "Viet Nam" came to mean almost endless war, death and destruction, crisis and corruption, and finally a questionable "peace with honor." But to the Vietnamese people the conflict has been going on for more than a generation; it has consumed their history and has affected them in a most intimate and personal way. To the Vietnamese people the war in their country against the French, against the United States and against each other has been a complex revolution.

Two of the most important elements in the Vietnamese Revolution have been the desire for national independence and a hatred of foreigners (xenophobia). From 1802, and throughout the first half of the 19th century, Viet Nam was a unified and centralized country. But with the French colonial wars of 1858–83 Viet Nam lost its name, its unity and its independence. For some eighty years it was, like Gaul, divided into three parts known as Tonkin (the north), Annam (the center) and Cochin China (the south). In 1897 it was lumped together with the ethnically and culturally distinct countries of Laos and Cambodia to form a territory known as Indochina—a name chosen as a semantic relief to soothe French wounds resulting from defeats in India and China. French colonial rule in Viet Nam was inefficient and unresponsive. Promised reforms were never realized. For example, the French built many prisons but only one university, while most Vietnamese children never received even elementary education. Another stark illustration is that in 1943 (to pick one year in which figures are available) the French spent five times as much on opium (distributed through a French monopoly) as it did on education, libraries and hospitals combined. Throughout this period a growing nationalism gained momentum until it finally burst forth in revolution in the 1940's led by Vietnamese Communists. The alternatives available to the Vietnamese at the time were fundamentally two: either they could follow the Communists and join the Revolution or remain under French colonial rule. It was hardly a choice for most of the population.

The protracted Vietnamese Revolution began in August, 1945 at the time of the collapse of Japan's wartime occupation of Indochina; in some respects it is still underway. The initial stage of the conflict, also known as the First Indochina War, 1947–54, centered on the elimination of colonial rule. It was not a war specifically to install communists in power; it was, instead, a war to establish freedom with the Communists happening to be in the forefront of the struggle. In this sense the war unleashed long submerged Vietnamese aspirations which the Viet Minh (i.e., the Communist-led League for the Independence of Viet Nam founded in 1941) harnessed into a revolution. That the Vietnamese would win was almost inevitable. The French were fighting for pride whereas for the Vietnamese it was a war for survival. The French had military superiority, but since the conflict was essentially political the Vietnamese, who enjoyed political superiority, had the long run advantage. And later, refusing to learn from history, the United States engaged in a limited war against a Vietnamese opponent for whom the conflict was total. Time was on the side of the Vietnamese. Battle victories meant little and body counts were a farce since this was not a war for territory, but for the minds and hearts of the people. American bombing was usually counter-productive; the more the Vietnamese lost to the United States the more they won from their own people. It is because the struggle in Viet Nam was a revolution that a village-based political movement could mobilize and maintain sufficient power in the face of stronger opponents. Because the conflict was a revolution foreign military intervention was self-defeating.

The Indochina War failed to solve the problem of which group would succeed France's many years of political control. The aim of this continuous revolution has been the establishment of a political order which would unify the Vietnamese people. After the Geneva Conference of 1954 the Revolution centered around two rival governments, each sharing an old culture and a history in common: the Democratic Republic of Viet Nam (in Hanoi, which is communist oriented) and the Republic of Viet Nam (in Saigon, which was western oriented). Each wanted a united Viet Nam, free from foreign control, and a modern economy and society. Each claimed to be the single legitimate government for the entire nation, although neither controlled much more than half of the territory.

After 1954 the West expected the two governments to act as separate states. But this was an absurd expectation from adversaries in a revolutionary war in which the goal was unification and, as such, the elimination of the political structure of the other. The differences between the two sides was not simply political, but social in the sense of a scheme for organizing a new, unified society. They disagreed about what the structure of society should be, the roles peoples should play, and what values should prevail.

The Vietnamese Revolution, first between the Viet Minh and the French-controlled state and then between two Vietnamese republics (with the South supported by the United States, and the North, aided by foreign communists), illustrates that an anti-colonial revolution does not have to be restricted to the elimination of an imperialist nation. It may also be, simultaneously, a civil war between opposing forces (in this case, forces with differing concepts of the political and social community) for a monopoly of state power. Thus, the Vietnamese Revolution has been an anti-colonial revolution followed by an international and civil war involving fundamental changes in the entire order of the nation.

The Vietnamese Revolution was launched by a small segment of the population, the thwarted intelligentsia. Its success depended, in part, on their being able to mobilize the less privileged portions of the population. This intelligentsia was educated by the French and had some opportunity for upward social mobility; but that mobility was constricted by the narrow, funnel shape of colonial society. Nevertheless, and unfortunately for the French, not only did this intellectual elite get to see what they were being deprived of but they got the opportunity to develop skills that made them, in time, able to compete for political power. Then, lacking the legitimate means to compete for that political power, they had no choice but to become revolutionists in order to achieve their ends. These Vietnamese revolutionists developed a strategy and established an organization which became the embryo of an alternative government. They were not merely trying to overthrow French rule, but to achieve basic changes in society by inaugurating new forms for mobilizing and harnessing power.

> The Vietnamese people's war of liberation was essentially a people's national democratic revolution carried out under armed force and had twofold fundamental tasks: the overthrowing of imperialism and the defeat of the feudal landlord class.[1]

> The Vietnamese people have clearly shown their anti-fascist spirit and their attachment to democracy.[2]

Nationalism, as employed by the revolutionists, not only meant driving out the French, but also allowing those who had gained social standing and political skills complete control over their own future.

From 1930, when the Indochinese (Vietnamese) Communist Party was founded in exile, to 1945 and the start of the Revolution, the ideological foundations of the revolutionists developed ways in which frustrated nationalist goals could be realized. As the Communists refined their techniques for acquiring and distributing power they successfully worked on gaining a strong position of revolutionary leadership in Viet Nam. But the majority of Vietnamese people did not become aware of the possibility for change until the Japanese occupation of their country during World War II. The comparative ease with which the Japanese subjugated the French destroyed the myth of French (and, for that matter, white) invincibility. During this period different national groups merged with the League for the Independence of Viet Nam (i.e., the Viet Minh), an organization founded by Ho Chi Minh (1892?–1969). The League was a mixture of nationalist, communist and other leftist groups. It was the only organization able to rise above provincialism and emerge as a complete national force. With it an alternative to French rule was available.

Ho Chi Minh was the leader of the Viet Minh and a father-figure to his people. He was primarily a man of action who had little interest in formulating revolutionary doctrine or theory, but he was a communist. It was a concern for his people in the face of French exploitation which drove Ho to Marxism and communism.

> At first, patriotism, not yet Communism, led me to have confidence in Lenin. . . . Step by step, along the struggle, by studying Marxism-Leninism

parallel with participation in practical activities, I gradually came upon the fact that only Socialism and Communism can liberate the oppressed nations and the working people throughout the world from slavery.[3]

As Paul Mus, the scholar and diplomat who was the last Frenchman to see Ho before France's defeat at Dien Bien Phu, wrote: "Ho had to build on what every Asian must build *per se,* a Western logic to deal with us Europeans. . . . An Asian must find this *logique* or be lost. Ho found it . . . in Marxism."[4] Ho's great gift was to maintain harmony and preserve stability within the Vietnamese Revolution. He played a vital role in bringing his country back to life, in constructing a state (or at least half a state) and in conducting two protracted revolutionary wars. And for the first time in his country's history Ho sought popular participation in politics. He did these things by appealing to nationalist sentiments and by linking the people and their traditions to the cause of revolution.

The Viet Minh provided a stimulus and a rationale for mass participation. Diverse groups of people, many with conflicting connections, could all identify with the Communist Party's revolutionary cause. The Viet Minh took advantage of the effects of the Japanese occupation to rally national feelings. Vietnamese people could therefore join the Viet Minh and identify with the cause of national independence without being directly affiliated with the Communists. However, invariably many of those attracted to the Viet Minh in time found their way into the Communist Party. While it may seem as if the primary purpose of the Viet Minh was to lure unsuspecting Vietnamese into the Communist Party, this was not the case. The principal function of the Viet Minh was to increase the legitimacy of the Party's evolving revolutionary structure and to enhance its national posture so that it would be recognized as the most important force seeking independence for Viet Nam. In this effort they were more successful than any other group or party.

The Viet Minh, with Ho as leader, established its supremacy over all rival nationalist groups and came to represent the spirit of resistance to French occupation and the will to be free. In fact, as French journalist Bernard Fall wrote: "given French policy . . . Ho Chi Minh could scarcely have acted differently if he had been a nationalist of the extreme Right."[5] To be sure, however, the leadership of the Revolution was communist, but the most important ideological component was nationalism—a nationalism that was no mere cover for communist activity.

The Vietnamese Revolution has been a mass, peasant-based revolution led more successfully by the Communist Party than any other group. Perhaps the most important reason for this communist influence has been the relevancy of their values to the lives of the peasant villagers, who comprise some three-fourths of the total population. The communist concept of society has been communal and has presented to the peasants a sense of community with which they could identify and in which they could easily participate, based on traditions from their past. For the Vietnamese peasants revolution has offered a chance to change the passive routines of their everyday lives and, by their own actions, gain a new position in society. Revolution has enabled them to participate in the political process.

The traditional upper classes of Viet Nam failed in their efforts to lead and direct the countryside. Especially in South Viet Nam these westernized upper classes became separated from their country's past and were unable to gain the allegiance that earlier Vietnamese elites had. Led first by an ex-emperor (Boa Dai) in a French regime, then a self-righteous dictator (Ngo Dinh Diem), and finally by an American supported president (Nguyen Van Thieu) the upper classes and their governments all depended upon foreign troops and money to sustain them. They failed to realize that the support gained by earlier elites was based on shared values. The old mandarins were respected because their achievements could be measured according to values by which the peasants lived. But the peasants had not shared the values of the westernized upper classes and their leaders. The values of the latter had been distant and foreign, and as a group they had been remote and elitist, concerned more with maintaining their privileges than with establishing a working relationship with the countryside.

For their part the rural based Communist revolutionists have developed and maintained power by connecting their strategy and values to peasant traditions and values. Thus, revolution in Viet Nam has come to mean an opportunity to participate in the political process. This has been a more potent force than the primarily military force placed against them. But support for the Communists was not widespread enough to guarantee that they would control all of their country, at least not all at once. This did not mean that another opposition party had developed or that the Western supported forces were especially influential. It did mean, however, that many Vietnamese people had no loyalty to any group or party outside their village. And until they did the success of the Revolution, especially as directed by the Communists, would remain in question.

The actual Vietnamese Revolution began with the defeat of Japan in 1945. The initial Viet Minh takeover in what is known as the "August Revolution" was a rapid and total change of authority, a new "Mandate of Heaven." The Vietnamese people have no tradition of reconciliation and compromise as we do in the West. Their traditions tell them that the single correct solution to social organization lies in individual ethics and governmental order. This tradition is known as the "Mandate of Heaven," by which they mean that heaven has revealed a way that groups can live in harmony with its will. As Paul Mus put it, this Mandate, "proceeding not by compromise as in the West . . . but by a total replacement, is the precise way [the Vietnamese are] . . . accustomed to represent history and to anticipate it. It can be seen as the cosmic or climatic concept of revolution. . . . At times of crisis, institutions, doctrines and the men in power change altogether, just as one season replaces another."[6] This concept is of great value in understanding the 1973 peace settlement as well as the future of Viet Nam, and we will return to it at the end of this chapter.

When Ho Chi Minh proclaimed Vietnamese independence on September 2, 1945 support for his regime became synonymous with the defense of the country. There simply was no viable non-communist alternative and, of course, voluntarily returning to French rule was unthinkable. Ho had previously made an effort to minimize the communism of his government to attract other groups. He had disbanded the Indochinese Communist Party and propagated the slogan "Fatherland Above All." The Declaration of Independence of the Democratic Republic of Viet Nam appealed to and quoted from the American Declaration of Independence and the French Declaration of the Rights of Man and Citizen. But the French would not yield gracefully. They moved back and reestablished control over parts of the country. The way was paved for a protracted revolution. In fact, the French and Viet Minh fought each other from one end of World War II until the former's defeat at Dien Bien Phu in 1954.

France utilized her superior military power but failed to offer or sponsor a government that would be an effective alternative to the Communists, capable of establishing new institutions for mobilizing power and maintaining connections with the countryside. The Vietnamese revolutionists sought to institute a political system involving mass participation. It was a new system capable of defeating the French and establishing a basis for national unity. Thus, in Viet Nam, there were men who had obtained some wealth and social standing from the colonial system but who had been denied the political power they believed to be due them. In their revolution they were attempting to create a system that would bind them to their society and at the same time overcome imperialism and its effects. This is what revolution symbolized for the Vietnamese Communists.

As much as Ho Chi Minh was the personification of the Vietnamese Revolution Vo Nguyen Giap was the personification of the evolving doctrine of the people's war. He was the military genius behind the Revolution and the victory at Dien Bien Phu. He was responsible for enlarging a guerrilla band of thirty-four men into a modern army capable of launching major military campaigns.

> The Vietnamese people's war of liberation was a just war, aiming to win back the independence and unity of the country, to bring land to our peasants and guarantee them the right to it. . . . That is why it was first and foremost *a people's war.* . . . A people's war is essentially *a peasant's war under the leadership of the working class.*[7]

Thanks to "Uncle" Ho and General Giap a revolutionary political structure, capable of mobilizing power—especially capable of organizing the countryside for military and political action—has been the chief characteristic of the Vietnamese Revolution. This mobilization has been due to the work of the Communist Party, but not especially to communist ideology. Instead, the Communists were successful because they developed a form of political organization uniquely suited to Viet Nam. They brought a new sense of community to the separate and comparatively backward areas of the nation; they brought new forms of political participation and equality, and with it the opportunity for progress.

During the 1945–54 phase of the Revolution against the French the Vietnamese rural oligarchy was overturned by significant social changes in land ownership and political influence. In 1954 (at Geneva) the country was partitioned. The new government in the South, instead of trying to take up the programs of the Viet Minh tried to crush them and the Revolution. Survival, as well as victory, became the order of the day for Communist. After 1954 the Revolution was not between incumbents and insurgents, between an old order and a new one, but between two separate, hostile political communities, each claiming sovereignty over the whole nation. The Revolution was a conflict between contrasting forms of political and social organization.

As in other revolutions, communist and non-communist alike, Vietnamese revolutionists have had enough of an eye to the future to see
at least the direction in which they wish to go.

> The Vietnamese people have shouldered a part of the responsibility to
> fulfill this mission [to develop democracy and build peace] side by side
> with the progressive and democratic forces struggling for a better world.
> Whether one likes it or not, the . . . Revolution is part of a great movement
> of mankind for the building of peace and democracy.[8]

By reordering the values which confer social standing the Revolution
has sought to motivate the once dispossessed masses to commit
themselves to new values beneficial for all.

The end of America's war in Viet Nam came in January, 1973. The
Communists considered it a "great victory" for their side despite
President Nixon's face-saving "peace with honor." The United States
agreed to leave the country and to abandon its position that South Viet
Nam was a separate nation (and thus the victim of "foreign" aggression). Instead, the United States acknowledged that Viet Nam was one
country and that it should be ruled by a single government, later to be
determined by the Vietnamese people themselves. Given the concept
of the "Mandate of Heaven" and given the history of Viet Nam it was
unlikely that reconciliation and compromise would be characteristics
of future activity. Viet Nam is a traditionalist society in which elections
and debates are only rituals glorifying the correctness of the regime in
power—communist or anti-communist. This is how the Vietnamese
have lived for generations and is not likely they will change.

NOTES

[1] Vo Nguyen Giap, *People's War, People's Army* (New York, 1962), pp. 27f.

[2] Truong Chinh (pseudonym for Dang Xuan Khu), *The August Revolution*
(1946) in C. R. Hensman (ed.), *From Gandhi to Guevara; The Polemics of
Revolt* (London, 1969), p. 95.

[3] Ho Chi Minh, "The Path Which Led Me To Leninism" (1960) in Bernard
Fall (ed.), *Ho Chi Minh on Revolution* (New York, 1968), p. 24.

[4] Quoted in Robert Shaplen, *The Lost Revolution* (New York, 1965), p. 49.

[5] Quoted in J. L. S. Girling, *People's War* (New York, 1969), p. 118.

[6] *Ibid.*

[7] Giap, *People's War, People's Army,* p. 27.

[8] Truong Chinh, *The August Revolution* in *From Gandhi to Guevara,* p. 98.

21

The New Left in America:
Marcuse and Mixed Company

What is the New Left? Like the Bible it is all things to all men. Like other amorphous terms or movements it might be easier to define in the negative, by saying what it is not rather than what it is (e.g., it is not a communist conspiracy to overthrow the government of the United States). However, stated simply and in general terms, the New Left is a non-structured movement for radical and revolutionary societal change. It is composed of students, intellectuals, minorities and the disaffected. It had its roots in the contradictions of contemporary society and the failure of the "Old" Left (i.e., communist, socialist and other left-wing parties and groups which originated in the United States and Western Europe between the two world wars) to resolve those contradictions. It emerged from the student movements of the early 1960's, particularly with the formation of the now defunct Student Nonviolent Coordinating Committee (SNCC) in 1960 and the Students for a Democratic Society (SDS) in 1962 (which subsequently factionalized and went underground). And it was inspired by the triumph of the Cuban Revolution (in which revolution was seen as a possible and, for many, desirable way to eliminate social evils) and the struggle of the Vietnamese and other Third World peoples.

The New Left has had its own constantly changing forms of struggle which have been manifested in multifarious ways: sit-ins, moratoria, demonstrations, riots, bomb planting, drug taking and communal living. The New Left has challenged everything and everybody, including itself, and it has had no formal leaders. Because it has been a revolutionary movement without a revolution there is no single, concrete, easily summarized concept of revolution that has been acceptable to all or even a majority within the movement. New Left groups have been as numerous as the splinters of a shattered piece of wood. The written works of or about New Leftists are usually either anthologies or polemics. Detached analyses have been rare.

Nevertheless, the New Left does have a theme, or a set of themes, which run more or less consistently throughout the published works of its adherents. Unlike the "Old" Left the New is more radical, even revolutionary, and is not willing to be a mere parliamentary opposition. Also unlike the "Old," the New not only challenges capitalist societies but, to some extent, totalitarian socialist societies as well. The New Left claims to be against the institutional authoritarianism of present day capitalist societies, against control from above, against rigid bureaucracies and bureaucratic decision making. It seeks anticapitalist reform which is different from mere reform in that the former is revolutionary in scope while the latter is essentially in support of the status quo. In short, the New Left seeks a radical reconstitution of capitalist society along socialist, participatory lines.

The New Left has not had a leader comparable to a Lenin or a Mao, a Gandhi or a Ho, a Castro or a Che. But it does have as its spiritual father the German-born American philosopher and revolutionary theorist Herbert Marcuse (1898–). To be sure, the works of others, such as Fanon and Debray, have been influential upon the ideology of the New Left but in Marcuse it has an old—but not "adult"—theorist who speaks the classical language of dialectics and who gives the movement a connection to the great tradition of revolutionary thought. Of equal importance, Marcuse has been a thinker who has not been restrained by the possible consequences of transforming revolutionary thought into revolutionary practice.

I

For Marx revolution would be a socialist revolution that would overthrow the capitalist system, introduce collective ownership of the means of production and control by the workers. Because of the internal contradictions inherent in capitalism the revolution would be initiated in the advanced industrial societies. It would occur at a time of economic crisis and be carried out by the organized mass action of the proletariat, resulting in a dictatorship of the proletariat as a transitory stage. But, claims Marcuse, this is not to be.

The century-old Marxian concept of revolution, according to Marcuse, needs rethinking in the light of new world-wide contradictions of advanced capitalism. There are ghetto populations, students, and national liberation movements in the Third World which pose a threat to the political, as well as the more obvious economic, stability of advanced capitalism. Thus, "the Marxian concept of revolution must comprehend the changes in the scope and social structure of advanced capitalism, and the new forms of the contradicitons characteristic of the latest stage of capitalism in its global framework." Then, following in the footsteps of Lenin and Mao, he surmises: "The modifications of the Marxian concept then appear, not as extraneous additions or adjustments, but rather as the elaboration of Marxian theory itself."[1]

Marcuse bases his ideas on developments in the United States. He sees a rich society in which scientific and technological progress has increased efficiency and created a constantly improving material standard of living. "It offers—or should offer—the greatest and most realistic possibilities for a pacified and liberated human existence. [But] . . . at the same time it is the society which very effectively suppresses these possibilities of pacification and liberation."[2] Most opposition to society is either limited, eliminated or absorbed into the system. Our needs and freedoms are manipulated by the mass media. This society is based upon an alliance between big business and big labor. The working class has been conditioned to increase its material holdings and its relative affluence allows workers to do so. In such a consumer society the working class is corrupted, tamed, non-revolutionary. It acquiesces in its own exploitation and even defends the capitalistic system. Society is one-dimensional; it does not result in the greatest rational use of productive forces, it does not eliminate war, and it does not minimize the struggle for existence.

Marcuse insists that the bourgeoisie and the proletariat are still the basic classes in capitalist society. But he deviates from Marx by asserting that

> Capitalist development has altered the structure and function of these two classes in such a way that they no longer appear to be agents of historical transformation. . . . [On the contrary] an overriding interest in the preservation and improvement of the *status quo* unites the former antagonists in the most advanced areas of contemporary society.[3]

The point reached by capitalist society, with its ability to satisfy material needs and its control over the media, constitutes the historical development which, says Marcuse, precludes the proletariat from playing its role as the chief agent of social revolution. Thus, he doubts that the working class can ever fulfill the role set out for it by Marx. He doubts it will ever overthrow capitalism and build a socialist society. Even the traditional Communist Parties in advanced capitalist countries have become part of the system.

A policy of formal cooperation with capitalist society is rejected by Marcuse. Constant negation if not outright confrontation is all that is acceptable. But that confrontation to change society will involve a long struggle. Since the state possesses overwhelming military and police power, and since the working classes are not to be trusted, a direct attempt at seizing power by assaulting the centers of political control is not practical. The alternative is to work within established institutions, learning from them, but not losing consciousness in working with others. Difficulties will invariably arise and such a strategy of the "long march through the institutions" may only lead to the further integration of the working class with capitalism. But there appears to be little choice. Thus, "the next revolution will be the concern of generations, and the 'final crisis of capitalism' may take all but a century."[4]

None of this, however, is to imply a relaxation of the revolutionary struggle. Society must be changed radically and qualitatively to achieve human liberation and this may result in violence. But revolutionary violence Marcuse judges to be "counterviolence, that is as violence necessary in order to secure higher forms of freedom against the resistance of the established forms."[5] It is violence that will secure freedom and, eventually one assumes, non-violence. Here he is distinguishing between revolutionary and reactionary violence; that is, between the violence of the oppressed and that practiced by the oppressors. It is the first kind that is justifiable as an attempt to break the established chain of "legal" violence.

The "average" man who is the product of advanced capitalist society, the man Marcuse calls "one-dimensional," will vacillate until the revolution presents him with two contradictory hypotheses: "(1) that

advanced industrial society is capable of containing qualitative
changes for the foreseeable future; (2) that forces and tendencies exist
which may break this containment and explode the society." But
Marcuse is uncertain which way "one-dimensional man" will proceed.

> The first tendency is dominant, and whatever preconditions for a reversal
> may exist are being used to prevent it. Perhaps an accident may alter the
> situation, but *unless the recognition of what is being done and what is
> being prevented subverts the consciousness and the behavior of man*, not
> even a catastrophe will bring about the change.[6]

The italicized words are crucial for understanding the way in which
Marcuse's analysis progresses. Some group must recognize the problems of advanced capitalist society and begin to do something about
it. If the bourgeoisie and the proletariat are excluded as agents for
social change, then which group or groups will it be? Beneath the
workers lies a substratum of the outcasts and outsiders of society, the
exploited and persecuted of other races and other colors, the unemployed and the unemployable. They will be the agent, but not alone.
To them Marcuse also adds the masses in the Third World and the
students and intellectuals in capitalist countries. These outsiders are
not a mere lumpenproletariat, but are a much larger, more esteemed
group.

  In youth especially Marcuse has faith because "they observe and
know how much sacrifice, how much cruelty and stupidity contribute
every day to the reproduction of the system. These young people no
longer share the repressive need for the blessings and security of
domination—in them perhaps a new consciousness is appearing; . . .
they have a feeling for a freedom that has nothing to do with, and wants
nothing to do with, the freedom practiced in senile society. In short,
here is the 'determinate negation' of the pervading system."[7] But
youth, and especially militant student revolutionists, are not by themselves revolutionary enough to change society radically and suddenly.
They are without effective organization and can only be an agent for
change in alliance with the forces which are resisting the system from
without. Youth can only become such an agent for change if it is
supported by a free working class, though this is not likely in the
capitalist West. A revolutionary proletariat does exist, according to
Marcuse, "where it is still the human basis of the social process of
production, namely in the predominantly agrarian areas of the Third
World, where it provides the popular support for the national liberation fronts."[8] Thus, the youth of the West and the proletariat of the

Third World can work together along with minorities in capitalist countries, to initiate revolution.

Marcuse is not saying that the student movement will replace the labor movement as a revolutionary subject. But he does say that students are catalysts who act as the vanguard of revolutionary struggle. Only a group whose needs and interests are not those of class society, a group which represents a new type of man and a radical reevaluation of values can take up a socialist revolution. Marcuse sees the beginning of this change in the youth of today, especially among militant students.

> I believe that all these defeatist assertions that a movement which to a large extent is limited to the universities and schools can't be a revolutionary movement, and that it is only a movement of intellectuals, a so-called elite—I believe that such assertions simply miss the facts. They miss the fact that in the universities and in the schools the cadre of the future society are now being educated and trained, and that therefore the development of consciousness, of critical thinking is a decisive task of the universities and schools.[9]

Marcuse is the prophet of a revolution that would not merely change institutions but human beings as well—their attitudes, instincts, goals and values. There are tensions and contradictions in contemporary society. The function of revolutionary action is to multiply and clarify them through analyses and confrontation to bring on the necessary revolution. Marcuse indicts modern industrial society, both capitalist and communist. He has no blueprint for the future, but revolution would yield a society characterized by collective ownership and collective control and planning of the means of production and distribution. Competitive ethics and gluttonous consumption would be absent. The world would be worthwhile and beneficial to all. Marcuse's vision has utopian elements, but he does not think it impossible to reach if approached properly.

Marcuse wants a society in which human beings would be able to act in solidarity with one another. He wants a society without men or institutions dominating one another. He wants a society in which science and technology are used to minimize the need for human labor. And he wants a society with only enough repression to keep things running smoothly. To be more specific, restraints imposed upon what Marcuse considered the elemental aggressiveness of man, upon the instinct for destruction and the death instinct would be necessary. Freedom of expression would be granted to all but aggressive and destructive groups and individuals, such as racists, neo-Nazis and anti-Semites. But this conjures up an element of elitism in Marcuse. Tolerance, he is convinced, cannot be indiscriminate nor should it protect false words and evil deeds which contradict and counteract the possibilities of liberation. Where freedom and happiness are at stake "certain things cannot be said, certain ideas cannot be expressed, certain policies cannot be proposed, [and] certain behavior cannot be permitted without making tolerance an instrument for the continuation of servitude."[10] Thus, Marcuse would withdraw tolerance from "repressive movements" before they can become active because tolerance for such groups merely destroys tolerance. "When tolerance mainly serves the protection and preservation of a repressive society, when it serves to neutralize opposition and to render men immune against other and better forms of life, then tolerance has been perverted."[11] Who is qualified to make these decisions? asks Marcuse. Those who have learned to think rationally and autonomously. But however simple this sounds Marcuse's position may represent an unreachable ideal or it may invariably encourage the formation of a new elite.

Still, Marcuse is hopeful that the society he envisions would create the conditions for the development of a new type of man who would enjoy the greatest possibilities for the development of rationality and happiness.

> The advent of a free society would be characterized by the fact that the growth of well-being turns into an essentially new quality of life. . . . Freedom would become the environment of an organism which is no longer capable of adapting to the competitive performance required for well-being under domination, no longer capable of tolerating the aggressiveness, brutality, and ugliness of the [presently] established way of life.[12]

In this sense the new man would be "biologically" (i.e., his nature) different.

The true liberation of man, Marcuse believes, can only come in society as he essentially envisions it. Even in modern America, in fact especially in modern America, where the majority of people live comfortably and with many material possessions, there is no liberation because the society that provides these comforts and benefits dominates by its very nature and cannot possibly liberate mankind. Freedom has been exchanged for security and affluence; as a result, we are controlled, regulated and dominated more than before. The American worker has been and wants to be integrated into society, and he shares too much with the dominant classes. No longer the antagonist of capitalism the worker is in collusion with it.

Marcuse insists upon the necessity of a two-fold revolution, a revolution in institutions *and* consciousness, in political life *and* personal life. Neither by itself will produce truly revolutionary change. Dropping out of society is not the answer because both political and personal liberation can only proceed within the political context. He sees future revolutions as stemming not from need but from loss of humanity, from dehumanization, and from the horror of the waste, brutality and ignorance of human beings. Revolution will therefore, for the first time in history, try "to find a truly dignified existence and to construct a wholly new form of life. It will be not only a matter of quantitative change, but really a qualitative one."[13]

To be effective, according to Marcuse, a revolution must calculate its chances by holding the future society up against the existing society with respect to human progress as it increases freedom and happiness. Potential revolutionists must weigh the cost of success in terms of victims and resources, and it must reveal that it has a chance to improve conditions making the cost worthwhile. Marcuse was aware that this was easier said than done, especially since we cannot evaluate a revolution until after the fact. That is why it is incumbent upon us to decide beforehand to accept or reject a revolution. We must be able to determine whether or not a revolution has a reasonable chance of being progressive.

> If conditions exist in which technological rationality is impeded or ever superseded by repressive political and social interests which define the general welfare, then the reversal of such conditions [by revolution] in favor of a more rational and human use of the available resources would also be a maximization of the chance of progress in freedom. Consequently, a social and political movement in this direction would . . . allow the presumption of historical justification.[14]

Marcuse is a Marxist who recognizes that Marx is out-of-date with regards to the progress of advanced capitalism. His modifications of the Marxian concept are not an invalidation, but what he calls an *Aufhebung,* an annulment, preservation and supercession all at once. The truth of the Marxian concept is preserved and reaffirmed on a level attained by historical development. Thus, the working class in capitalist societies has become an aristocracy of labor; it is passive, conservative and even counterrevolutionary. The new opposition in the cities of the West are the outsiders (i.e., the unemployed, the unemployable and the minorities) acting together with the students and intellectuals, in whom resides the inspiration and understanding of the nature of the needed changes. The proletarian ally of these forces is the exploited masses of the Third World. A synchronization of all these forces must come about both naturally and through organization. For Marcuse, like Marx, liberation both precedes and is a consequence of revolution.

Marx believed in the necessity of the transition to a higher stage of human development; moreover, it was an inevitable process. Marcuse believes in the same transition but questions its inevitability by adding the distinct possibility of failure. His concept of revolution keeps in mind the possibility of the total subordination of man to machine unless the counterforces are strong enough to prevent it. An awareness of this possibility should strengthen and solidify the opposition to capitalism. It is, he claims, the only hope.

II

Marcuse may be the most prominent and distinguished of New Left revolutionists, but he is certainly not alone in expressing a new or modified concept of revolution. To do justice in this short space to all other components is impossible. What follows, therefore, is a jagged summary of what "revolution" has meant to the New Left in America.

The concept of revolution has been transformed from the Marxian ideal. The SDS showed its awareness of this in its "Port Huron Statement":

> The vast majority of our people regard the temporary equilibrium of our society and world as eternally functional. . . . In this is perhaps the outstanding paradox: we ourselves are imbued with urgency, yet the message of our society is that there is no viable alternative to the present.

The history of the New Left in the 1960's was a process of continuous radicalization to a point where, by the late 60's and early 70's, significant sections of it became increasingly revolutionary. It was concerned with the development of a conceptual framework to capture the reality of American society, as well as to be appealing. It rejected the idea of a revolutionary vanguard per se, and it imagined a decentralized mass movement that would experiment with a democratic community it sought to institutionalize. But this failed and many turned to other and/or older forms (e.g., Maoism and Leninism). Thus, the New Left has been a movement of self-transformation, moving from little ideology to classical doctrine, and back and forth again and again.

At the same time the New Left has been faced with several problems. First, there is no precedent for successful revolution in an advanced industrial society. Second, opposition often becomes reformist since it is permitted and even encouraged to struggle within the system. Third, the State has the advantage of being able to claim that it alone has the capacity to solve technological problems and is thus best suited to satisfy the needs of society. Fourth, the New Left is a minority and revolutions against a majority generally fail. Finally, much New Left activity has been negative (e.g., against racism, imperialism, militarism) and thus has offered little by way of concrete proposals for a new order. Claiming that a program will emerge as the revolution develops is not enough to create a mass following. Moreover, self-proclaimed "Maoists" who see revolution as an end in itself will also get nowhere. In addition, it is difficult for the American New Left to be revolutionary because it is not an oppressed class or group in the classical sense, whereas its influence among the oppressed is minimal.

Although the economic goals of the New Left are socialistic, its revolution is to be more than a class struggle in the old Marxian sense. The heart of its revolution is the reconstruction of civil society and culture. Its aim is to force the institutions of society to serve and be governed by the people, and not merely the corporate system and the state. Thus, it can be seen as a cultural revolution within advanced capitalist countries to repoliticize society. "Community" is a key word implying a sense of individual being and relationships with others. It is a revolution against dehumanization. Revolution is "what you do all day, how you live." It is "doing your own thing," a state of mind, a life style, a "revolution in consciousness."

> [The revolution] will originate with the individual and with culture, and it will change the political structure only as its final act. It will not require violence to succeed, and it cannot be successfully resisted by violence. . . . It promises a higher reason, a more human community, and a new and enduring wholeness and beauty—a renewed relationship of man to himself, to other men, to society, to nature, and to the land.[15]

There is one other factor of revolutionary movements that has created a problem for the New Left in America: nationalism and a search for identity. In the face of the revolutionary nationalism of liberation movements in the Third World the American New Left more often than not rejects nationalism—not only chauvinism or jingoism but domestic revolutionary nationalism as well—as a vehicle for change in the United States. This was a problem the Old Left had as well, with many seeing themselves as world revolutionists whose primary task was the support of the socialist mother country (USSR), Not America. Today the New Left has identified more with the Chinese, Cuban or Vietnamese revolutions. White middle class American leftists see their role as revolutionists to be that of a small, elite, auxiliary force for Third World revolutions or minority groups at home. The result has been a hatred of "Amerika" and the majority of her people. But, as has been pointed out elsewhere, no revolutionists have ever made a revolution in a country they hated. It is not likely that the New Left will succeed until it realizes this. The future of justice and freedom lies with and not against the majority. Revolutionists, it seems, must be nationalists to have a hope for success.

The revolution that the New Left has tried—and, one suspects, will try—to create is not a simple, single insurrection, nor is it an all-out civil war. Instead, it has been a long, continuous conflict, with all facets of it inextricably intertwined. It has not been, nor is it likely to be, a traditional socialist revolution in which society will be overturned suddenly. The New Left has sought a revolution in which vital decision making will be placed in the hands of those people whose lives are affected by those decisions. The revolution will aim not simply at seizing power, but at dispersing it. As much as anything else this is the ideal of revolution for the New Left; the splintering and problems of the movement have come over questions of strategy and tactics.

Postscript: The Continuing Potential For Revolution In America

Any consideration of the continuing potential for revolution must include a discussion of the various social and psychological factors related to the instability of a society's basic institutions. Many factors can be disruptive to a society if conditions and circumstances are such as to make the usual institutional safeguards or protective mechanisms and processes ineffective. In other words, if the institutional systems of society are not able effectively to integrate into the power structure those groups that are self-conscious, organized, interested and capable of exercising power, trouble will begin to develop. Rhetorical attacks, protest demonstrations, and eventually physical force will occur. These confrontations will sooner or later reduce the viability of the institutions and bring them into disrespect (i.e., weaken them), thereby making them incapable of meeting the demands of society to which the majority of its members have become accustomed. If these conditions continue long enough the way is opened for individuals or groups who may wish to make radical or revolutionary changes.

In the Western industrial world of the 20th century, attacks explicitly directed against the "system" have occurred. By contrast, earlier revolutionists often appeared to direct their force at a specific ruler or ruling elite, such as a king and/or his nobles. But revolutionary activists, in the 1960's and 70's particularly, defined their enemies as diffuse and embodied in the concept "system." This practice may not, however, represent as great a change from the past as would at first appear since in earlier eras a king and his nobles could be described as an institution. In any case, they certainly represented the institution of government. In some European countries today the king and nobility are still regarded as comprising an important institution having great symbolic meaning if nothing else. Consequently, whether the system is seen as represented by the king as in the past or by the state-government and its various representatives as is true today, the attacks of revolutionists are still directed toward essentially the same source—that which is believed to be a diffuse, unbending, unsympathetic system of corrupt officialdom and unjust laws.

Often the hatred and attacks of the revolutionists are not motivated solely because the system is corrupt and unjust per se. In other words, lofty ideals of truth and justice are not the only things that motivate revolutionists. On the contrary, to some degree people become revolutionists in direct proportion to which they individually, or as members of a group, are denied economic, social, psychological, and religious rewards in comparison with other groups or individuals whom they perceive otherwise to be similar to themselves.

Related to the continuing potential for revolution in the 20th century, specifically during the decade of the 60's, is the phenomenon of collective violence. Collective violence in the 60's in the U.S. and elsewhere in the Western world was noteworthy for its increasingly political implications. In the past this political emphasis had been less prominent, particularly with regard to collective violence as it occurred in the U.S. The lack of political emphasis in the violence of America's past can be explained as a result of four important social factors. First, given America's federal, capitalistic structure, state institutions have historically been less important than private or public institutions in other societies. Capitalism pitted labor against industry, farmers against the railroads or an impersonal market system. Only rarely was violence directed against the state and when it was, it was quickly and often easily put down.

Second, in America unparalleled radical and ethnic pluralism has always existed. Frequently collective violence has been intergroup in nature. Group frustrations generated displaced aggression against racial and ethnic scapegoats. Having readily available scapegoats may have served to provide objects against which to express aggression. Consequently, this has minimized the likelihood of the frustrations and accompanying aggression becoming politically oriented and thus having revolutionary potential.

Third, America has been an affluent society. If we relate political apathy to national wealth, it can be seen that an increase in the latter has been paralleled by a general decline of voter participation. When people are reasonably well off economically and experience a degree of economic security the desire to challenge or change their system of government is usually minimized. Possession of an abundance of wealth then, is one important reason why most Americans not only are uninterested in revolutionary change but why only two-thirds of qualified 20th century Americans bother to vote, even in presidential elections. Contrast this with the extremely high percentage of voting that characterizes the impoverished Latin American nations where demands upon and challenges to those in power are a continual source of disruption. Their poverty and economic insecurity drives people to action against the source perceived as most logically able to provide some relief of and improvement in their situation. Hence, acts of collective violence and political instability in Latin America are endemic.

Fourth, American material progress reinforces faith in the legitimacy of the system and sanctifies the dominant institutions of the state. "It has been a faith of astonishing tenacity, deeply rooted in the wisdom of the Founders; the American Dream of a New Jerusalem, of a City on a Hill; the Fetish of Consitution worship; the rags to riches . . . [has been called] the sense of 'giveness' of American institutions."[16]

Since World War II society has come to accept, or at least understand violence as having a political dimension. Nevertheless, we have been unwilling to apply this understanding and acceptance to the riots and rebellions of the 60's. Much less threatening to a middle class way of life is to attribute violence to the fault of individuals. In other words, if *individuals* are responsible for violent acts, and not just the injustice and inequality existing in society, then *individuals* should be punished by the mechanisms society provides. This relieves people of responsibility for the violence. But if the society is experiencing a crisis its members are forced to accept some of the responsibility for what happens.

Consequently, while there were definite indications of a general loss

of regard for the customary social institutions of society during the
60's—including an increased use of violence—society avoided facing
the possibility that the violence had taken on a measure of political
significance. Various theories arose to explain that the politicizing of
the violence was only apparent, but in the end none of the theories
proved very satisfactory. Among the most loudly proclaimed was the
notion that communists or "outside agitators" with links to Hanoi,
Peking, Havana, if not Moscow, were behind the acts of disruption and
destruction. In reality, however, the American Communist Party was
aging, old fashioned, and ineffective, having little impact on young
people or minorities.

A closely related argument blamed the violence on riffraff, incorrigi-
ble mischief-makers and no-gooders who would sweep responsible
and law abiding bystanders into a vortex of violence. They were the
participants in the riots and violence on college campuses, in the
streets, and in the ghettos, an infinitesimal fraction of the people
actually present. Hence the belief that only a small fraction of the black
population actively participated in the street riots of American cities
in the 1960's. Furthermore, went the argument, the rioters, far from
being representative of the black community, were principally unat-
tached, unskilled, unemployed, uprooted, criminal outside agitators.
In fact, the majority of the black population, it was held, unequivocally
opposed and deplored the riots. But studies of American ghetto riots
in the 60's dispute these assumptions. They indicate that substantial
numbers of the people actively participated in the riots, and that as
high as 72% of high-income blacks thought the urban riots were positive factors of social revolutionary protest.

Further evidence of the unwillingness to face the political and revolutionary implications of the violence of the 60's is seen in another
explanation. The collective and individual violence in America's past
has been used to justify or explain its presence today. The frontier
required, so it was said, that people occasionally take the law into their
own hands. When the frontier closed people tended to perpetuate the
violence of their cultural heritage in vigilantism and gangsterism. Slavery, too, was a system based on violence. The whole history of property
rights, labor-management relations, interstate disputes, and nationality and racial relations has been steeped in violence. But the frontier
theory of violence is contradicted by experiences of other frontier
nations, such as Australia. Although Australia's frontier period was
marked by violence, when compared with the U.S. experience Australia has for some time enjoyed relative peace and tranquility.

Closely related to the frontier hypothesis is the gun theory which argues that the very prevalence of privately owned weapons increases the use of violence. For example, assassination, sniping, and shoot-outs with the police are common, in part because people can easily obtain the necessary weapons. All of this leads to private paramilitary groups with revolutionary potential, such as the white Minute Men or the black Deacons of Justice. The gun theory is attractive because the solution seems so simple; that is, banish the possession of guns by ordinary citizens and the incidence of weapon related violence will disappear. But this argument is erroneous, regardless of whether violence is or is not politically inspired, since other means of creating violence are readily available. Many are sincere in their belief that possession of guns inspires violent insurrection. Others clutch to the argument as a means of *avoiding* the possibility that the violence of the past decade was politically inspired and thus implying a condemnation of America as a social system.

Other fascinating explanations which attempt to explain politically inspired collective violence are available. There is, for example, the theory of repressed sexuality related to America's puritan past and the Protestant ethic, thus implying that repressed social and physical needs must find violent expression in some form. Another argument relates violence to the return of the "killer instinct." But again, the significance of all these theories which attempt to explain the violence of the 60's is that they revealed a general unwillingness to accept fully the political seriousness and, consequently, the revolutionary potential which existed in some of the social and political problems facing America and the Western world.

Obviously violence is not a new phenomenon in society. The only new element was the politicizing of it. The political nature of the violence, though it was expressed in a variety of ways, came to be most effectively revealed in a general movement in American society. This movement involved mostly persons, organizations, world views and activities located on what is conventionally called the Left and acting in radical judgment upon the prevailing patterns (political, economic, social, and moral) of American life. The "Movement" was obviously not primarily a violent revolution. But it did reveal the existence of a revolutionary consciousness in American life. It was a mood and, to a lesser extent, a program. It was the feeling that times had brought things to a head and that things cannot go on as they are. It was a signal that some people, primarily youth, wanted immediate changes in society that were radical enough to be called a revolution—a revolution of consciousness, a cultural revolution , a revolution to overthrow the existing order, violently if necessary.

Presumably, the major concern of the movement was for a better, more equalitarian, even perhaps, more humanitarian society, with justice for all. But on this score the movement rated some serious criticism, not because of its revolutionary significance and potential, but because it seemed to favor only changes which would fit its ideology. In this respect it was anti-humanist or at best selectively humanist. For example, there was little objection to deliberate acts of violence against "deserving" people and objects as long as it was they (the movement people) who instigated the violence.

To what extent did the politicizing of violence in America imply a potential for revolution? To pursue that question further we now turn to a discussion of the trends and changes in the nature of violence since the 1960's. The politicizing of violence and the potential for revolution during the 60's quite suddenly became remote in the U.S. as the country moved into the 70's. While America's incidence of violence continued unabated, the character of the violence, its collective nature, and its political and revolutionary significance greatly receded. While no single factor appeared to dominate in the changed character of the violence a number of things undoubtedly contributed to returning it to its previous apolitical nature. These would include, first, President Lyndon Johnson's ineptness in the handling of the Viet Nam War, protest demonstrations (some of them violent), and the president's decision not to seek reelection. Shortly before the official end of that unofficial war the political nature of much of the violence began to recede.

A second factor to be considered in the depoliticizing of collective violence in the early 70's was that some changes appeared to take place in the thinking of America's racial minorities. The strategy of power through the political process, rather than through political violence, came to occupy a more prominent role among many minority people in the U.S. As a consequence, greater emphasis upon seeking political positions by minorities was evident. There was a new emphasis by them to exert political and social pressure in lieu of revolutionary force to obtain rights. Increased interest in and demands for higher education by them indicated an awareness of the fact that real power in the long run belongs to those who are trained, and not to those who must rely on physical force. The cost of collective violence in the lives and property of minorities themselves, relegated its use to a last resort strategy. However, minorities have not been unwilling to use violence and confrontation, even after the 1960's. But the new urban minorities were willing to try a wider variety of political approaches than their elders. The violence, changed from the large scale variety, therefore had distinctly less significance politically and as revolutionary force. The psychological benefits of large-scale riots were perceived as not offsetting their terrible cost to the minority community. The violence of the early 70's tended to be limited to guerrilla type attacks upon the police and other establishment agents.

Third, the fact that some progress was made toward meeting the demands of minority people undoubtedly contributed to the lessening of violence as a political tool in America's ghettos. The extent to which progress was made in meeting minority demands was a source of some dispute between minorities and whites. Whites claimed tremendous progress in this respect, only to have these claims heatedly rejected by the minority communities. Actually, the rejection of claims of progress may have been used by the minorities as a tactic to resist complacency toward racial problems among both groups. Then, too, for those who are suffering there is a tendency to underevaluate *any* degree of progress. It is difficult to to be content when one does not have essentially the same as others.

A fourth factor which should not be overlooked in sustaining the changed, more moderate mood among activists was a socio-psychological one. After intense involvement by people in protest and violence of a revolutionary nature, a period of emotional exhaustion appears characteristically to set in. Furthermore, the harsh realities of the real world are ever present and, while they may be pushed into the background for a time, soon reassert themselves and must be given consideration. The ardor, passion, and ideals of the revolutionary ideologue tend to be dimmed as he is forced to contend with the persistent demands of survival.

Violent revolution in the U.S. became a more remote consideration because of a number of other things, some of which have been discussed previously. For example, the essential stability of American institutions provided strong support for the view that revolution was unlikely at the beginning of the 1970's. We have also noted the ability of the system to integrate into the power structure some of the dissident groups that were self-conscious, organized, interested, and capable of exercising power. To some extent this did happen among minorities. And certainly, the question of whether white America and its institutions had had a sincere change of heart could not be easily determined, as ugly incidents of racial discrimination continued to occur.

Finally, an important socio-psychological factor reducing the potential for violent revolution in America was the traditional emotional commitment to and belief in the American way. Although forms of violent collective behavior were still evident, the political character of violence dramatically present during the 60's had become relatively insignificant. The riots and other forms of collective violence began to lack concrete political issues, goals, and grievances. They appeared to be simply expressions of delinquent behavior, not associated with any significant political cause, revolutionary or otherwise. The intensely discontented groups which perpetrated the rebellions of the earlier period degenerated to ineffective, self-survival clubs, or they disappeared completely.

Hence, revolution in America became unlikely at the outset of the 1970's. How the Watergate affair and the energy crisis will affect the politics of America in any significant (i.e., revolutionary) manner is unclear at the time this book goes to press. Does it mean that not only activist leftists but, for the first time in the history of America, the silent majority will begin to suspect that the institutions of government are faltering, their credibility seriously undermined, and that a radical change is called for? Or will these startling developments be seen as merely revelations of corrupt men trying to secure their own personal gain and not as an indication of underlying weaknesses in the American system and its institutions? The latter is the anticipated outcome of these crises. In other words, we expect that a repeat of the revolutionary protests of the 60's against the system will not occur even though corruption has been laid bare for the whole nation and the world to observe.

This belief is based upon rather subjective reasons. They are first, that emotionally, most people are not ready, nor will they be, to launch into a full scale protest and to experience again the trauma of the 60's. Second, young people for the most part have turned to the business of living and working within the system. The cost of the psychological and physical effort needed to redirect these activities will be greater than the motivation to do so. Our predictions are not much more than guesses. Only history will provide the final answer.

NOTES

[1] Herbert Marcuse, "Re-Examination of the Concept of Revolution" (1969) in A. Lothstein (ed.), *"All We Are Saying . . ." The Philosophy of the New Left* (New York, 1971), p. 281.

[2] "Revolution or Reform: Herbert Marcuse and Karl Popper," *University Review,* 21 (November 1971), p. 11.

[3] Marcuse, *One-Dimensional Man* (Boston, 1964), p. xiif. Also see Marcuse, *An Essay on Liberation* (Boston, 1969), p. 15.

[4] Marcuse, *Counterrevolution and Revolt* (Boston, 1972), p. 134.

[5] Marcuse, "Ethics and Revolution" (1966) in Edward Kent (ed.), *Revolution and the Rule of Law* (Englewood Cliffs, 1971), p. 51. Also see Marcuse, "Repressive Tolerance" (1965) in Robert Paul Wolff, *et al, A Critique of Pure Tolerance* (Boston, 1969).

[6] *One-Dimensional Man,* p. xv. (Our italics)

[7] Marcuse, "The Question of Revolution," *New Left Review* (September-October 1967), p. 7.

[8] "Re-Examination of the Concept of Revolution" in Lothstein, *"All We Are Saying",* p. 278.

[9] "Revolution or Reform: Herbert Marcuse," p. 36.

[10] "Repressive Tolerance" in Wolff, *A Critique,* p. 88.

[11] *Ibid.,* p. 111.

[12] *An Essay on Liberation,* pp. 4f.

[13] "Revolution or Reform: Herbert Marcuse," p. 36.

[14] "Ethics and Revolution" in Kent, *Revolution and the Rule of Law,* p. 57.

[15] Charles A. Reich, *The Greening of America* (New York, 1970), p. 2.

[16] Hugh Davis Graham, "The Paradox of American Violence: A Historical Appraisal," quoted in James F. Short, Jr. and Marvin E. Wolfgang (eds.), *Collective Violence* (Chicago, 1972), pp. 203–05.

22

Conclusion:
Some Observations

The idea that is common to all the different people, places and periods covered in this book, the idea that cements the mixture together and gives it an organic unity is the great dream and the frightening reality of revolution. From the end of the 18th century both the dream and the reality have been central to the history and the hopes first of Western and then non-Western people. The dream of revolution incorporates the wish of a people to be masters of their fate and to create a much improved if not entirely new kind of community, or even a new world altogether. Freedom, liberty and equality are among the key words for the resulting society in which people will express themselves freely and individually as never before. The dream of revolution involves the perfection of humanity. But dreams, though they are not always forgotten, are disturbed by an awakening to reality and a reluctant return to earth as revolutions discover their limitations in chronology, geography and human weaknesses. Nevertheless, any attempt to analyze modern revolutions solely in terms of their political, economic and social panaceas is incomplete.

Virtually all of the revolutions with which we have dealt have been products of a variety of historical, social and political situations. Their solutions to societal ills differ and their philosophies have been expressed in many ways. Yet, from our study it appears that they clearly indicate, among other things, many people's massive discontent with the status quo. Although such discontent is most often expressed in terms of a criticism of political, economic and social factors its source is more fundamental and its goal is more inclusive. Revolutions are as much concerned with the spiritual, psychological and ethical conditions of man as with the material; filling stomachs, clothing bodies, protecting families, and providing freedom and education are the external prescriptions for curing a more penetrating ailment: dehumanization. In other words, as Bakunin insisted, we must "transform completely the milieu in which we live." Not only must man's environment be changed but so must his moral condition. Man must be made anew, he must be recreated. This, as much as anything else, is the most unique feature common to modern revolutionary movements.

Modern revolutions have sought to recast society according to patterns that have been unprecedented in the context of those societies or in history as a whole. They have espoused a new social order, one based on such concepts as "the rights of man and citizen," "self-determination," or the principle "from each according to his ability, to each according to his needs." In the revolutions we have examined conscious efforts were made to reconstruct society along such conceptual and ideal lines. Common to the literature of revolution was a humanitarian impulse, the idea of progress, an irreverence and even contempt for what appeared to be outdated institutions, and a messianic sense that the time for revolution was now. This is what revolutions have meant since the late 18th century, and not the Greek reference to changes in the form of government nor the early modern references to the circular movement of history. From the late 18th century, revolution came to mean the creation of a new order and a new man, the beginning of history anew. The modern revolutionists with whom we have dealt, from Marx to Marcuse, from Ghandi to Guevara, and from Paine to Fanon, all envisioned a similar future, however much their suggested means for getting there may have differed. They all agreed as well that unless a new man is created man's domination of man will remain, regardless of what we choose to call it. It is clear that the new man has yet to appear; but then again, the struggle for perfection and salvation has never been easy.

Flip the coin of revolution and on the reverse of the ideal side will be a pragmatic one. Whatever else they may share in common the thought of successful revolutionists is deeply rooted in the realities of their own nations. With a little improvisation and experimentation they correctly assess their enemies and employ tactics which are effective. Although each revolutionary situation is different this has not prevented revolutionists from learning from one another. The wise revolutionists make themselves aware of the dynamics of social upheaval. They simultaneously evaluate what is different in their own situations. They then act to create a positive revolutionary situation, one in which the revolutionists begin with and maintain the greatest advantage possible. Thus, at the start of a successful revolution society is presented with an ideal which not only condemns, but insists that people must be ready to fight against oppressive conditions. Moreover, it specifies a variety of ways that can be utilized for liberation. For example, if poverty and famine stand in the way of fulfillment then private property and wealth are denounced while a redistribution of land and wealth are promised. If liberty has been limited then it too is promised. But again, the specific, concrete form this pragmatic side will take depends upon the conditions of time and place.

There are other, related factors to consider. The language of revolution must be provocative enough to motivate people in a new direction. Regular, everyday language and expressions lack the psychological impact and controversial associations necessary to incite people to action. Old speech is only a series of trite cliches and meaningless sounds, but revolutionary language should create strong emotional response. Specifically, it is slogans that are especially effective. The slogans of a revolution are often derived from more complex ideas, but their utility lies in their relevance to the revolutionists' understanding of the situation and in providing signals for action. Slogans, and revolutionary speech in general, are verbal reminders of the causes and nature of discontent. When used they serve to evoke instinctively all the sentiments associated with the revolution. People are susceptible to the appeal of revolution, as embodied in speech and slogans, if they are aware of the problems and believe change is possible. The appeal does not create the problems, but it draws attention to them and suggests solutions. Slogans and speech intensify expectations, but a people's acting upon them is a function of the intensity of their discontent. Indeed, behind every revolutionary ideal can be found the conviction, or one similar to it, that men have become slaves to their tools and that they must be valued for themselves.

Revolutions are not necessarily times for reason and common sense, but for faith. Reason is often relegated to a position of secondary importance and is not considered a guiding light. This is not at all to imply that revolutions are unreasonable or unjustified; but rather to suggest the view that a future society and the new man do not need to be rationally demonstrated. A dependence upon reason, as the word is conventionally used, is not a part of the revolutionary ideal. With this in mind it therefore follows that a revolution will have a chance to succeed if its supporters can be persuaded to put their whole beings behind it, if they can be convinced that without the continuation of the revolution all will be lost. The leaders of revolution need to recognize that a fanatical faith in the necessity of the new order is vital. Success will come much easier if followers find in the revolutionary ideal the quintessence of all their values. That ideal must not only promise a new vision, but also at the same time, be congruent with the old culture; it must be both chiliastic and contemporary, promising for the future as well as the more immediate present. The ideal must communicate a message of faith and it must elucidate the direction that needs to be followed; it must be an ideal of hope and fulfillment.

With this in mind we return to a theme which we have alluded to in several earlier chapters: religion and revolution. We have already dealt with the modern revolutionary goals of the creation of a new man and a new order, of beginning anew and of faith, all of which have clear religious overtones. Now we want to turn our attention to what Eric Hoffer called the art of "religiofication"—the art of turning practical purposes into holy causes.[1] Extreme discontent with existing conditions, however eloquently expressed by leaders and reinforced by promises, will virtually never bring forth a successful revolution. Inherent in such success must be a religious force. Men will invariably fight better if, in addition to "bread," their struggle is presented as a crusade for "liberty," "freedom," and "redemption."

Most of the revolutions we have discussed were "religious" in the sense that they were engineered by men who felt themselves to be the tools of a Supreme Being, an Ultimate Power or a Universal Law however conceived. The goals of various religious movements have been called the Kingdom of God, Salvation and Nirvana. Revolutionists have labeled their goals as some kind of earthly paradise or more recently, Communism. Georges Sorel called this spiritual dynamic of revolution the "social myth." The social myth grows from a fusion of the ideas expressed by the intellectual revolutionists with the needs of society. From the criticisms of contemporary conditions and the hopes of the future there gradually emerges a new myth of ideal. The ideal creates a vision of the future in order to give reality to the hopes of the present.

Often there are elements within the ideal which are unrealistic, irrational and even contradictory; the ideal may even be a terrible delusion. But that is not important. The power of the revolutionary ideal, as with the power of religion, stems from the intensity of the faith with which it is believed. In order to believe that a revolution will create a new world and a new man the motives of credibility must be of a mystical, religious character. It is essential for revolutionists to believe that they are "doing God's work," or "altering the course of history," or "fulfilling history." The ideal is faith, not reason. The principles of a revolution are its dogma; its saints are its heroes and martyrs. Revolutions have had ceremonial similarities with religions; the hammer and sickle and the swastika have their parallels in the cross. For Protestant revolutionists, such as Luther and Calvin, "justification by faith" and "predestination" were the ideals that propelled their followers. The English Puritans were going to have a "rule of the saints." The ideal of the French Revolution was summed up in the slogan "Liberty, Equality, Fraternity"; French revolutionists believed that they were the apostles of a new faith which was destined to regenerate the world. Marx and his followers envisaged for man a goal that involved his total transformation; by changing the physical world man would himself be changed. Marxists, to be sure, are not men and women of religion, but there can be little question as to the religious quality of their revolutionary ideal.

It may also be stated that just as a religion that begins in one country and spreads and takes root in other countries, so too can a revolutionary ideal. This can occur even when the initial spread is through conquest and forced conversion. Such was the case during the French Revolution as it has been of Marxism.

Finally, in religion as in revolution, there is usually present an optimism bordering on naïveté. In foreseeing a new and better world, a utopia, a golden age, revolutionists seemingly take little account of such apparently human characteristics as greed and selfishness. But this does not mean that revolutionists are ignorant of human foibles;

rather, they generally believe that in the revolution itself there will occur an inexplicable metaphysical reaction that will rid man of his weaknesses. This is a religious faith which must be effective even when people are not wholly ignorant of the difficulties involved in their monumental task.

Another factor common to many revolutions is the desire for that vague, relative word "equality." Those who have—or think they have —been denied some kind of equality have been most responsive to joining the ranks of revolutionists who demand it. Aristotle wrote that "Inferiors revolt in order that they may be equal, and equals that they may be superior. Such is the state of mind which creates revolutions."[2] From that time on, whether the language was Lutheran, Rousseauean, Jeffersonian or Marxian, the unsatisfied expectation of equality and the dissatisfied state of mind have been major causes of revolution. Still it takes two sides to make a revolution. Edmund Burke's comment in 1769 about a possible revolution in America illustrates the nature of many revolutionary conflicts.

> The Americans have made a discovery or think they have made one, that we [the English] mean to oppress them: we have made a discovery, or think we have made one, that they intend to rise in rebellion against us. . . . We know not how to advance; they know not how to retreat. . . . Some party must give way.[3]

The two most important influential revolutions of modern times have been the French (1789) and the Russian (1917). European, and even world politics from 1789 to 1917 was largely the struggle for and against the principles of the French Revolution. More than any other country it was France which provided the concepts and ideas for liberal and radical politics everywhere else. It was France which first gave the example of fighting nationalism, and nationalism has been a copious source of enthusiasm ever since. Much of modern European history is a result of the legacy of the French Revolution. In this century most revolutions have been revolutions of underdevelopment; that is, they have often occurred in economically backward countries and have become long-term efforts to overcome their underdevelopment. In this sense they have been revolutions of modernization and thus a result of the legacy of the Russian Revolution and the doctrines of Marxism-Leninism. Interestingly, with the Russian Revolution the Bolsheviks came to power on an anti-war, and in effect, an anti-national Russian platform. Instead of nationalism the Bolsheviks advocated internationalism. Lenin's efforts to transform what he considered an imperialist war into a number of revolutionary civil wars which would best serve the interests of all workers were ignored. It was only after the 1917 Revolution, especially under Stalin, that Russian communism became more nationalistic.

The followers of Marx, like those of Christ, as we wrote at the end of Chapter 9, have been virtually innumerable. This has been because Marx was sometimes inconsistent, inaccurate and vague and because of the absolute necessity to bend Marxism to suit local needs. Thus, what is called "Marxism" today is really many different, sometimes conflicting "isms." In this sense the concept of revolution among the spiritual descendents of Marx, as it has been and no doubt will be for other deities, has undergone changes somewhat like the initial message in the game of "telephone." From Marx to Lenin to Che to Marcuse (among others) the Marxian concept has been modified, sometimes intentionally, sometimes not, according to the interests of those involved. Each change has induced further adjustments. The transmitted message is sometimes garbled, sometimes improved but always different from the original. The resultant changes have been useful and instructive since, unlike "telephone," the original message (of Marx) is always available. And also unlike "telephone," the whole process has hardly been a game. Revolutions are for keeps.

From our study it appears that there are four basic types or categories of revolutionists. (1) There are those who participate in revolutions for negative, often destructive ends, for lack of anything else to do. Those who see revolution only for its own sake and those who can see no farther than the next confrontation fall in this grouping. These "negative revolutionists," as we choose to call them, can be dismissed as the least historically and socially significant and, although the revolutionary movements discussed in this book were composed of numbers of them, we do not think that they started or controlled any revolution. They are an important group, to be sure, since they sometimes influence the outcome of certain revolutionary episodes or may even occasionally determine the fate of a revolution. But "negative revolutionists" neither lead nor direct revolutions and thus least influence their nature and character. (2) There are those who take part in a revolution as a last resort, because they are driven to it by oppression, injustice and an unresponsive government. These "reluctant revolutionists" would rather be left alone by society at large, but they are compelled out of necessity, for the sake of survival as they understand it, and often to preserve what they cherish to join in a revolution. The mass of participants in most revolutions, the colonists in our own

American Revolution, Fidel Castro, Ho Chi Minh, many black and brown American militants all belong in this category. As George Washington wrote in 1776: "Our cruel and unrelenting enemy leaves us only the choice of a brave resistance, or the most abject submission. We have, therefore to resolve to conquer or to die." (3) There are next those who encourage revolution to serve their own selfish purposes, to achieve power and gain wealth. These "destructive revolutionists" are often extreme right-wingers (though the Right does not have a monopoly of them), fascistic and reactionary. Hitler, Mussolini, and many of the military leaders of coups in Latin America and the Middle East are of this type. They are probably the least attractive to the world at large and may actually be called regressive or even counterrevolutionary. (4) Finally, there are those who advocate revolution as a necessary means to achieve an ideal or even utopian goal or end; that goal may be considered inevitable or it may be desired as the best for all concerned. These "ideal revolutionists,"such as Calvin, Cromwell, Robespierre, Marx, Lenin, Mao, Che and Fanon, proceed out of an unusual conviction—some would say a blind or compulsive conviction. They proceed believing, even knowing, that their revolutions are part of the inevitable course of history or the divine order of things. This type of revolutionist is the leader who shows and/or leads the way. These are the rare individuals who change the course of history.

Admittedly, to distinguish among these types by labeling a given revolutionist as one or another or, for that matter, characterizing an entire revolution as being motivated by people supposedly of one type or another, is a difficult task and one that involves a certain amount of moralizing. Moreover, this typology is not perfectly distinct and clear-cut; one or more types often overlap in the same persons. A Freudian might say that the second type is the only real type and the others are merely variations. It would also be safe to say that virtually all revolutions are initiated by and attract all four types, but invariably one type comes to dominate in the end and determines the ideal of a given revolution. Thus, typologizing revolutionists in this fashion may be a useful tool.

The liberation of the human race appears to be the ultimate aim of most revolutions. Such an aim, however, is apparently—at least at this juncture in history—unattainable, especially since freedom and liberty have almost always come for one or more groups or people at the expense of others. However much revolutions seek to be for all mankind, in practice they have never been able to be such. As soon as a revolution overthrows the old order and establishes a new regime the revolutionists usually cease revolting and seek to preserve and protect their advances without proceeding much further or too quickly. They tend to place dogma before people and secure national freedom without guaranteeing individual freedom. This does not mean that revolutionists waste their energy. Revolutions may fail to reach their ideals but they otherwise change the world and, as long as the nature of man remains the same, they probably will continue to occur.

Can the human race in stepping up to the liberation of all do so without stepping on the rights of some groups? The answer to this question has been and will continue to be the test for the validity of revolution. Ideally, the freedom that revolution seeks must not only be for all but must stem from the conviction that it is the essence of morality. Liberty and freedom must be viewed as absolutes, not to be enjoyed by the majority only, but by all because, as John Stuart Mill said, it is intrinsically right.

Looking ahead to the future of revolution we conclude with an appropriate statement from Che Guevara.

> It does not matter what the results of today's struggles are. It does not matter, as far as the final result is concerned, whether one movement or another is momentarily defeated. What is definitive is the determination to fight, . . the awareness of the need for revolutionary change, and the certainty that the latter is possible.[4]

As long as there are human beings who are able to struggle for a better life and as long as such struggles are resisted by governments then, we suspect, there will always be revolutions.

NOTES

[1] See Eric Hoffer, *The True Believer; Thoughts on the Nature of Mass Movements* (New York, 1951).

[2] Quoted in Paynton and Blackey, *Why Revolution?*, p. 11.

[3] Quoted in Bailyn, *The Ideological Origins of the American Revolution*, pp. 158f.

[4] Che Guevara, "Guerrilla Warfare: A Method" (1963) in John Gerassi (ed.), *Venceremos! The Speeches and Writings of Ernesto Che Guevara* (New York, 1968), p. 279.

Suggestions for Further Reading

BIBLIOGRAPHY

Blackey, Robert. *Modern Revolutions and Revolutionists: A Bibliography.* Santa Barbara, Calif.: ABC-Clio Press, 1976.

CHAPTER 1. BACKGROUND OF THE CONCEPT

Arendt, Hannah. *On Revolution.* New York: The Viking Press, 1963.

Calvert, Peter. *Revolution.* New York: Praeger Publishers, 1970.

Davies, James C. (ed.). *When Men Revolt—And Why.* New York: The Macmillan Company, 1971.

Dunn, John. *Modern Revolutions; an introduction to the analysis of a political phenomenon.* New York: Cambridge University Press, 1972.

Edwards, Lyford P. *The Natural History of Revolution.* Chicago: The University of Chicago Press, 1927.

Ellul, Jacques. *Autopsy of Revolution.* Trans. by P. Wolf. New York: Alfred A. Knopf, Inc., 1971.

George, Charles H. *Revolution: European Radicals from Hus to Lenin.* Glenview, Ill.: Scott, Foresman and Company, 1971.

Johnson, Chalmers. *Revolutionary Change.* Boston: Little, Brown and Company, 1966.

Kaplan, Lawrence (ed.). *Revolutions: A Comparative Study.* New York: Random House, Inc., 1973.

Mazlish, Bruce, *et al* (eds.). *Revolution: A Reader.* New York: The Macmillan Company, 1971.

Paynton, Clifford T., and Robert Blackey (eds.). *Why Revolution? Theories and Analyses.* Cambridge, Mass.: Schenkman Publishing Company, Inc., 1971. *New York Times Magazine* (January 17, 1971).

Pettee, George. *The Process of Revolution.* New York: Harper and Row, Publishers, 1938.

Rosenstock-Hussy, E. *Out of Revolution.* New York: W. Morrow and Co., 1938.

CHAPTER 2. VIOLENCE AND STRATEGY IN REVOLUTION

Brinton, Crane. *The Anatomy of Revolution.* Englewood Cliffs: Prentice-Hall, Inc., 1965.

Edwards, Lyford P. *The Natural History of Revolution.* Chicago: The University of Chicago Press, 1927.

Feuer, Lewis S. "Generations and the Theory of Revolution," *Survey* (Summer 1972), 161–188.

Hendin, Herbert. "A Psychoanalyst Looks at Student Revolution," *The New York Times Magazine,* (January 17, 1971).

Hoffer, Eric. *The True Believer.* New York: The New American Library, 1951.

Hopper, Rex D. "The Revolutionary Process: A Frame of Reference for the Study of Revolutionary Movements" in Clifford T. Paynton and Robert Blackey (eds.). *Why Revolution? Theories and Analyses.* Cambridge, Mass.: Schenkman Publishing Company, Inc., 1971.

Nieburg, H. L. *Political Violence: The Behavioral Process.* New York: St. Martin's Press, 1969.

Oberschall, Anthony. *Social Conflict and Social Movements.* Englewood Cliffs: Prentice-Hall, Inc., 1973.

Rejai, Mostafa. *The Strategy of Political Revolution.* Garden City: Doubleday and Company, Inc., 1973.

Rudé, George. *The Crowd in the French Revolution.* London: Oxford University Press, 1959.

Short, Jr., James F., and Marvin E. Wolfgang (eds.). *Collective Violence.* Chicago: Aldine-Atherton, 1972.

Weber, Max. *The Theory of Social and Economic Organization.*Trans. by Talcott Parsons. London: Collier-Macmillan Limited, 1964.

Willner, Ann Ruth, and Dorothy Willner. "The Rise and Role of Charismatic Leaders" in Roland Ye-Lin Cheng (ed.). *The Sociology of Revolution.* Chicago: Henry Regnery Company, 1973.

CHAPTER 3. SOCIAL INSTITUTIONS AND REVOLUTION

Apter, David E. (ed.). *Ideology and Discontent.* Glencoe: The Free Press of Glencoe, 1964.

Berk, Richard A. "The Emergence of Muted Violence in Crowd Behavior" in James F. Short, Jr. and Marvin E. Wolfgang (eds.). *Collective Violence.* Chicago: Aldine-Atherton, 1972.

Cheng, Ronald Ye-Lin. *The Sociology of Revolution: Readings on Political Upheaval and Popular Unrest.* Chicago: Henry Regnery Company, 1973.

Gurr, T. R. "Sources of Rebellion in Western Societies: Some Quantitative Evidence" in James F. Short, Jr. and Marvin E. Wolfgang (eds.). *Collective Violence.* Chicago: Aldine-Atherton, 1972.

Kent, Edward (ed.). *Revolution and the Rule of Law.* Englewood Cliffs: Prentice-Hall, Inc., 1971.

Kuper, Leo. "Theories of Revolution and Race Relations," *Comparative Studies in Society and History,* 13, 1 (January 1972), 87–107.

McPherson, William. *Ideology and Change: Radicalism and Fundamentalism in America.* Palo Alto: National Press Books, 1973.

Nieburg, H. L. "Agonistics: Rituals of Conflict" in James F. Short, Jr. and Marvin E. Wolfgang (eds.). *Collective Violence.* Chicago: Aldine-Atherton, 1972.

CHAPTER 4. SOCIAL-PSYCHOLOGICAL FACTORS IN EXPLANATIONS OF REVOLUTION

Davies, James C. "Toward A Theory of Revolution" in Clifford T. Paynton and Robert Blackey (eds.). *Why Revolution?* Cambridge, Mass. Schenkman Publishing Company, Inc., 1971.

Hopper, Rex D. "The Revolutionary Process" in Clifford T. Paynton and Robert Blackey, *Why Revolution?* Cambridge, Mass.: Schenkman Publishing Company, Inc., 1971.

Johnson, Chalmers. *Revolution and the Social System.* Stanford: The Hoover Institution, 1964.

Lang, Kurt, and Gladys E. Long. *Collective Dynamics.* New York: Thomas Y. Crowell Co., 1961.

Rejai, Mostafa. *The Strategy of Political Revolution.* Garden City: Doubleday and Company, Inc., 1973.

Sorokin, Pitirim A. *The Sociology of Revolution.* Philadelphia: J. P. Lippincott, 1925.

Tsurutani, Taketsuger. "Stability and Instability: A Note in Comparative Political Analysis" in Ronald Ye-Lin Cheng (ed.). *The Sociology of Revolu-*

tion: Readings on Political Upheaval and Popular Unrest. Chicago: Henry Regnery Company, 1973.

Urry, John. *Reference Groups and The Theory of Revolution.* London: Routledge and Keegan Paul Ltd., 1973.

CHAPTER 5. URBANIZATION AND REVOLUTION

Beyer, Glenn H. (ed.). *The Urban Explosion in Latin America: A Continent in Process of Urbanization.* Ithaca: Cornell University Press, 1967.

Breese, Gerald (ed.). *The City in Newly Devoloping Countries: Readings on Urbanism and Urbanization.* Englewood Cliffs: Prentice-Hall, Inc., 1969.

Freedman, Ronald (ed.). *Population: The Vital Revolution.* Garden City: Doubleday and Company, Inc., 1964.

Hatt, Paul K. and Albert J. Reiss, Jr. *Cities and Society: The Revised Reader in Urban Sociology.* New York: The Free Press of Glencoe, Inc., 1957.

Herrick, Bruce H. *Urban Migration and Economic Development in Chile.* Cambridge: Cambridge University Press, 1971.

Millikan, Max F., and Donald L. M. Blackmer (eds.). *The Emerging Nations: Their Growth and United Policy.* Boston: Little Brown and Company, 1961.

Rostow, W. W. *The Stages of Economic Growth: A Non-Communist Manifesto.* Second edition. Cambridge: Cambridge University Press, 1971.

Simic, Andrei. *The Peasant Urbanites: A Study of Rural-Urban Mobility in Serbia.* New York: Seminar Press, 1973.

"Urbanization: Development Policies and Planning," *International Social Development Review,* I. New York: United Nations, 1968.

CHAPTER 6. ON THE EVE OF THE MODERN CONCEPT: THE GREEKS TO THE GLORIOUS REVOLUTION

Aristotle. *Politics and Poetics.* Trans. by B. Jowett and T. Twining. New York: The Viking Press, 1957.

Brinton, Crane. *The Anatomy of Revolution.* New York: Random House, Inc., 1965.

Cohn, Norman. *The Pursuit of the Millennium.* New York: Harper and Row, Publishers, 1961.

Forster, Robert, and Jack P. Greene (eds.). *Preconditions of Revolution in Early Modern Europe.* Baltimore: The Johns Hopkins Press, 1970.

Koenigsberger, H. G. *Estates and Revolutions; Essays in Early Modern European History.* Ithaca: Cornell University Press, 1971.

Locke, John. *Two Treatises of Government.* Ed. by Peter Laslett. Cambridge: Cambridge University Press, 1960.

Merriman, Roger Bigelow. *Six Contemporaneous Revolutions*. Hamden, Conn.: Archon Books, 1963.

Milton, John. *The Tenure of Kings and Magistrates* in *Complete Prose Works of John Milton*. Vol. III. New Haven: Yale University Press, 1962.

Pinkham, Lucille. *William III and the Respectable Revolution*. Cambridge, Mass.: Harvard University Press, 1954.

Straka, Gerald M. (ed.). *The Revolution of 1688*. Lexington, Mass.: D. C. Heath and Company, 1963.

Thucydides. *The Peloponnesian Wars*. Trans. by B. Jowett. New York: Washington Square Press, Inc., 1963.

Walzer, Michael. *The Revolution of the Saints*. New York: Atheneum, 1968.

CHAPTER 7. AGE OF THE DEMOCRATIC REVOLUTION

Alden, J. R. *The American Revolution, 1775–1783*. New York: Harper and Row, Publishers, 1954.

Amann, Peter (ed.). *The Eighteenth-Century Revolution—French or Western?* Lexington, Mass.: D. C. Heath and Company, 1963.

Bailyn, Bernard. *The Ideological Origins of the American Revolution*. Cambridge, Mass.: The Belknap Press of Harvard University Press, 1967.

Gershoy, Leo. *The French Revolution, 1789–1799*. New York: Holt, Rinehart and Winston, 1932.

Godechot, Jacques. *France and the Atlantic Revolution of the Eighteenth Century, 1770–1799*. Trans. by H. H. Rowen. New York: The Free Press, 1965.

Hobsbawm, E. J. *The Age of Revolution, 1789–1848*. New York: The New American Library, Inc., 1962.

Lefebvre, Georges. *The Coming of the French Revolution*. Trans. by R. R. Palmer. Princeton: Princeton University Press, 1947.

Lefebvre, Georges. *The French Revolution from Its Origins to 1799*. Trans. by E. M. Evanson, J. H. Stewart and J. Friguglietti. 2 vols. New York: Columbia University Press, 1962, 1964.

Maier, Pauline. *From Resistance to Revolution; Colonial Radicals and the Development of American Opposition to Britain, 1765–1776*. New York: Alfred A. Knopf, Inc., 1972.

Palmer, R. R. *The Age of the Democratic Revolution; A Political History of Europe and America, 1760–1800*. 2 vols. Princeton: Princeton University Press, 1959, 1964.

CHAPTER 8. REVOLUTION IN THE 19th CENTURY

Duveau, Georges. *1848: The Making of a Revolution.* Trans. by A. Carter. New York: Random House, Inc., 1967.

Hamerow, Theodore S. *Restoration, Revolution, Reaction; Economics and Politics in Germany, 1815–1871.* Princeton: Princeton University Press, 1958.

Jellinek, Frank. *The Paris Commune of 1871.* London: Victor Gollancz Ltd., 1937.

Joll, James. *The Anarchists.* New York: Grosset and Dunlap, 1966.

Kranzberg, Melvin. *The Seige of Paris, 1870–1871.* Ithaca: Cornell University Press, 1950.

Langer, William L. *The Revolutions of 1848.* New York: Harper and Row, Publishers, 1969.

Lougee, Robert W. *Midcentury Revolution, 1848; Society and Revolution in France and Germany.* Lexington, Mass.: D. C. Heath and Company, 1972.

Namier, Lewis. *1848: The Revolution of the Intellectuals.* Garden City: Doubleday and Company, Inc., 1964.

Nomad, Max. *Apostles of Revolution.* New York: Collier Books, 1961.

Robertson, Priscilla. *Revolutions of 1848; A Social History.* Princeton: Princeton University Press, 1952.

Runkle, Gerald. *Anarchism: Old and New.* New York: Dell Publishing Co., Inc., 1972.

Thomas, Emory M. *The Confederacy As A Revolutionary Experience.* Englewood Cliffs: Prentice-Hall, Inc., 1971.

Williams, Roger L. *The French Revolution of 1870–1871.* New York: W. W. Norton and Company, Inc., 1969.

Woodcock, George. *Anarchism.* Cleveland: The World Publishing Company, 1962.

CHAPTER 9. REVOLUTION ACCORDING TO KARL MARX

Avineri, Shlomo. *The Social and Political Thought of Karl Marx.* Cambridge: Cambridge University Press, 1970.

Berlin, Isiah. *Karl Marx: His Life and Environment.* New York: Oxford University Press, 1959.

Carr, Edward H. *Studies in Revolution.* New York: Grosset and Dunlap, 1964.

Davis, Horace B. *Nationalism and Socialism; Marxist and Labor Theories of Nationalism to 1917.* New York: Monthly Review Press, 1967.

Eastman, Max. *Marx and Lenin: The Science of Revolution.* New York: Albert and Charles Boni, 1927.

Hunt, R. N. Carew. *The Theory and Practice of Communism.* Revised and enlarged edition. London: Geoffrey Blas, 1957.

Lichtheim, George. *Marxism: An Historical and Critical Study.* Second edition. New York: Praeger Publishers, 1965.

Marx, Karl. *On Revolution.* Ed. with intro. by Saul K. Padover. New York: McGraw-Hill Book Company, 1971.

Meyer, Alfred G. *Marxism; The Unity of Theory and Practice* Cambridge, Mass.: Harvard University Press, 1954.

Tucker, Robert C. (ed.). *The Marx-Engels Reader.* New York: W. W. Norton and Company, Inc., 1972.

Tucker, Robert C. *The Marxian Revolutionary Idea.* New York: W. W. Norton and Company, Inc., 1969.

Ulam, Adam. *The Unfinished Revolution: An Essay on the Sources of Influence of Marxism and Communism.* New York: Random House, Inc., 1960.

CHAPTER 10. LENIN'S CONCEPT OF REVOLUTION

Christman, Henry M. (ed.). *Essential Works of Lenin.* New York: Bantam Books, Inc., 1966.

Connor, James E. (ed.). *Lenin on Politics and Revolution.* New York: Pegasus, 1968.

Conquest, Robert. *V. I. Lenin.* New York: The Viking Press, 1972.

Deutscher, Isaac (ed.). *The Age of Permanent Revolution: A Trotsky Anthology.* New York: Dell Publishing Co., Inc., 1964.

Fischer, Louis. *The Life of Lenin.* New York: Harper and Row, Publishers, 1964.

Meyer, Alfred G. *Leninism.* New York: Praeger Publishers, 1962.

Morgan, Michael. *Lenin.* Riverside, N. J.: The Free Press, 1973.

Page, Stanley W. *Lenin and World Revolution.* New York: McGraw-Hill Book Company, 1972.

Possony, Stefan T. *Lenin: The Compulsive Revolutionary.* Chicago: Henry Regnery Company, 1964.

Shub, David. *Lenin: A Biography.* Garden City: Doubleday and Company, Inc., 1948.

Shukman, Harold. *Lenin and the Russian Revolution.* New York: G. P. Putnam's Sons, 1967.

Treadgold, Donald W. *Lenin and His Rivals.* New York: Praeger Publishers, 1955.

CHAPTER 11. THE RUSSIAN REVOLUTION

Abramovich, Raphael R. *The Soviet Revolution.* New York: International Universities Press, 1962.

Carr, Edward H. *The Bolshevik Revolution.* 3 vols. Baltimore: Penguin Books, 1966.

Carr, Edward H. *The October Revolution.* New York: Random House, Inc., 1971.

Daniels, Robert V. *Red October: The Bolshevik Revolution of 1917.* New York: Charles Scribner's Sons, 1967.

Hill, Christopher. *Lenin and the Russian Revolution.* Middlesex, Eng.: Penguin Books Ltd., 1971.

Katkov, George. *Russia 1917, The February Revolution.* New York: Harper and Row, Publishers, 1967.

Liebman, Marcel. *The Russian Revolution.* New York: Random House, Inc., 1972.

Melgunov, S. P. *The Bolshevik Seizure of Power.* Trans. by J. S. Beaver. Santa Barbara, Calif.: ABC-Clio Press, 1972.

Pipes, Richard (ed.). *Revolutionary Russia.* Garden City: Doubleday and Company, Inc., 1969.

Russell, Bertrand. *The Practice and Theory of Bolshevism.* London: George Allen and Unwin Ltd., 1920.

Ulam, Adam B. *The Bolsheviks: The Intellectual and Political History of the Triumph of Communism in Russia.* New York: The Macmillan Company, 1965.

Wolfe, Bertram D. *Three Who Made A Revolution.* New York: Dell Publishing Co., Inc., 1964.

CHAPTER 12. NON-LEFT REVOLUTIONS: THE IRISH REVOLUTION, GANDHI'S REVOLUTION, THE NAZI REVOLUTION

Bondurant, Joan V. *Conquest of Violence: The Gandhian Philosophy of Conflict.* Revised edition. Berkeley: University of California Press, 1965.

Dhawan, Gopinath. *The Political Philosophy of Mahatma Gandhi.* Ahmedabad: Navajivan Publishing House, 1957.

Fischer, Louis. *The Life of Mahatma Gandhi.* New York: Harper and Row, Publishers, 1950.

Gandhi, M. K. *Non-Violent Resistance.* New York: Schocken Books, 1961.

Holborn, Hajo (ed.). *Republic to Reich: The Making of the Nazi Revolution.* New York: Random House, Inc., 1973.

McCaffrey, Lawrence J. *The Irish Question, 1800–1922.* Lexington, Ky.: University of Kentucky Press, 1968.

Mansergh, Nicholas. *The Irish Question, 1840–1920.* Revised edition. Toronto: University of Toronto Press, 1966.

O'Farrell, Patrick. *Ireland's English Question: Anglo-Irish Relations, 1534–1970.* New York: Schocken Books, 1971.

Schoenbaum, David. *Hitler's Social Revolution.* Garden City: Doubleday and Company, Inc., 1966.

Snell, John L. (ed.). *The Nazi Revolution.* Lexington, Mass.: D. C. Heath and Company, 1959.

Wheaton, Eliot B. *The Nazi Revolution.* Garden City: Doubleday and Company, Inc., 1968.

Williams, Desmond (ed.). *The Irish Struggle, 1916–1926.* Toronto: University of Toronto Press, 1966.

CHAPTER 13. CHINA IN REVOLUTION: SUN YAT-SEN, MAO TSE-TUNG, AND THE CULTURAL REVOLUTION (I)

Bianco, Lucien. *Origins of the Chinese Revolution, 1915–1949.* Trans. by M. Bell. Stanford: Stanford University Press, 1971.

Chow Tse-tung. *The May Fourth Movement.* Cambridge, Mass.: Harvard University Press, 1960.

Franke, Wolfgang. *A Century of Chinese Revolution, 1851–1949.* Trans. by S. Rudman. New York: Harper and Row, Publishers, 1971.

Gasster, Michael. *Chinese Intellectuals and the Revolution of 1911; The Birth of Modern Chinese Radicalism.* Seattle: University of Washington Press, 1969.

Holcombe, Arthur N. *The Spirit of the Chinese Revolution.* New York: Alfred A. Knopf, Inc., 1930.

H̄seuh, Chun-tu (ed.). *Revolutionary Leaders of Modern China.* New York: Oxford University Press, 1971.

Lee, Ta-ling. *Foundations of the Chinese Revolution, 1905–1912.* New York: St. John's University Press, 1970.

Liang, C. T. *The Chinese Revolution of 1911.* New York: St. John's University Press, 1962.

Mende, Tibor. *The Chinese Revolution.* London: Thames and Hudson, 1961.

Robottom, John. *China in Revolution; From Sun Yat-sen to Mao Tse-tung.* New York: McGraw-Hill Book Company, 1969.

Simone, Vera (ed.). *China in Revolution; History, Documents, and Analysis.* Greenwich, Conn.: Fawcett Publications, Inc., 1968.

Ssu-yü Teng and John K. Fairbanks (eds.). *China's Response To The West; A Documentary Survey, 1839–1923.* Cambridge, Mass.: Harvard University Press, 1961.

CHAPTER 14. CHINA IN REVOLUTION: SUN YAT-SEN, MAO TSE-TUNG, AND THE CULTURAL REVOLUTION (II)

An, Tai Sung. *Mao Tse-tung's Cultural Revolution.* Indianapolis: Pegasus, 1972.

Bulletin of the Atomic Scientists, The. *China After the Cultural Revolution.* New York: Random House, Inc., 1969.

Ch'ên, Jerome. *Mao and the Chinese Revolution.* London: Oxford University Press, 1965.

Cohen, Arthur A. *The Communism of Mao Tse-tung.* Chicago: The University of Chicago Press, 1964.

Harrison, James Pinckney. *The Long March to Power; A History of the Chinese Communist Party, 1921–72.* New York: Praeger Publishers, 1972.

Hinton, William. *Turning Point in China; An Essay on the Cultural Revolution.* New York: Monthly Review Press, 1972.

Hsiung, James C. *Ideology and Practice; The Evolution of Chinese Communism.* New York: Praeger Publishers, 1970.

Johnson, Chalmers A. *Peasant Nationalism and Communist Power; The Emergence of Revolutionary China, 1937–1945.* Stanford: Stanford University Press, 1962.

Karol, K. S. *China; The Other Communism.* Trans. by T. Barstow. Second edition. New York: Hill and Wang, 1968.

Rejai, M. (ed.). *Mao Tse-tung on Revolution and War.* Garden City: Doubleday and Company, Inc., 1969.

Robinson, Thomas W. (ed.). *The Cultural Revolution in China.* Berkeley: University of California Press, 1971.

Schram, Stuart R. *Mao Tse-tung.* Baltimore: Penguin Books, Inc., 1967.

Schram, Stuart R. (ed.). *The Political Thought of Mao Tse-tung.* Revised and enlarged edition. New York: Praeger Publishers, 1969.

Snow, Edgar. *Red Star Over China.* Revised edition. New York: Grove Press, Inc., 1968.

CHAPTER 15. LATIN AMERICAN REVOLUTIONS AND REVOLUTIONISTS: MEXICO

Burr, Robert N. (ed.). *Latin America's Nationalistic Revolutions.* Philadelphia: The American Academy of Political and Social Science, 1961.

Cline, Howard F. *Mexico; Revolution to Evolution, 1940–1960.* London: Oxford University Press, 1952.

Cumberland, Charles C. (ed.). *The Meaning of the Mexican Revolution.* Lexington, Mass.: D. C. Heath and Company, 1967.

Cumberland, Charles C. *Mexican Revolution; Genesis Under Madero.* Austin: University of Texas Press, 1952.

Cumberland, Charles C. *The Struggle for Modernity.* New York: Oxford University Press, 1968.

Edelmann, Alexander T. *Latin American Government and Politics; The Dynamics of a Revolutionary Society.* Revised edition. Homewood, Ill.: The Dorsey Press, 1969.

Ferguson, J. Halcro. *The Revolutions of Latin America.* London: Thames and Hudson, 1963.

Quirk, Robert E. *The Mexican Revolution, 1914–1915.* New York: W. W. Norton and Company, Inc., 1970.

Ross, Stanley R. (ed.). *Is the Mexican Revolution Dead?* New York: Alfred A. Knopf, Inc., 1966.

Tannenbaum, Frank. *Mexico: The Struggle for Peace and Bread.* New York: Alfred A. Knopf, Inc., 1962.

Tannenbaum, Frank. *Peace By Revolution: Mexico After 1910.* New York: Columbia University Press, 1933.

Villegas, Daniel Cosío. *Change in Latin America: The Mexican and Cuban Revolutions.* Lincoln, Neb.: The University of Nebraska Press, 1961.

Wilkie, James W., and Albert L. Michaels (eds.). *Revolution in Mexico: Years of Upheaval, 1910-1940.* New York: Alfred A. Knopf, Inc., 1969.

Womack, Jr., John. *Zapata and the Mexican Revolution.* New York: Random House, Inc., 1968.

CHAPTER 16. LATIN AMERICAN REVOLUTIONS AND REVOLUTIONISTS: CUBA, CASTRO, CHE

Draper, Theodore. *Castroism; Theory and Practice.* New York: Frederick A. Praeger, Publishers, 1965.

Draper, Theodore. *Castro's Revolution; Myths and Realities.* New York: Praeger Publishers, 1962.

Goldenberg, Boris. *The Cuban Revolution and Latin America.* New York: Frederick A. Praeger, Publishers, 1965.

Green, Gil. *Revolution, Cuban Style.* New York: International Publishers, 1970.

Guevara, Che. *Guerrilla Warfare.* Trans. by J. P. Morray. New York: Random House, Inc., 1969.

Huberman, Leo, and Paul M. Sweezy. *Cuba; Anatomy of a Revolution.* Second edition. New York: Monthly Review Press, 1968.

James, Daniel. *Che Guevara.* New York: Stein and Day, Publishers, 1969.

Karol, K. S. *Guerrillas in Power; The Course of the Cuban Revolution.* Trans. by A. Pomerans. New York: Hill and Wang, 1970.

Lockwood, Lee. *Castro's Cuba; Cuba's Fidel.* New York: The Macmillan Company, 1967.

MacGaffey, Wyatt, and Clifford Barnett. *Twentieth Century Cuba: The Background of the Castro Revolution.* Garden City: Doubleday and Company, Inc., 1965.

Matthews, Herbert L. *Fidel Castro.* New York: Simon and Schuster, 1969.

Mills, C. Wright. *Listen Yankee; The Revolution in Cuba.* New York: Ballantine Books, Inc., 1960.

Ruiz, Ramon Eduardo. *Cuba; The Making of a Revolution.* New York: W. W. Norton and Company, Inc., 1970.

Sinclair, Andrew. *Che Guevara.* New York: The Viking Press, 1970.

CHAPTER 17. LATIN AMERICAN REVOLUTIONS AND REVOLUTIONISTS: CHE IN BOLIVIA, DEBRAY, CHILE

Alba, Víctor. *The Latin Americans.* New York: Frederick A. Praeger, Publishers, 1969.

Alexander, Robert J. *The Bolivian National Revolution.* New Brunswick: Rutgers University Press, 1958.

Calvert, Peter. *Latin America: Internal Conflict and International Peace.* New York: St. Martin's Press, 1969.

Debray, Régis. *The Chilean Revolution; Conversations with Allende.* New York: Random House, Inc., 1971.

Debray, Régis. *Revolution in the Revolution? Armed Struggle and Political Struggle in Latin America.* Trans. B. Ortiz. New York: Grove Press, Inc., 1967.

Debray, Régis. *Strategy For Revolution; Essays on Latin America.* Ed. by R. Blackburn. New York: Monthly Review Press, 1970.

The Diary of Che Guevara; Bolivia: November 7, 1966–October 7, 1967. Ed. by R. Scheer. New York: Bantam Books, 1968.

Feinberg, Richard E. *The Triumph of Allende: Chile's Legal Revolution.* New York: The New American Library, 1972.

González, Luis, and Gustavo Sánchez Salazar. *The Great Rebel: Che Guevara in Bolivia.* New York: Grove Press, Inc., 1969.

Gott, Richard. *Guerrilla Movements in Latin America.* Garden City: Doubleday and Company, Inc., 1971.

Harris, Richard. *Death of a Revolutionary; Che Guevara's Last Mission.* New York: The Macmillan Company, 1971.

Huberman, Leo, and Paul M. Sweezy (eds.). *Régis Debray and the Latin American Revolution.* New York: Monthly Review Press, 1968.

Mallin, Jay (ed.). *"Che" Guevara On Revolution.* New York: Dell Publishing Co., Inc., 1969.

Morris, David J. *We Must Make Haste—Slowly: The Process of Revolution in Chile.* New York: Random House, Inc., 1973.

CHAPTER 18. AFRICAN REVOLUTIONS AND REVOLUTIONISTS: GUINEA-BISSAU AND CABRAL

Blackey, Robert. "Fanon and Cabral: A Contrast in Theories of Revolution for Africa," *The Journal of Modern African Studies,* XII, 2 (June 1974), 191-209.

Cabral, Amilcar. *Revolution in Guinea.* Trans. and ed. by R. Handyside. New york: Monthly Review Press, 1969.

Cameron, James. *The African Revolution.* New York: Random House, Inc., 1961.

Chaliand, Gérard. *Armed Struggle in Africa.* Trans. by D. Rattray and R. Leonhardt. New York: Monthly Review Press, 1969.

Davidson, Basil. *The Liberation of Guiné; Aspects of an African Revolution.* Baltimore: Penguin Books, 1969.

Gibson, Richard. *African Liberation Movements.* New York: Oxford University Press, 1972.

Grundy, Kenneth W. *Guerrilla Struggle in Africa.* New York: The Viking Press, 1972.

Howe, Russell Warren. *The African Revolution.* New York: Harper and Row, Publishers, 1969.

Miller, Norman, and Roderick Aya (eds.). *National Liberation; Revolution in the Third World.* New York: The Free Press, 1971.

Nasser, Gamal Abdul. *Egypt's Liberation; The Philosophy of the Revolution.* Washington: Public Affairs Press, 1955.

Nkrumah, Kwame. *Consciencism; Philosophy and Ideology for De-Colonization.* Revised edition. New York: Monthly Review Press, 1970.

Rothberg, Robert I. (ed.). *Rebellion in Black Africa.* London: Oxford University Press, 1971.

Sigmund, Paul E. (ed.). *The Ideologies of the Developing Nations.* Revised edition. New York: Frederick A. Praeger, Publishers, 1967.

CHAPTER 19. AFRICAN REVOLUTIONS AND
REVOLUTIONISTS: ALGERIA AND FANON

Bourdieu, Pierre. *The Algerians.* Trans. by A. C. M. Ross. Boston: Beacon Press, 1962.

Caute, David. *Frantz Fanon.* New York: The Viking Press, 1970.

Clark, Michael K. *Algeria in Turmoil; The Rebellion, Its Causes, Its Effects, Its Future.* New York: Grosset and Dunlap, 1960.

Fanon, Frantz. *Toward the African Revolution.* New York: Grove Press, Inc., 1967.

Fanon, Frantz. *The Wretched of the Earth.* New York: Grove Press, Inc., 1966.

Geismar, Peter. *Fanon; The Revolutionary as Prophet.* New York: Grove Press, Inc., 1971.

Gendzier, Irene L. *Frantz Fanon; A Critical Study.* New York: Pantheon Books, 1973.

Gillespie, Joan. *Algeria; Rebellion and Revolution.* New York: Frederick A. Praeger, Publishers, 1960.

Gordon, David C. *The Passing of French Algeria.* London: Oxford University Press, 1966.

Henissart, Paul. *Wolves in the City; The Death of French Algeria.* New York: Simon and Schuster, 1970.

Humbaraci, Arslan. *Algeria: A Revolution That Failed.* New York: Frederick A. Praeger, Publishers, 1966.

Ottaway, David and Marina. *Algeria; The Politics of a Socialist Revolution.* Berkeley: University of California Press, 1970.

Quandt, William B. *Revolution and Political Leadership: Algeria, 1954–1968.* Cambridge, Mass.: The M.I.T. Press, 1969.

Trevelyan, Humphrey. *The Middle East in Revolution.* Boston: Gambit, 1971.

CHAPTER 20. THE VIETNAMESE REVOLUTION

Bain, Chester A. *Vietnam: The Roots of Conflict.* Englewood Cliffs: Prentice-Hall, Inc., 1967.

Burchett, Wilfrid. *Vietnam: Inside Story of the Guerrilla War.* New York: International Publishers, 1965.

Buttinger, Joseph. *A Dragon Defiant: A Short History of Vietnam.* New York: Praeger Publishers, 1972.

Buttinger, Joseph. *Vietnam: A Dragon Embattled.* New York: Frederick A. Praeger, Publishers, 1967.

Duncanson, Dennis J. *Government and Revolution in Vietnam.* New York: Oxford University Press, 1968.

Fall, Bernard (ed.). *Ho Chi Minh on Revolution.* New York: Signet Books, 1968.

Halberstam, David. *Ho.* New York: Random House, Inc., 1971.

Lacouture, Jean. *Ho Chi Minh; A Political Biography.* New York: Random House, Inc., 1968.

McAlister, Jr., John T. *Viet Nam: The Origins of Revolution.* Garden City: Doubleday and Company, Inc., 1971.

McAlister, Jr., John T., and Paul Mus. *The Vietnamese and Their Revolution.* New York: Harper and Row, Publishers, 1970.

Purcell, Victor. *The Revolution in Southeast Asia.* London: Thames and Hudson, 1962.

Race, Jeffrey. *War Comes to Long An; Revolutionary Conflict in a Vietnamese Province.* Berkeley: University of California Press, 1972.

Shaplen, Robert. *The Lost Revolution: Vietnam, 1945–1965.* New York: Harper and Row, Publishers, 1965.

Vo Nguyen Giap. *People's War, People's Army.* New York: Frederick A. Praeger, Publishers, 1962.

CHAPTER 21. THE NEW LEFT IN AMERICA:
MARCUSE AND MIXED COMPANY

Aya, Roderick, and Norman Miller (eds.). *The New American Revolution.* New York: The Free Press, 1971.

Berger, Peter L., and Richard J. Neuhaus. *Movement and Revolution.* Garden City: Doubleday and Company, Inc., 1970.

Cranston, Maurice (ed.). *The New Left: Six Critical Essays.* New York: The Library Press, 1971.

Hope, Marjorie. *The New Revolutionaries.* Boston: Little, Brown and Company, 1970.

Howe, Irving (ed.). *Beyond the New Left.* New York: The McCall Publishing Company, 1970.

Keniston, Kenneth. *Youth and Dissent: The Rise of a New Opposition.* New York: Harcourt Brace Jovanovich, 1971.

Lasch, Christopher. *The Agony of the American Left.* New York: Random House, Inc., 1969.

Lothstein, Arthur (ed.). *"All We Are Saying . . ." The Philosophy of the New Left.* New York: Capricorn Books, 1971.

Marcuse, Herbert. *An Essay on Liberation.* Boston: Beacon Press, 1969.

Marcuse, Herbert. *Counterrevolution and Revolt.* Boston: Beacon Press, 1972.

Sears, David O., and John B. McConahay. *The Politics of Violence: The New Urban Blacks and the Watts Riot.* Boston: Houghton Mifflin Company, 1973.

Short, Jr., James F., and Marvin E. Wolfgang (eds.). *Collective Violence.* Chicago: Aldine-Atherton Inc., 1972.

INDEX

Adams, John, 76-77
Administrator-Executive, see Leaders, Types of
Africa (Africans), 2, 51-52, 56, 59, 123, 141, 208-18, 225-32
Agitator, see Leaders, Types of
Agrarian Revolution, see Revolution, Types of, Rural (Agrarian) Revolution
Aleppo, 52
Algeria (Algerians), 14, 46, 83, 212-13, 221-26
Algerian Revolution, 14, 46, 142, 209, 221-26, 230
Algiers, 224
Allende, Salvador, 190, 203-05
Amann, Peter, 6
America (American), 2, 31-32, 49, 55, 74-78, 81, 83-84, 108, 152, 160, 183-84, 187, 190, 203, 234, 238, 241, 244, 249, 251-57, 259-60, 267, 269
American Civil War, 6, 45, 90-91
American Communist Party, 256
American Revolution, 2, 46, 74-84, 173, 269
Anabaptist, 66
Anarchism, Anarchists, 1, 45, 90, 93, 94-98, 111-12
Angola, 213, 219
Annam, 233
Anti-colonial Revolution, see Revolution, Types of
Arabs, 209, 222, 226
Argentina, 183, 191
Aristocracy (Nobility, Privileged Classes, Upper Class), 63, 68, 70, 74, 80, 87-89, 105, 134, 182, 190, 198, 203, 205, 238, 254
Aristotle, 63-64, 72; *Politics*, 63, 86, 267
Army, see Military
Army of National Liberation (ALN), 224
Aryan, 148
Asia (Asians), 2, 52-53, 56, 123, 141, 157, 210, 237
Astronomy Phase of Revolution, see Revolution, Phases of
Augsburg, Peace of, 66
August Revolution, 239
Australia, 256
Austria, 88

Backward Countries (Areas), see Underdeveloped Areas
Bacon, Frances, 72
Bakunin, Mikhail, 95-97, 110, 263

Batista, Fulgencio, 22, 175, 183-86, 189-90, 193
Belgium, 79
Ben Bella, Mohammed, 225
Bernstein, Eduard, 115-16, 118
Biafra, 212
Bible, 104, 243
Black Africa, 226
Blacks (American), 12, 14, 32-33, 143, 228, 256, 269,
Blanqui, Louis, 92-94, 106, 120
Boa Dai, 238
Bolivia, 15, 22, 174-76, 191-94, 196-98, 206
Bolivian Revolution, 25-26, 174-76, 183, 196-97
Bolsheviks, Bolshevik Party, 107, 112, 120-21, 134-36, 138, 267
Bourgeois Revolution, see Revolution, Types of
Bourgeoisie (Middle Class), 21-23, 33, 55, 68, 80, 87-89, 91, 93-94, 96, 98-99, 104-09, 112, 114-15, 118-19, 122-23, 125-26, 130-36, 151, 159-63, 169, 174-75, 183-86, 190, 192, 199-200, 203-05, 210, 217-18, 221, 230-31, 245, 247, 252
Brinton, Crane, 43
British, 141-43
Burke, Edmund, 83, 267
Cabral, Amilcar, 209, 214-19, 227, 229-31
Calvin, John, 66, 69, 116, 266, 269
Calvinism, 68, 157
Cambodia, 53, 234
Canada, 14
Cape Verde Islands, 214
Capitalism, Capitalist, 68, 94, 102-03, 106-07, 109-10, 112, 114-17, 119, 122-23, 124, 126, 130-32, 136, 138, 153-54, 156, 160-61, 166, 168-69, 171, 177, 179-80, 187, 190, 199, 210-11, 213, 216, 226, 228, 244-52, 254
Cárdenas, Lázaro, 178
Caribbean, 226
Castro, Fidel, 4, 21, 25, 176, 184-91, 193-94, 199-201, 206, 244, 269
Castroism, 188-89
Catalonia, 66-67
Catholic, 141-43
Catholic Church, 65-66, 173, 177, 183
Charisma, 18-19, 21, 26, 50, 188-89, 191

Charismatic Leader, see Leaders, Types of
Chartists, 109
Charles II, 72
Chiang Kai-shek, 155-56
Chile, 174, 190, 202-06
Chilean Revolution, 203-06
China (Chinese), 46, 54, 83, 112, 149-58, 159-71, 185, 199, 217-18, 229, 234, 252
Chinese Communist Party (CCP), 8, 154-57, 161-70
Chinese Communist Revolution, 25, 46, 134, 154-58, 160-70, 175, 252
Chinese National Revolution (1911), 23-24, 151-55
Christ, Jesus, 112, 144, 268
Christian, 143, 212
Christianity, 140
Churchill, Winston, 19
Cities, see Urbanization
Civil Disobedience, 143-45
Class, 6, 13, 21-23, 33-34, 37, 40, 42, 46, 51, 57, 60, 64, 68, 86, 91-92, 95, 97-98, 102, 104-12, 114-19, 121, 123, 125-26, 135, 138, 154, 157, 160, 162, 166, 169, 176-77, 184-86, 188, 200, 203-04, 211, 216-18, 228-31, 245-46, 248-49, 252
Cleaver, Eldridge, 225
Cochin China, 233
Cold War, 184, 211
Colonial, Colonization, Colonialism, 174, 215-18, 224, 226-32, 234-35, 240
Colons, 222-25
Colony, Colonies, 123-24, 143, 159-60, 167, 174, 222, 224-25, 227-29
Committee of Public Safety, 81
Communism, Communists, 29, 71, 94, 97, 102, 105, 110-11, 124, 131, 138, 154, 169-70, 185-87, 190-91, 204, 210-13, 228, 234-41, 243, 248, 256, 266, 268
Communist Party, 105, 169, 189, 191, 197, 199-200, 211, 246
Communist Revolution, see Revolution, Types of
Communist Youth League, 168, 170
Communocracy, 211
Condorcet, 82
Confucian, 153, 155, 167
Congo, The, 213
Consciencism, 211
Conservatives, 13, 65-68, 70, 88-89, 90, 103, 155, 173, 205, 250

Conspiracy, 86, 94, 106, 118, 120, 145, 243
Constitution of 1917 (Mexico), 179
Contagion, 74, 87, 95
Copernicus, Nicholas, 72
Counterrevolution, 46-47, 88, 135, 145, 169, 190, 197, 205, 250, 269
Countryside, see Rural Activity
Coup d'etat, 46, 119, 172-74, 189, 197, 203-05, 213
Cromwell, Oliver, 69, 269
Cuba (Cubans), 25, 83, 174-76, 182-94, 197-200, 206, 252
Cuban Communists, 184-85, 187, 189, 191, 200
Cuban Revolution, 25-26, 174-76, 182-94, 196, 199, 202, 206, 244, 252
Cultural Revolution, 161, 168-71
Damascus, 52
Davis, Jefferson, 91
Deacons of Justice, 257
Debray, Regis, 196, 198-203, 206, 215, 219, 230, 244; Revolution in the Revolution?, 198, 200, 202
Declaration of Independence, 77, 239
Declaration of Independence of the Democratic Republic of Viet Nam, 239
Declaration of the Rights of Man and the Citizen, 81, 239
Déclassés, see Lumpenproletariat
Decolonization, 227-29, 232
De Gaulle, Charles, 19
Dehumanization, 13-14, 15, 162, 211, 250, 252, 263
Democracy, Democratic, 115, 120, 125, 135, 136, 144, 150-52, 155, 159-63, 173, 175-76, 178, 180-81, 185-86, 189, 197, 199, 204, 206, 224, 236, 241, 251
Democratic Republic of Viet Nam (North Viet Nam), 235
Democratic Revolution, see Revolution, Types of
Destructive Revolutionists, see Revolutionists, Types of
Developing Nations, see Third World
Diaz, Porfirio, 176-78
Dien Bien Phu, 237, 239-40
Dutch Revolt, 66-68, 78

East, Eastern, 149, 167, 211
Easter Rebellion, 141-42
Economics, 7, 13, 33-34, 37, 40-41, 47, 50-51, 53-54, 56, 59-60, 64, 67-68, 72, 94-95, 98, 102, 107, 109, 111-12,

116-17, 121-24, 131-32, 136, 138, 141, 145, 152-53, 155, 160, 163-64, 168-70, 172-75, 177-81, 183-84, 186-90, 193, 197-98, 203, 205-06, 209-10, 212-13, 215-16, 223, 226-27, 231, 235, 245, 252, 254-55, 257, 263
Edwards, Lyford P., 43
Egypt, 62, 211
  1848, Revolutions of, 87-90, 102, 108
  1830, Revolutions of, 87
Elite (Revolutionary) Party, 80, 93-94, 104-05, 116-17, 119-22, 127, 130-31, 133-35, 138, 162, 164, 167, 192, 199-201, 212, 229-30, 249
Ellwood, Charles, 7
el Moudjahid, 225-26
Engels, Friedrich, 1, 5, 101-02, 104, 108-09, 118, 125-26, 132
England (English), 8, 14, 67, 69, 72, 75-78, 83, 108-09, 131, 141, 179, 222, 266-67
English Revolution, see Puritan Revolution
Enlightenment, 78-81, 94, 105
Established Authority, see Government
Estates General, 80
Europe (Europeans), 2, 49, 53, 65, 71, 81-82, 87-88, 92, 94, 96, 109, 116-17, 122-23, 124, 136-37, 143, 157, 160, 173, 209-10, 213, 218, 225-26, 230-32, 237, 243, 254, 267
Evian, 225
Fall, Bernard, 237
Fanon, Frantz, 12, 14, 209, 212, 218-19, 225-32, 244, 263, 269; *The Wretched of the Earth*, 226-27
Facism, Fascist, 71, 91
February Revolution, see Russian Revolution (1917)
Feudalism, Feudal, 103, 109, 132, 160-61, 163, 168, 224, 236
First Indochina War, 234-35
First International, 108
Foco, 192, 198-202, 206, 215
Followers, Followership, 7, 15, 16, 18-19, 21-24, 25, 36, 45, 59
Florence, 65
Fort Moncada, 184, 191
France (French), 5, 6, 47, 66, 70, 80, 82-83, 84, 88, 92, 109, 131, 173, 198, 221-27, 233-40, 266-67
Frankfurt Parliament, 89
Frei, Eduardo, 204
French Revolution (1789), 2, 6, 24, 46, 74-84, 85-88, 93-94, 105, 109, 131,

160, 173, 266-67
French Revolution (1830), 45, 87, 109
French Revolution (1871), see Paris Commune
Freudain, 269
Fronde, 66-67
Fundamental Rights of the German People, 89

Galileo, 72
Gandhi, Mohandas, 19, 141, 143-47, 244, 263
General Strike, 99, 133
Gėneva, 78
Geneva Conference of 1954, 235, 240
German Revolution (1848), 88-89
Germany (Germans), 65-66, 88-89, 92, 136, 147-48, 222, 244
Ghana, 211, 213
Glorious Revolution, 67, 70-71, 72-73, 79
Goldman Emma, 97
Gottschalk, Louis, 6
Government, State, Ruling Class, Established Authority, 4, 6-7, 16, 27-28, 36, 40-41, 45-46, 48, 50, 55, 57, 63-64, 67-68, 71-72, 74, 76-78, 80-81, 83, 85-86, 88, 90, 92, 95-99, 105-08, 112, 114-16, 120, 123, 125-27, 130-135, 137, 141-43, 145-47, 150-52, 154-55, 159-61, 164-66, 170-71, 173-81, 182-83, 185-86, 188-90, 192-93, 197-200, 202-06, 213, 216-18, 222, 224, 235-41, 243, 246, 252, 254-55, 260, 263, 268, 270
Great Britain, 141, 143, 152, 166, 227
Greeks, 1, 49, 62-65, 263
Guerrilla Warfare, Guerrillas, 31, 60, 143, 145, 156-57, 164-65, 185-86, 189, 192-93, 197-206, 214-15, 224, 227, 230, 240, 259
Guevara, Ernesto "Che", 12, 15, 22, 174, 188, 190-94, 196-201, 205-06, 215, 219, 229-30, 244, 263, 268-70; *Guerrilla Warfare*, 192
Guinea, 211
Guinea-Bissau, 208-09, 211-15, 217, 219
Guinea-Bissau, Revolution in, 215-19
Hanoi, 235, 256
Hegel, 103
Haiti, 173
Havana, 184, 187, 198, 256
Hitler, Adolph, 19, 91, 147, 269
Hobbes, Thomas, 72
Ho Chi Minh, 188, 194, 236-37, 239-40,

244, 269
Hoffer, Eric, 34, 265
Hoffman, Abbie, 17, 31
Holland, 68
Home rule, 90, 141-42
Holy Roman Empire, 65
Hopper, Rex, 43-44
Hsing Chung-hui, 151
Hugo, Victor, 6
Humanistic Phase of Revolution, see Revolution. Phases of Hunan, 163
Hungary, 88

Ideal Revolutionists, see Revolutionists, Types of Ideology, 2, 17, 24-26, 28, 33, 43, 45-46, 77-78, 92-93, 104, 109, 117, 130-31, 140-41, 143, 147-48, 154, 161, 166, 168, 175, 177, 179, 186-87, 189, 191, 200-01, 210-12, 225, 228-30, 236-37, 240, 251, 258
Imperial Knights, Revolt of, 65-66
Imperialism, Imperialist, 123-24, 130-31, 152-53, 157, 160-61, 166, 168, 175, 183, 186-87, 190, 200, 209, 213, 215-19, 221, 226-27, 235-36, 240, 252, 268
India (Indians), 143-47, 234
Indian National Congress, 146
Indians (American), 75
Indochina, 234
Indochinese (Vietnamese) Communist Party, 236-40
Industrial Revolution, 85, 94, 102
Institutions (Social), 1, 13, 20, 22, 24, 29-37, 40, 44, 77, 79, 82, 96, 110, 114, 150-51, 169-70, 180, 183, 189, 239, 244, 246, 248, 250, 252-56, 260, 263
Intellectuals, 87, 93-94, 99, 105-06, 112, 118-19, 131, 138, 150, 154-55, 160, 164, 199-200, 210, 221, 227, 229, 235, 243, 247-48, 250, 266
Iraq, 52
Ireland (Irish), 14, 46, 141-43
Irish Free State, 141
Irish Republican Army (I.R.A.), 14, 142
Irish Revolution, 46, 78, 140-43
Iskra, 118
Islam, 211-13, 223, 225
Islamic Revolutionists, see Revolutionists, Types of
Israel, 52
Italy, 65-66, 72, 88

Jacobin Communist Revolution, see Revolution, Types of
Jacobins, 81-82, 93

Jacquerie, 45
Japan (Japanese), 23, 134, 150-51, 161, 165-66, 234, 236-37, 239
Jefferson, Thomas, 64, 77
Jeffersonian, 267
Jews, 148
Johnson, Chalmers, 45
Johnson, Lyndon, 12, 258
Jordan, 52

Kamenka, Eugene, 7
Kashmir, 146
Kautsky, Karl, 4
Kazakhstan, 54
Kennedy, John F., 19
Khrushchev, Nikita, 131
Kropotkin, Peter, 95-96
Kuomintang, 151-52, 154-56, 165-66, 170
Kuwait, 52

Labor, 98, 123
Language of Revolution, 264-65
Laos, 234
Latin America, Latin Americans, 2, 46, 52-53, 55-56, 83, 123, 141, 172-76, 182-83, 185-86, 188-92, 194, 198-206, 209-10, 255, 269
Leaders, Leadership, 4, 7, 15, 16-21, 22, 25-28, 36, 44-45, 46, 50, 56-57, 67-68, 89, 93, 95, 105, 111, 118, 120, 130, 133, 144, 150, 154, 160, 162, 164-66, 169-70, 173, 175-77, 180, 183, 185, 188-89, 191-92, 199-200, 208, 210, 215, 217, 219, 223, 229, 231, 237-38, 265, 269
Leaders, Types of
  Administrator-Executive, 21, 188
  Agitator of Man of Words, 20, 33-34, 47, 52-53, 88, 256
  Charismatic Leader, 18-19, 21
  Practical Man of Action, Reformer or Statesman, 20-21, 188
  Prophet or Fanatic, 13, 20, 188
League for the Independence of Viet Nam, see Viet Minh
Leary, Timothy, 225
Lebanon, 52
Lee, Robert E., 91
Left, 140, 204, 206, 230, 243-44, 252, 257, 260
Legitimacy, 35-36, 41, 78, 162, 176, 190, 237, 255
Linin, V. I., 25, 92, 103, 106-07, 112, 114-27, 129-38, 154, 156-57, 160-64, 167, 188, 191-92, 194, 205, 227-29,

236, 244-45, 267-69; *State and Revolution*, 125, 127
Leninism Leninist, 118, 123, 130, 153, 156, 188, 199, 251
Leopoldville, 59
Lippman, Walter, 49
Lisbon, 214
Locke, John, 64, 69-71, 76-77, 86, 131; *Two Treaties of Government*, 70, 72
Long March, 165, 170, 201, 246
London, 108
Louis XVI, 5, 82
L'Ouverture, Toussaint, 173
Lumpenproletariat, 106, 218, 230, 247
Luther, Martin, 66, 266
Lutheran, 267

Maceo, Antoneo, 186
Machiavelli, 65, 72
Madero, Francisco, 175-78
Mali, 213
Manchu, 149-53, 156
Maoism, Maoists, 157, 188, 194, 251-52
Mao Tse-tung, 11, 122, 148, 154-58, 159-71, 188, 191, 194, 229, 244-45, 269
Marcuse, Herbert, 244-51, 263, 268
Marian Exiles, 69
Martí, José, 186
Martinique, 226
Marx, Karl, 1, 5, 25, 41, 84, 86-87, 92-94, 101-12, 114-18, 121-27, 129-30, 132-33, 135-38, 140, 156-57, 162-63, 191-92, 204, 211, 227-30, 245-46, 250-51, 263, 266, 268-69; *Communist Manifesto*, 104-05, 121; *Theses on Feuerbach*, 5
Marxism, 40, 90, 93, 98, 101-12, 114-18, 121-24, 129-30, 133, 154, 156-57, 161-62, 167, 204, 206, 225, 229-30, 236-37, 266, 268
Marxism-Leninism, 121, 125, 154-58, 161-64, 167, 169, 189, 191, 194, 201, 211, 228, 236, 266
Marxist, Marxian, 92-93, 97, 115, 117, 122, 124-26, 132, 159, 163, 186-87, 194, 198-201, 203-04, 218, 228, 245, 250-52, 266-68
Marxist-Leninist Revolutionists, see Revolutionists, Types of
Mary Tudor, 69
May Fourth Movement, 155
Medici, 65
Mediterranean Sea, 222
Mensheviks, Menshevik Party, 112, 120, 132-34

Mexican Revolution, 25-26, 46, 174-81, 183, 187, 206
Mexico (Mexicans), 174-81, 187, 190-91
Middle Ages, 64
Middle Class, see Bourgeoisie
Middle East, 46, 52, 141, 269
Military, 63, 70, 135, 151-52, 157, 164-65, 167, 173, 175-77, 182-83, 185-86, 192-93, 196-206, 213-15, 219, 221, 223-24, 234, 238-40, 246, 252
Mill, John Stuart, 270
Millenarianism, 45, 71, 94
Milton, John, 69, 76, 86
Minorities (Ethnic Groups), 13-15, 32-33, 35, 42, 46, 54-55, 57, 143, 243, 248, 250, 253, 256, 258-60
Minute Men, 257
Mode of production, 103, 110-11, 209
Modernization, 51, 109, 151-52, 154, 168, 189, 209-10, 267
Morocco, 222
Moscow, 135, 256
Moslem, 209, 213, 222
Movimiento Nacionalista Revolucionario, 196
Mozambique, 213, 219
Münster, Kingdom of, 66
Mus, Paul, 237, 239
Mussolini, 91, 269
Myth, 99, 266

Nacheyev, Sergei, 96
Naples, 66-67, 72
Napoleon, 6, 82
Napoleon III, 91
Nasser, Gamal Abdul, 158, 211-12
National Assembly (France), 91, 93
National Assembly (Guinea-Bissau), 215
National Convention (France), 81, 83
National Guard (Paris), 91
National Liberation Front (FLN), 223-25
National Liberation Revolutionists, see Revolutionists, Types of
Nationalism, Nationalist, 45-46, 85, 90-92, 115, 119, 125, 134, 141-42, 150-55, 157, 161, 167, 174-75, 183-84, 186, 194, 197-98, 210-12, 215, 217, 221-23, 225, 227, 230-31, 234, 236-37, 252-53, 267-68
Nationalist Revolution, see Revolution, Types of
NATO, 214
Natural Phase of Revolution, see Revolution, Phases of
Nazi, Nazism, 91, 141, 147-48, 248
Nazi Revolution, 141, 147-48

291

Negative Revolutionists, see Revolutionists, Types of
Neru, Jawaharlal, 146
Neo-colonial, Neo-colonialism, 187, 215-18, 227
Netherlands Revolution, see Dutch Revolt
Neumann, Sigmund, 7, 124
New Democracy, 160-61
New Left, 7, 228, 243-44, 251-53
New Man, 76, 98, 121, 147, 168, 171, 193, 216, 228, 232, 248-49, 263-66
New Model Army, 70
New Order (or Society), 103, 105, 108, 110-11, 117, 121, 126, 130, 147, 165, 169, 193, 200, 216, 229, 232, 235, 252, 262-63, 265-66
Ngo Dinh Diem, 238
Nguyen Van Thieu, 238
Nigeria, 212
Nixon, Richard, 12, 241
Nkrumah, Kwame, 158, 211-12
Nobility, see Aristocracy
Non-recognition, 15
Non-violence, 102, 143-47, 203

Obregón, Alvaro, 178
October Revolution, see Russian Revolution (1917)
Organization, 15-16, 19-21, 26, 57, 67, 71, 93, 96, 105-06, 108, 117-19, 121, 125, 127, 130-32, 134-35, 152, 154, 156, 163-67, 177, 187, 192, 197, 201, 212-15, 219, 223-24, 228-29, 235-36, 239-41, 245, 247, 251, 253

PAIGC, 214-15, 217
Paine, Thomas, 82, 84, 86, 263; *The Rights of Man,* 84
Pakistan, 146
Palermo, 66-67
Palestine, 14, 52
Pan-Africanist, 212, 227, 231
Pan-Arabist, 212
Paris, 91, 93
Paris Commune, 6, 90-94, 102
Parliament, 69, 71
Party, see Elite (Revolutionary) Party
Passive Resistance, 144, 146
Patriotism, 68, 92, 123, 166, 198, 236
Peace of Versailles, 153
Peasants, Peasantry, 15, 22, 33, 50, 53, 67, 88-89, 102, 106, 112, 117, 121-22, 124-25, 132, 134-35, 156-57, 159-65, 167-68, 175, 185-86, 192-94, 197-200, 202, 205-06, 215, 217-19, 221, 229-31, 238
Peasants' Revolt, 65
Peking, 256
People's War, 240
Permanent Revolution, 124-25, 147, 162, 194
Peron, Juan, 183
Petrograd, 135
Petrograd Soviet of Workers, 134
Petty Bourgeoisie, 160, 217-19
Pettee, George, 6
Phillips, Wendell, 79
Plan of San Luis Potosi, 177-78
Plato, 63, 72
Platt Amendment, 183-84
Poland, 79
Political Revolution, see Revolution, Types of
Polybius, 64, 72
Popular Socialist Party (Cuba), 183-84, 200
Popular Unity Coalition (Chile), 203
Port Huron Statement, 251
Portugal (Portuguese), 66-67, 208, 213-15, 218-19
Practical Man of Action, see Leaders, Types of
Privileged classes, see Aristocracy
Progress, 67, 95, 263
Proletarian Revolution, see Revolution, Types of
Proletariat (Workers), 22, 33, 40, 49-50, 88-89, 91-92, 93, 96-99, 102-09, 112, 114-26, 129-38, 154-57, 159-64, 167-68, 175, 180-81, 183-86, 190, 192-94, 196, 199-200, 203, 205-06, 211, 215-19, 230-31, 240, 245-50, 268
Prophet, see Leaders, Types of
Protestant, 141-43, 257, 266
Protestant Revolution, 65
Proudhon, Pierre-Joseph, 95-98, 102
Provisional Government (Russian Revolution), 134, 136
Puritan Revolution, 8, 67-70
Puritans (English), 266

Race, Racial, Racism, 13, 15, 32-33, 35, 91, 141, 148, 176, 222, 228, 247, 252, 254-56, 258-60
Radicals, 31, 59, 78, 158, 166, 189
Realistic Phase of Revolution, see Revolution, Phases of
Red Army, 124, 156, 164-65
Red Guards, 169

Reformation, 2, 65-66
Regional Revolutionary Nationalists, see Revolutionists, Types of
Relative Deprivation, 36-37
Religion, 5, 50, 60, 65, 68, 71, 80, 104, 112, 141-42, 147, 212-13, 224, 254, 265-67
Religious Revolution, see Revolution, Types of
Reluctant Revolutionists, see Revolutionists, Types of
Renaissance, 2, 49, 65, 69
Republic of Viet Nam (South Viet Nam), 235, 238, 240-41
Republicanism, 78
Restoration, 8, 65, 70-73, 91
Revision, Revisionism, Revisionist, 115-16, 118, 129, 168-70
Revolution, Definitions of, 6-8
Revolution, passim
Revolution, Phases of
Humanistic or Romantic Phase, 5, 189
Natural or Astronomy Phase, 5, 43-45, 71-72
Scientific or Realistic hase, 5, 72
Revolution, Types of
Anti-colonial Revolution, 68, 78, 90, 123, 140-43, 172-74, 208-11, 213, 215, 221, 223, 225-27, 235-36, 240
Bourgeois Revolution, 96, 106, 108, 112, 121-22, 124-26, 132-33, 136-37, 180, 185
Communist Revolution, 107, 110-11, 124, 129, 132-33, 136-38, 186, 200, 215, 217, 221, 231, 245, 248, 253
Conservative Revolution, 147
Democratic Revolution, 1, 71, 74-84, 87, 98, 129, 132, 136-37, 160, 226
Jacobin Communist Revolution, 45
Minority Revolution, 141
Nationalist (or National) Revolution, 8, 45, 108, 125, 137, 140, 143, 151, 161, 163, 166, 175-76, 180, 190, 209, 211
Peasant Revolution, 135, 163, 185, 238
Political Revolution, 86, 95-96, 103-04, 109, 131, 147, 182
Proletarian Revolution, 92, 104, 107-09, 112, 115, 117, 121-26, 130, 132-33, 135, 137, 155, 159, 185
Religious Revolution, 86, 177
Rural (Agrarian) Revolution, 164, 180

Social Revolution, 78, 86, 92, 95-96, 103-04, 109-11, 155, 166, 168, 172, 174, 177, 182, 187, 191, 196, 209, 211, 213, 226, 246
World Revolution, 109, 131, 137
Revolution, Typologies of, 43-47, 86
Revolutionary Ideal, passim
Revolutionary Nationalists, see Revolutionists, Types of
Revolutionary Pan-nationalists, see Revolutionists, Types of
Revolutionists, Types of
Destructive Revolutionists, 269
Ideal Revolutionists, 269
Islamic Revolutionists, 213
Marxist-Leninist Revolutionists, 212-13
National Liberation Revolutionists, 213
Negative Revolutionists, 268
Regional Revolutionary Nationalists, 212
Reluctant Revolutionists, 268-69
Revolutionary Nationalists, 212
Revolutionary Pan-nationalists, 212
Rhodesia, 213
Right, 141, 147, 203-04, 237, 269
Ritual, 30-31, 49
Robespierre, Maximilien, 81-82, 269
Roman Empire, 64
Romanov, 133
Romantic Phase of Revolution, see Revolution, Phases of
Roosevelt, Franklin D., 19
Rousseauean, 267
Rubin, Jerry, 17, 31
Rural Class, see Government
Rural (Countryside, Agrarian) Activity, 49-55, 58, 60, 103, 163-64, 167, 192, 198-200, 205-06, 214-15, 218, 230, 238-40, 247
Russia (Russian), 6, 29, 54, 83, 112, 116-18, 120-22, 124-25, 129, 131-38, 154, 156, 163, 165-66, 169, 185, 187, 199, 205, 252, 267-68
Russian Revolution (1905), 121, 124, 131
Russian Revolution (1917), 6, 7, 25, 46, 75, 79, 82, 87, 118, 124, 127, 129-38, 154, 156-57, 167, 175, 267-58

Saigon, 235
Sartre, Jean-Paul, 189
Satyagraha, 143-47
Saudi Arabia, 52
Scientific Phase of Revolution, see Revolution, Phases of

Sectarian Groups, 42-43, 59, 140
Sepoy Mutiny, 6
Serfs, 109, 111
Siberia, 54, 133
Sicily, 66
Siéyès, Abbe, 80; *What Is The Third Estate?*, 80
Slaves, Slavery, 75, 90, 97, 103, 109, 111, 126, 173, 237, 256, 265
Social Democratic Labor Party (Russia), 120
Social Myth, see Myth
Social Revolution, see Revolution, Types of
Socialist Party (Chile), 203
Socialist Revolution, see Communist Revolution
Socialism, Socialists, 92-94, 98, 101-03, 105, 109, 112, 116-20, 125-27, 130-37, 140, 145, 155, 159-62, 166, 168-70, 184, 189-90, 192-93, 199, 202-05, 210-11, 213, 217, 221, 223, 225, 227, 237, 243-44, 244, 252
Sorel, George, 12, 98-99, 266
Sorokin, Pitirim, 43
Soummam Congress, 224
South Africa, 213
South America, see Latin America
Southeast Asia, 141, 233
Soviet Communist Party Congress, 131
Soviet Union, see Russia
Soviets, 127, 134, 165
Spain, 66
Spanish-American War, 183
Spontaneity, 121, 200
Stalin, Joseph, 124-25, 163, 268
State, see Government
Strategy, 16-28, 236, 253
Student Nonviolent Coordinating Committee, 243
Students, 14, 22-23, 199-200, 243, 245, 247-48, 250
Students for a Democratic Society (SDS), 31, 243, 251
Sukarno, Achmed, 158
Sun Yat-sen, 148, 151-53, 155
Switzerland, 134, 136
Syndicalism, 90, 98-99
Syria, 52

Taiping Rebellion, 6, 149
Tanzania, 213
Target, 46-47
Teller Amendment, 184

Terror, Terrorism, 106, 142, 170, 184, 186, 189, 203, 224
Thermidor, 82
Third Estate, 80
Third World, 33, 37, 50-53, 55, 59-61, 122, 141, 143, 209-11, 225-27, 231, 244-45, 247-48, 250, 252-53
Thoreau, Henry David, 144
Three Principles of the People, 152-54
Thucydides, 63
Tocqueville, Alexis de, 41-42, 46, 83, 86-87; *L'Ancien Regime*, 42
Tolstoy, Leo, 144
Tonkin, 233
Totalitarianism, 133
Touré, Sékou, 211-12
Trade Unions and Unionism, 98-99, 119
Trotsky, Leon, 6, 124-25, 132-33, 162, 194
T'ung-meng-hui, 151
Tunisia, 222
Tupamaros, 206

Ulster, 142
Underdeveloped Areas, 117, 121-22, 124, 129-31, 138, 141, 143, 156, 167, 190-92, 203, 208-10, 228, 231, 267
Uninterrupted Revolution, 161-62, 170
United Nations, 52, 215
United States, 12, 15, 19, 32, 59, 83, 90, 143, 166, 173, 183, 187, 190, 206, 233-35, 241, 245, 252, 254, 256, 258-59
United States Congress, 184
Upper class, see Aristocracy
Urban, Urbanization, 48-61, 88, 102, 135, 156-57, 163, 167, 184-86, 192-93, 198-200, 206, 214, 218, 224, 229-31, 250, 256, 259
Urban guerrillas, 142
U.S.S.R. see Russia
Utopia, Utopian, 5, 42, 45, 66, 92-94, 97-99, 103, 108, 111, 115, 126, 179, 231, 248, 266, 269

Vendee, 47
Versailles, 80, 91
Viet Minh, 234-37, 239-40
Viet Nam (Vietnamese), 46, 53, 205, 225, 229, 233-41, 244, 252
Viet Nam War, 258
Vietnamese Revolution, 46, 233-41, 252
Villa, Pancho, 178
Violence, 1, 7, 11-28, 30-31, 34-35, 37,